John Channon and
brass-inlaid furniture
1730–1760

John Channon and brass-inlaid furniture 1730–1760

CHRISTOPHER GILBERT AND TESSA MURDOCH

1993
Yale University Press · New Haven and London
IN ASSOCIATION WITH
Leeds City Art Galleries
AND
The Victoria and Albert Museum

Copyright © 1993 by Yale University
All rights reserved. This book may not be reproduced, in whole
or in part, in any form (beyond that copying permitted by
Sections 107 and 108 of the U.S. Copyright Law and except by
reviewers for the public press), without written permission from
the publishers.

Designed by John Trevitt
Set in Linotron Baskerville by Best-set Typesetter Ltd., Hong Kong
Printed in Hong Kong through World Print Ltd.

Library of Congress Cataloging-in-Publication Data

Gilbert, Christopher.
John Channon and brass-inlaid furniture, 1730–1760 / Christopher
Gilbert and Tessa Murdoch.
  p. cm.
Includes bibliographical references and index.
ISBN 0-300-05812-8
1. Channon, John—Criticism and interpretation. 2. Brass-inlaid
furniture—England—London—History—18th century.
3. Furniture, Rococo—England—London. I. Murdoch, T. V.
II. Title.
NK2542.C48G56   1994
749.22—dc20   93-8447   CIP

Contents

	Preface	*page* vii
1	Introduction	1
2	The Channon family of London and Exeter	5
3	Channon's rivals and the London market for brass-inlaid furniture	13
4	The continental context: Germany *Helena Hayward and Sarah Medlam*	24
5	The continental context: France *Carolyn Sargentson*	37
6	Furniture manufacture and workshop organisation *Josephine Darrah, Sarah Medlam, Anthony North and Kevin Rogers*	46
	Trade practices	46
	Woods	49
	Other materials	51
	Joints and construction	53
	Inlaid brass and brass mounts	55
7	Furniture survey	59
	Bureau-cabinets	59
	Tables and desks	74
	The 'nymph and satyr' group	86
	Cabinets on stands	99
	The Powderham bookcases	106
	Pillar and claw tables	113
	Tea-chests and dressing-boxes	121
	Chairs	126
	Miscellaneous furniture	131
8	Workshop groups	135
Appendixes		
1	The wills of John and Martha Channon	138
2	Accounts, letters and inventories	140
3	John Channon's fire-insurance policy	143
4	The inlaid room at Mawley Hall	144

Notes	146
Select bibliography	152
Notes to the plates and figures	153
Index	162

Preface

It is now well over ten years since a major study devoted to the work of a leading firm of London cabinet-makers active during the mid-eighteenth century appeared. Books on Thomas Chippendale (1978) and William and John Linnell (1980) are available and another on Ince & Mayhew is in course of preparation. Despite fresh discoveries made during research and fieldwork for *The Dictionary of English Furniture Makers* (1986), there is probably not yet enough material to justify separate monographs on Giles Grendey, Seddons or Vile & Cobb. Chippendale the Younger awaits a modern biographer and there is, to be sure, capital scope for a book-length survey of work by the dynasty of royal cabinet-makers stretching from Jensen and Moore & Gumley to Charles Elliott. However, one of the most gripping challenges for the present generation of furniture historians is a re-investigation of the tradition of brass-inlaid furniture by John Channon and his rivals who were responsible for creating, during the reign of George II, many ravishing masterpieces embellished with engraved brass inlay and lavish mounts. The pieces are all of outstanding quality, are made of exotic woods and often display a flamboyant rococo personality – they are among the most richly styled examples of English furniture.

Any approach worthy of this subject demands a knowledge of French and German sources, the metalworking trades, printed designs, dealers' and auctioneers' records, estate archives, genealogy, timbers and much else besides. The theme is really too daunting to be tackled by an individual, so it seemed a sound idea for the two major decorative-art museums who have, over the years, collected examples of brass-inlaid furniture, to combine forces on a Channon project. Happily, the suggestion was warmly welcomed by academics, collectors and antique dealers. As the idea was discussed and took shape, it was decided that Leeds City Art Galleries and the Victoria and Albert Museum should collaborate on an exhibition supported by a major scholarly publication. Since 1993 happens to be the centenary year of Leeds City Council some extra money was available to stage an important show at Temple Newsam House, so the display opened in Leeds in the autumn of 1993 and moved to London in 1994.

A team of seven curators with interlocking specialist interests was recruited from both museums, and Helena Hayward, a former Secretary of the Furniture History Society, was also invited to participate because of her wide knowledge of both English and German furniture. The authors have received invaluable help from colleagues in the profession, especially John Kitchin, Michael Snodin, John Styles and Christopher Wilk of the Victoria and Albert Museum; among the fraternity of dealers Ronald Lee has been outstandingly generous in making available copious material from his legendary photographic albums, while John Partridge has provided vital energy and practical help over fund-raising for the venture; Asprey, John Bedford, Christopher Claxton-Stevens of Norman Adams Ltd, Apter Fredericks Ltd, Jeremy Ltd, Christian Jussel, John Keil, Malletts, Alan Rubin of the Pelham Galleries, Nicholas Somers,

James Graham Stewart of Carlton Hobbs, Jonathan Cook (Phillips), Giles Ellwood (Sotheby's) and John Hardy (Christie's) have also been uncommonly generous in supplying photographs. Many other individuals, firms and institutions are acknowledged in the captions and notes.

The support and encouragement of everybody approached for assistance has been very heartening: these include Lord Courtenay, Colonel Delforce, Tim Faulkner and Frank MacBratney at Powderham Castle; Hugh Harrison, the staff of the Devon Record Office, the Devon and Exeter Institution, and the West Country Studies Library; the parish priest of St Mary's Church, Hornby; Susanna Avery, Francie Downing, Christian Baulez and Peter Fuhring in Paris and Winfried Baer and Burkhardt Göres in Berlin. Roy Baxter, Dr Lindsay Boynton, Sebastian Edwards, Peter Van Gerbig, Sir Nicholas Goodison, John Harris, David Learmont, Sigrid Sangl, Larry Sirolli, Anne Stevens, Karin Walton and Lucy Wood have all provided assistance with research, and in particular Janet Halton of the Moravian Church Library. At the Victoria and Albert Museum Malcolm Baker, Philip Barnard, Frances Collard, Philippa Glanville, Ken Jackson, Linda Lloyd Jones, Tim Miller, John Murdoch, Albert Neher, Charles Saumarez Smith, Madeleine Tilley, Nick Umney, Gareth Williams, and James Yorke deserve a special mention.

The Paul Mellon Centre for Studies in British Art provided a most welcome grant for preliminary fieldwork and research, and the Monument Trust, Carlton Hobbs and Sir Emmanuel Kaye contributed handsomely towards the exhibition. Additional support for the Victoria and Albert Museum showing of the exhibition was generously provided by Herbert Black, James Bourlet & Sons (Museum and Fine Art Packers), John Bryan, B. Everli, S. Jon Gerstenfeld, the J. Paul Getty Trust, Harry Hyams, Philip Hewat-Jaboor, Robin Kern of Hotspur Ltd, Neil Sellin and Sotheby's. We are infinitely grateful to all the owners of furniture who have allowed us to examine and illustrate their pieces. Many well-wishers supplied welcome information and provided generous help with photographs, often at short notice. Sarah Medlam's contribution to the writing and editing of this publication has been particularly valuable. We hope that everyone who has been involved with this collaborative project will feel that the outcome is worth while. The subject has definitely been advanced on many fronts and we have done our best to provide a first-class photographic record of this memorable group of furniture.

1. Introduction

When Ralph Edwards and Margaret Jourdain came to prepare the first edition of *Georgian Cabinet-Makers* in 1944, either they were unaware that a tradition of brass-inlaid furniture flourished during the reign of George II or they failed to grasp its significance. Over the next ten or fifteen years matters changed greatly, owing almost entirely to the exertions of R.W. Symonds, the most energetic furniture historian of his generation who, between 1945 and his death in 1958, published seven articles on what is now widely regarded as the most challenging family of English eighteenth-century cabinet furniture. The story of how this exceptional group emerged and was researched in spasmodic bursts of scholarly activity reaching a peak of intensity with the present publication deserves to be told, even though investigations have by no means yet run their course.

Symonds first wrote about 'the variety of "tip-up table" ... that has a dished top and is decorated with engraved brass and mother of pearl inlay' in 1945, when replying to a Collector's Question in *Country Life*.[1] He was aware of some half-dozen examples and, drawing on his unrivalled knowledge of press notices, crucially linked them with the now celebrated announcement which Frederick Hintz placed in the *Daily Post* of 22 May 1738 advertising: 'A Choice Parcel of Desks and Book-Cases of Mahogany, Tea-Tables, Tea-Chests, Tea-Boards, etc. all curiously made and inlaid with fine Figures of Brass and Mother of Pearl'. Strangely, Symonds seems never to have devoted an article to this numerous class of tripod table, despite the fascinating wisps of mystery that surround its exact social function.

The next milestone came in 1948,[2] when Symonds discussed a Palladian desk and bookcase then owned by Mr and Mrs Joseph Steinberg but later acquired for Kenwood (Pl. 61) and an ambitiously styled serpentine writing-cabinet formerly in Lord Leverhulme's collection and now in Portugal (Pl. 103–5). He reckoned that they were made in different workshops. Both featured engraved brass inlay and were published as outstanding specimens of mahogany cabinet furniture 'adorned with brass', but at this time Symonds did not display any great intellectual excitement about this distinctive decorative technique.

A year later he was clearly astonished and thrilled when Sir William Keith Murray of Ochtertyre, Perthshire, sold at Christie's a spectacular rococo writing-cabinet of strikingly similar design to the Leverhulme version, but with flamboyant ormolu corner mounts instead of carved trusses and brass inlay of a 'more intricate and elaborate character' (Col. pl. XVII–XVIII). His article[3] on this 'far richer and more splendid' masterpiece described as 'a *tour de force* of the English cabinet-maker's craft' radiates enthusiasm and admiration. The vitality of the prose shows that he was intensely stimulated by this piece of furniture.

Six years later, Symonds wrote[4] about an exceptional dressing-table which 'demanded craftsmanship of almost unbelievable skill and ingenuity' and, on the evidence of the fire-gilt mounts and technical construction 'came from the same workshop as the two writing cabinets' (Pl. 106). He suggested that the maker 'would probably be a German who went to Paris to learn his trade and then came to England to better his position', and speculated that the mounts were cast and chased in France – thus perceptively pin-pointing two of the most challenging problems posed by this ensemble. Symonds would have been interested to discover that the dressing-table was one half of a twin unit, since in the same year he wrote an article on 'Back-to-Back Writing-Tables'.[5]

No sooner had this 'magnificent dressing table' been purchased by the Victoria and Albert Museum than Symonds heard of an 'incomparable mahogany commode' which displayed 'the same high quality in its cabinet work... the same curious, un-English characteristics... the same handwriting... and the use of identical mounts' (Pl. XXII). He was, in an old-fashioned way, coy about disclosing details of provenance, but after it had been bought by Temple Newsam enquiries revealed that it came originally from Southwick Park, Hampshire, and was almost certainly commissioned by Alexander Thistlethwayte, who subscribed to the first edition of Chippendale's *Director* in 1754. 'I had not got over the excitement of finding this commode,' he continued,[6] 'when I came across a photograph of a cabinet... it will be seen that the same woman's head and bearded man's head mounts are used as on the dressing table.' Happily this photograph, taken when Moss Harris & Sons advertised the piece in 1924, survives among the Symonds papers at Winterthur (Pl. 112), although the cabinet's present whereabouts is still unrecorded.

Five 'exceptional pieces of English furniture... from the same workshop' had now been identified, but Symonds was forced to admit that 'we are no nearer solving the mystery of who was the maker. In fact the problem has become even more baffling...'. He continued to be haunted by the ensemble, publishing in the last year of his life (1958, 2) a second article on the Temple Newsam commode and another (1958, 1) comparing the arabesque decoration on a walnut bureau-cabinet by Samuel Bennett (Pl. 44) with the delicate engraved brass inlay on a superb rosewood secretaire which H. Blairman & Sons then had in stock (Pl. IV). The fact that Symonds first identified this spectacular group and researched it so perceptively enhances his reputation as an outstanding furniture historian: he set a high standard for others to follow.

The next scholar to advance the study of English brass-inlaid furniture dating from the reign of George II was John Hayward, Deputy Keeper of the Department of Furniture at the Victoria and Albert Museum (1951–66), who was also an international authority on firearms, metalwork, jewellery, horology, ceramics and design. During his time, the museum acquired six outstanding specimens enriched with engraved brass inlay work. It was the purchase in 1964 of a cabinet on stand, described as 'one of the most sumptuous surviving pieces of English furniture' that inspired Hayward to re-examine this celebrated group. The two resulting articles published in the short-lived *Victoria and Albert Museum Bulletin* for January 1965 and April 1966 have become classic statements. He concentrated on pieces in the museum collection, but discussed them in the context of other known examples, which now numbered a dozen all told.

Hayward explored the strong Continental (more specifically German and French) influence on their design and embellishment. Abraham Roentgen, founder of the famous cabinet-making business at Neuwied on the Rhine, who worked 'for some of the most skillful cabinet makers' in London *c.*1733–1738, was suggested – without much conviction – as a possible author, although Hayward thought that he might have made a dished-top tea table inlaid with brass and pearl shell bequeathed to the Museum by Claude Rotch in 1962 (Pl. 153). Frederick Hintz of Newport Street (who, as Symonds noted, advertised in 1738 'Desks and Book-Cases of Mahogany, Tea-

Tables, Tea-Chests, Tea-Boards etc all curiously made and inlaid with fine Figures of Brass and Mother of Pearl') was also mentioned as a possible foreign immigrant creator of the group, but Hayward dismissed his claim to authorship as 'improbable'. A third candidate was proposed: J. Graveley, whose name had been discovered branded under the base of a mahogany bureau-cabinet adorned with characteristic brass inlay (Pl. 50–2). Unfortunately nothing further has emerged about this individual, although the chances are that he was a tradesman.

A rapid survey of Hayward's article can at best only indicate its scope and significance. He pointed out that the brass inlay, like similar decoration on gun stocks, might have been sub-contracted to specialist workshops, and helpfully observed that whereas early pieces fall within the normal range of main-stream London cabinet-making, the later, more opulent work – the pieces which Symonds so admired – were much more ambitious in design, with profuse inlay and sculptural brass mounts drawing on a far wider vocabulary of rococo ornament. Obviously eager to identify the maker, he argued ingeniously that the 'ram pendant from two entwined serpents' engraved on the four hinges of the Victoria and Albert Museum cabinet on stand might represent the 'Golden Fleece' displayed outside a cabinet-maker's shop 'on the pavement' in St Martin's Lane. However, in the concluding paragraph he honestly admitted that 'the identity of the makers of this group of furniture must for the present remain unsolved' while suggesting that their 'workshop, probably in the vicinity of St Martin's Lane... was probably founded by a German immigrant' who 'continued to welcome immigrant German craftsmen'.

In 1966 all students of English furniture were given a heartening sense of progress when John Hayward triumphantly announced that the group of English furniture embellished with brass inlay which he had discussed in the first *Victoria and Albert Museum Bulletin* was produced by John Channon, an Exeter cabinet-maker, who came to London in or before 1737 and set up his workshop on the west side of St Martin's Lane. The vital connecting link was a towering pair of bookcases displaying affinities with Continental baroque design and lavish Berainesque brass inlay at Powderham Castle, near Exeter, Devon (Pl. XXIII). Each bears a brass tablet engraved in Gothic script 'J. Channon Fecit 1740' (Pl. 6). These bookcases and relevant payments among the Courtenay papers had been published by Mark Girouard in a series of articles on Powderham for *Country Life* in July 1963. However, Edwards and Jourdain had briefly reported their existence in 1944 (although the J was initially misread as T) and they are referred to again in the *Dictionary of English Furniture*, 1954. Nevertheless, John Hayward was the first person to realise their crucial significance. His second article contained valuable background information about the Channon family culled from sources in Exeter and London and he attributed three more pieces to the Channon workshop, including a collector's cabinet on stand of 'unparalleled prodigality' which Bristol Art Galleries had been persuaded to buy (Pl. XIX–XX).

In his final paragraph the author toyed with the notion that Abraham Roentgen might have produced some brass-inlaid furniture during his stay in London and made 'other pieces of a distinctly English type and construction' on his return to Germany about 1738. The large group of often rather coarse dished-top tripod tables with brass and mother-of-pearl inlay was tentatively ascribed to Roentgen's hand. However, in the best tradition of experienced researchers Hayward wisely concluded that the identification of other makers 'remains a task for the future'. Despite this note of caution it was almost inevitable that very soon all George II brass-inlaid furniture, whether ostentatiously splendid or shoddy and insipid, was being described by dealers, collectors and the compilers of sale catalogues as coming from the Channon workshop. Channon had suddenly become nearly as famous as Chippendale, Vile & Cobb, Ince

4 INTRODUCTION

& Mayhew or Robert Adam. Hayward's carefully researched articles seemed to be so comprehensive and definitive that for the next twenty years they discouraged serious re-investigation of the subject, except for a single article published six months later by two colleagues.

In 1966 Desmond Fitz-Gerald and Peter Thornton revived the idea, floated but rejected by Hayward, that during his sojourn in London Roentgen 'may have been engaged by John Channon for the making of the engraved inlaid brasswork with which much of his furniture was embellished'. They even argued that he could have returned to England in 1740 to produce 'the engraved plates which now decorate the superb bookcases at Powderham'. Their suggestion that Roentgen 'was associated as engraver and technician with John Channon' is improbable and speculative, despite a loose claim that 'the more one looks into the matter, the more likely it seems that he must have done'. However, the not particularly helpful linking of these two famous names quickly became part of the Channon mythos and it is now increasingly hard to remember that it has no place in the historical record – although a feeling lingers that it just might contain a germ of truth.

The foundation of the Furniture History Society in 1965 inspired a period of intense academic activity; however, no fresh published work on Channon and his circle appeared. Anthony Coleridge summarised existing knowledge in his *Chippendale Furniture* (1968), but it was the acquisition as recently as 1985 by Leeds City Art Galleries for Temple Newsam of the ravishing Murray writing-cabinet that led to a revival in Channon studies. This is not to say that no progress or important discoveries were made in the intervening years. The dealer Ronald Lee assembled a pictorial anthology of brass-inlaid furniture which has been of inestimable value in the preparation of this work, while the furniture archive at the Victoria and Albert Museum recorded transcripts of letters and bills associated with two of the firm's late commissions at Hornby Hall, Lancashire (1766–9), and the London home of Richard Crosse, miniature painter (1773), together with a few additional advertisements (appendix 2). In 1982 Helena Hayward published a Continental engraved source for some elaborate brass inlay on the slope of a mahogany bureau-cabinet, thus opening up a fresh line of attack that has proved most rewarding. The methodical trawl of source material undertaken for Beard and Gilbert's *Dictionary of English Furniture Makers* (1986) disappointingly yielded only a single fire-insurance policy taken out in 1760 (appendix 3) and one bank-account payment.

The renewed wave of activity resulted in articles by James Lomax (1988), James Yorke (1989) and Christopher Claxton-Stevens (1990) and various lesser contributions, all of which synthesised previous work gingered up with one or two additional facts and illustrations of newly recorded pieces. Their chief importance was to stimulate a new cycle of scholarly activity, one result being Donald Johnston's commendable thesis *John Channon and the German Community in London* (1990). This new climate also inspired the present broad survey of what is once again perceived to be the most thrilling challenge for historians of elite eighteenth-century furniture. Instead of lumping all brass-inlaid furniture together as being 'in the manner of Channon', this census sets out to identify various house styles and attribute them to different workshops; it also explores design sources, looks again at techniques and materials, and attempts to place the English tradition within a European context.

2. The Channon family of London and Exeter

In 1742 two London daily papers announced the presence of a cabinet-maker by the name of John Channon, whose premises were in St Martin's Lane in the parish of St Martin's-in-the-Fields. On 24 July *The Craftsman* carried the following advertisement:

this is to give notice That FURBER's Collection of twelve monthly Flower Prints are now reprinted, and to prevent the Publick being imposed on, by spurious Copies sold about the Town, the original Plates are Sixteen Inches and a Quarter by Twelve, with a handsome Title Plate of the Subscribers Names, and under each Plate is engraved these Words, from the Collection of Robert Furber, Gardener, at Kensington; design'd by P. Cassteels, and engraved by H. Fletcher; and now sold colour'd for Two Guineas a Set by Samuel Sympson, Engraver and Printseller, in Maiden-Lane, Covent Garden; John Channon, Cabinet-Maker and Frame-Maker, in St Martin's Lane; and George Lacy, who colours the said Flowers, in Red Lyon-Court, Long-Acre. N.B. At the above Places are sold Mr. Furber's Collections of Fruit Pieces'.[1]

The Daily Advertiser informed the public on 23 November that 'Mr Eade having left off his publick School in St Martin's Lane, continues to teach (only abroad) some few Persons writing, Arithmetic, and Merchants Accounts, in a very short and easy Method. His Lodgings are at Mr. Channon's, a Cabinet Warehouse, upon the Pavement in St Martin's Lane.'[2]

The advertisement in *The Craftsman* is the first public announcement of John Channon's presence in London. Robert Furber's *Twelve Months of Flowers* was first published in 1730 and the list of subscribers included the name Otho Channon (Pl. 1).[3] This is likely to be John Channon's master and may also prove to be the Otho Channon whose daughter Frances was baptised on 24 April 1725 at St Martin's-in-the-Fields, when his wife was named as Elizabeth.[4]

John Channon, described as the son of Otho Channon of Exeter, sergemaker (fig. A), was apprenticed in 1726, on payment of a fee of £8, to another Otho Channon, also of Exeter, joiner, who has been described as John's elder brother.[5] However, instead of the usual seven years' apprenticeship, John only obtained his freedom on 15 September 1740.[6] It is possible that John Channon's master, although of Exeter origins, had moved to London by 1726. It is certain that John served at least part of his apprenticeship in London, for by 1737 he was recorded in the Rate Books for St Martin's Lane (Pl. 2).[7] However, his master was trained in Exeter; in 1714 he was apprenticed to William Culme, joiner, also on payment of £8, and he obtained his freedom eight years later on 26 February 1722.[8] John Channon's master Otho was described on his apprenticeship in 1714 as the son of Otho Channon of Exeter,

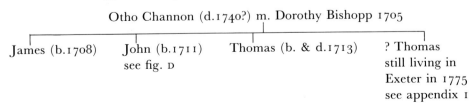

A The family of Otho Channon of Exeter, serge-maker

1. Title-page to Robert Furber's *Twelve Months of Flowers and Fruit*, folio, London, c.1732. The subscribers included Otho Channon. *The Trustees of the Victoria and Albert Museum*

2. Page from the rate book of the parish of St Martin's-in-the-Fields, showing the first entry for John Channon in St Martin's Lane, Bedfordbury Ward, in 1737. *Westminster Local History Library*

innholder (fig. B).[9] If John and his master Otho shared the same father then Otho Channon senior must have changed his occupation from that of innholder to serge-maker in the course of fourteen years.

THE CHANNON FAMILY OF LONDON AND EXETER

Otho Channon (d.1740?) m. Anne Soanes 1697

Otho (b.1698, d.1756) see fig. C | William —(twins b.1699)— John

B The family of Otho Channon of Exeter, innholder

The Otho Channon who married Anne Soanes of Exeter in October 1697[10] is usually described as the father of both Otho Channon, junior, joiner, and John Channon, cabinet-maker. The evidence is as follows: on 4 November 1698 Otho, 'son of Otho Channon' was baptised at the church of St Sidwell's, Exeter, and twin brothers, William and John, were baptised there on 12 November in the following year.[11] However, the St Sidwell's Marriage Register also records that one Otho Channon married Dorothy Bishopp on 5 October 1705.[12] Was this Otho Channon senior's second marriage? If so, Otho Channon junior is more likely to be John Channon's half-brother. Thus three boys, James, 'son of Otho Chonon', baptised on 31 October 1708, John 'son of Otho Channon', baptised on 21 May 1711 and Thomas, baptised 13 September 1713 (who died five months later) are as likely to have been children of this later marriage.[13]

The presence of the Channon family in St Sidwell's parish is recorded from at least 1677, when Hanah Chaninge, daughter of Otho Chaninge, was baptised there.[14] The church of St Sidwell's was rebuilt in 1812 to the designs of William Burges and contains no further evidence of the family.[15] However, the records of the Exeter Poor Rate in the Exeter City Library confirm that Otho Channon senior held property in the parish in 1708, 1715 and 1732.[16] In December 1719 Otho Channon, innkeeper, is granted a lease of Exeter market tolls and in 1724 Otho Channon of St Sidwell, sergemaker, is granted the privilege of collecting wheelage in the City.[17] Sergemaking was one of the principal occupations in eighteenth-century Exeter (Pl. 3); out of a population of some twelve thousand inhabitants, four out of five earners derived their income from the wool trade.[18] When Celia Fiennes visited Exeter during the reign of

3. Plan of the city of Exeter by John Rocque, 1744, showing the location of St Sidwell's parish. *British Library*

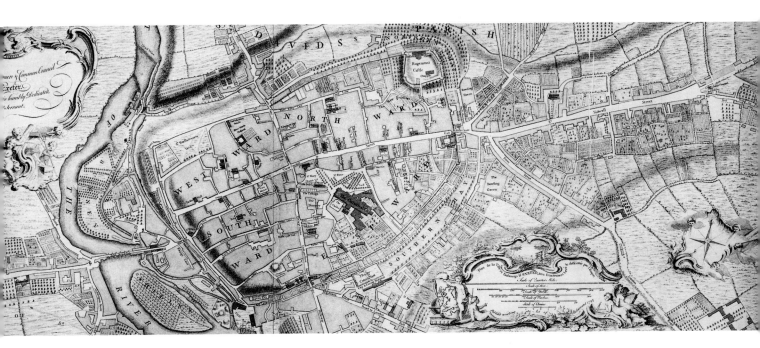

```
Otho Channon (1697–1756) m. Elizabeth
┌──────────┬──────────┬──────────┬──────────┬──────────┬──────────┬──────────┬──────────┐
Frances    Otho       Caligula   Anne       Dorothy    Otho       Titus      Tiberius
(b.1725)   (b.1726–7) (b.1728)   (b.1729,   Maria      (b.1733)   Vespasian  (b.1735)
                                 d.1730)    (b.1731,              (b.1734,
                                            d.1736)               d.1735)
```

c The family of Otho Channon (1697–1756) of Exeter and London(?), joiner

William III she noted, 'The whole town and country is employed for at least twenty miles around in spinning, weaving, dressing and scouring of serges. It turns the most money in a week of anything in England.'[19] It has been suggested that the Channon family were of German origin, which now seems unlikely. However, by the early eighteenth century Exeter enjoyed a flourishing overseas trade and exported substantial quantities of wool and serge to North Germany and succeeded in attracting a growing community of continental merchants the first of whom, John Baring (1697–1748), founder of the distinguished line of merchant bankers, arrived from Bremen in 1717 and by 1723 had taken up British citizenship. He became one of the richest merchants in the West Country, his fortune being based on the Exeter wool trade.[20]

Both Otho Channon (b.1698) and John Channon (b.1711) maintained their Exeter connections. There is no evidence that Otho married in Exeter and it is therefore possible that he married in London, where a daughter was baptised at St Martin's-in-the-Fields in 1725. On 7 March 1726/7 Otho, son of Otho junior, was baptised at St Sidwell's, Exeter (but he was buried there on 22 September 1730). Otho junior's other children (fig. C) included Caligula, baptised in May 1728; Anne (baptised 17 September 1729, buried 20 October 1730), Dorothy Maria baptised in March 1731 at St Stephen's, Exeter (two children of this name were buried at St Sidwell's in 1736 and 1738) and Otho, who was christened in September 1733. Another son, Titus Vespasian, was buried in November 1735. In 1735 Otho Channon junior was a churchwarden of St Stephen's, Exeter. It is probable that the Otho Channon who died in Exeter in January 1756 was John Channon's master.[21]

John Channon's fellow apprentices included Charles Morgan, who was taken on in 1729 and obtained his freedom in 1738, John Stone, free in 1745, and John Burnett, free in 1747.[22] John Channon's earliest recorded work is the pair of elaborate brass inlaid bookcases supplied in 1740 to Sir William Courtenay for the library upstairs at Powderham Castle, near Exeter, (Pl. 4, 132–43) although they are now located in the ante-room to the downstairs library, to which position they were moved in about 1830. Otho Channon is traditionally credited with the ornamental and carved wooden mantelpiece in the old library at Powderham (Pl. 5), although the accounts do not substantiate this claim. The authorship of a curious screen with applied pilasters and carved head which flanks the two door-cases at the entrance to the old library has not been determined; although idiosyncratic in design, it is likely to be contemporary with both the mantelpiece and John Channon's bookcases. They are unusual in that both pieces bear brass plaques with the inscription 'J. Channon fecit 1740' (Pl. 6). The inscription is substantiated by a payment in Sir William Courtenay's account books dated 29 April 1741 'to Jno Channon part on Acct £50'.[23] No other records of payments to John Channon from Courtenay survive for the 1740s, although a human note is provided by an undated letter contained in the same account book from one Ann Reading to her brother, who was Sir William Courtenay's butler, which reads 'Mr Courtenay has sold his mare to Mr Channon & he is to leave ye monny with you'.[24]

Otho Channon also worked for Courtenay and was paid 'in full of all demands' £27 13s on 25 March 1743, and on 12 October 1748 £14 5s for a cabinet-maker's bill which was originally submitted in 1745 and on this occasion he is described as 'chairmaker'.[25]

4. Bookcase, one of a pair, supplied by John Channon in 1740 for the library, Powderham Castle. *The Trustees of the Victoria and Albert Museum*

5. Overmantel in the old library (now the Gold Drawing Room), Powderham Castle, attributed to Otho Channon, c.1740. *The Trustees of the Victoria and Albert Museum*

6. Brass plaque from one of the bookcases supplied by John Channon for Powderham Castle. *The Trustees of the Victoria and Albert Museum*

The introduction to Courtenay may well have come from Culme the joiner, whose name occurs in the Powderham accounts between 1727 and 1742 'for carving ye Shipp' in 1733, 'on account of Joyners work in ye shipp' in 1734 and in 1739 when he was paid over £40 by Captain Teague (who is referred to elsewhere as having taken charge of the ship named appropriately the *Powderham Castle*).[26] Both Otho and John Channon continued to work for Sir William Courtenay in the 1750s. In 1751 an entry in the Powderham accounts for 23 August records that Otho was paid £33 10s 'in full for a Mahogany Table & Chairs'.[27]

John's name occurs in the 'Ledger of the Accounts of the Honble Sir William Courtenay Bart with Tradesman & others in London' when he was paid £45 8s 4d 'By his Bill deliver'd beginning 20 Feb 1756 and ending ye 31st of July following'. It seems probable that this latter payment was for cabinet-maker's goods supplied for Courtenay's new 'House in Grosvenor Square' as the upholsterer John Price was paid in 1754–5 for moving goods from Courtenay's previous house in Pall Mall.[28] Unfortunately no inventories of the contents of Courtenay's London houses have come to light, so it is not yet possible to identify what John Channon, cabinet-maker, was paid for on this occasion.

Little is known about John Channon's London workshop, although he occupied the same site for over forty years. He took over premises formerly occupied by a John Humphries in 1737 which he occupied until his death in 1779. He is recorded as paying £25 in rates from 1737 to 1740, £22 in 1741 and £32 from 1742 to 1749.[29] In 1749 he is listed in the Westminster Poll Book as 'George Chanon, St Martin's Lane Cabinet maker'.[30] In 1750 Channon's rate payment increased to £40, in 1756 to £64 and from 1757 to 1764 £50. In 1765 the payment decreased to £34, and it remained constant until 1778. In that year Channon was paying rates on two properties of £23 and £11 respectively, and in 1779, the year of his death, he paid rates on the smaller property only.[31] His widow Martha Channon continued to occupy the premises until 1784, when the additional name Hughes occurs. Martha evidently moved away from St Martin's Lane, and is described, at the time of her death, as of Sloane Square.[32]

Only three apprentices are recorded: Stephen Fryer who joined him in 1741 on payment of £25, Rowland Jackson in 1752 on payment of £15 and Edward Henry Williamson in 1762 on payment of £50.[33] It seems likely that his master Otho Channon had returned to Exeter, where most of his apprentices were taken on. In 1742 Otho Channon took on an additional apprentice, Thomas Parker.[34] Both 'Channon, Senr and Channon, Jnr' subscribed to the 1754 edition of Chippendale's *Director*, but yet another Channon, cabinet-maker, is recorded in 1758 – a Thomas Channon, of Taunton, who took Richard Tucker as an apprentice on payment of £20.[35] This is almost certainly John Channon's younger brother described as Thomas Channon of Exeter, who was the main beneficiary of his will drawn up in 1775.[36]

John Channon's fire insurance policy with the Sun Fire Insurance Company dated 9 January 1760 (see appendix 3) covered a total valuation of £1,000, including £500 for household goods, utensils and stock in trade, £100 for glass in trade, and £150 for household goods, utensils and stock-in-trade in a house behind the St Martin's Lane premises. Additional stock-in-trade held in the shop only in the yard behind was insured for £150.[37]

John was married to Martha Bishop on 18 December 1757 at St Martin's-in-the-Fields at the rather late age of forty-six, although his wife was only twenty-four. They had five children baptised between 1758 and 1767 (fig. D): John born in 1758, Otho in 1759, twin daughters, Anne Jane and Dorothy Martha born in 1766, and another John, born in 1767. The birth and progress of the last son John is referred to in correspondence from Martha Channon to Mrs Fenwick dated from June 1767 to

D The family of John Channon (1711–79) of Exeter and London, cabinet-maker

John Channon (1711–1779) m. Martha Bishop 1757

| John (b.1758) | Otho (b.1759) | Anne Jane | Dorothy Martha | John (b.1767) |

—(twins b.1766)—

December 1768 which provides revealing evidence for the state of Mrs Channon's health and also that her fifth-born was the only child still living in 1768.[38] Judging from the evidence of the wills of both parents, not even he survived childhood.[39]

There is tantalisingly little information on Channon's business activity during the years which must have been dominated by domestic matters. It is significant that John Channon's wife Martha wrote business letters for him. The fact that Channon did not apparently employ a book-keeper, like Haig who worked for Chippendale, suggests that his business was modest by comparison.[40] The main source for Channon's business practice is the correspondence with Mrs Anne Fenwick which survives in the archives from Hornby Hall, Lancashire (see appendix 2).[41] This shows that Channon was dealing in paintings as well as furniture and even supplying lottery tickets. Indeed, the fact that John Channon also worked as a 'Frame Maker' may have encouraged him to deal in paintings.[42] In 1766 Channon supplied Mrs Fenwick with 'two pictures in Carv'd and Gilt frames' for five guineas and 'a Small pr of Jourandoles painted flack-white with Brass Nossells Holdfasters and Screws to do' for 15s 6d. In the same year his wife informed Mrs Fenwick 'Mr Channon has been in pursuit of Some Vast Curious and Valuable pictures which at last he has purchased its our Bless'd Savour [sic] and Six of his Apostles Supposed by the best Judges to be done by Raphel Urbin'. Channon had purchased the paintings in anticipation that Mrs Fenwick would buy them from him, but in the event they were returned, the frames having been damaged in transit.

Other documentary evidence (transcribed in appendix 2) records that John Channon was paid £9 14s by Thomas Treslove on 18 June 1768 (entry in Treslove's bank account with Drummonds of Charing Cross – although there is no evidence that this was the cabinet-maker, it seems likely).[43] A bill from John Channon dated 18 November 1769 records that Channon supplied Walter Scott of Harden with a walnut-tree chest of drawers on castors for £3 10s, a mahogany sideboard table for £3, twelve 'Beach Chaires Carrott feet dyed with Matted seates' for £3 18s and six high wooden chairs for 12 shillings. Walter Scott was Member of Parliament for the County of Roxburgh from 1747 to 1765, and appointed Receiver General of Customs in 1765.[44] In 1773 Channon supplied Richard Crosse, miniature-painter, of Henrietta Street, Covent Garden, with a mahogany-pillared bedstead and accompanying hangings of crimson moreen for £21 and repaired a mahogany clock-case. This bill shows that he was also involved in upholstery and could muster three men to fix a bedstead.[45] This is a sparse record for a cabinet-maker who was operating in London for over forty years, and although it shows that Channon was attracting both London and country customers, it indicates that his business may not have been as prolific as the numerous recent attributions to him might suggest.

The content of his will (appendix 1) reinforces this interpretation of Channon's career. Drawn up in 1775 when he is described as being 'sick in Body but of perfect mind memory and understanding' it records modest legacies of £100 to his brother Thomas and £300 in trust for his brother's three children.[46] Interestingly the original executors appointed in 1775 were both in the furnishing or allied trades. John Cambridge, cabinet-maker of St Martin's Lane, is also recorded as having premises at 12 Ranelagh Street, Pimlico.[47] The other executor, Edward Crace (1725–99), founder of the distinguished Crace firm of decorators, set up business as a decorative house painter to the nobility and gentry.[48] However, a note on the Will in John Channon's hand reads 'Mr Ed Crace desired to be excused I have appointed George Palmer in his room'. John Channon died in October 1779 and was buried at St Mary Abbot's Burial Ground in Kensington.[49] The will was proved on 3 November 1779.

John Channon's wife Martha outlived him by eighteen years. Her will (appendix 1) was drawn up in 1791 and in it she requested 'to be buried in Kensington Church Yard as near my late husband John Channon as possible'.[50] Her will provides more detail of her household effects which she had presumably inherited from her husband. To one executor, a Miss Anne Towne, she left 'my Silver Soup Ladle' and to the other, a Miss Margaret Towne 'my four tooth and egg Candlesticks my best Snuffers and Snuffer pan my two Silver plated Candlesticks and flatt and chamber do with Snuffers and Extinguisher belonging to it'. The other beneficiary was James Scadding 'of the Parish of St Mary Magdalen in Taunton, Somerset, carpenter and joiner, but now of London' and his wife Elizabeth and their three children.[51] It seems likely that James Scadding was connected with the James Scadding whose marriage at St Mary Abbot's Kensington John Channon attended as a witness in 1776.[52] Martha Channon died in July 1797 and was buried, as requested, in Kensington Church Yard on the 17th of that month.[53] Her will was proved on 29 August 1797.

3. Channon's rivals and the London market for brass-inlaid furniture

This chapter seeks to place John Channon in the context of the other London workshops which are known from documentary evidence to have produced brass-inlaid furniture during the period from 1730 to 1770. It examines the evidence for earlier London workshops producing metal-inlaid furniture and also seeks to explain the taste for such furniture in England. Contemporary sale catalogues show that French Boulle furniture remained a popular luxury in England throughout this period. Boulle furniture is decorated with brass and tortoiseshell and was a technique perfected by the Paris cabinet-maker André-Charles Boulle (1642–1732). Such furniture provided the inspiration for brass-inlaid furniture produced in England during the eighteenth century.

The opportunities which greeted John Channon when he set up in London's St Martin's Lane must have formed a dramatic contrast to the limited scope of the cabinet-maker's trade in Exeter. Not a great deal is known about the Exeter furniture-making trades, but it is probable that they were sometimes closely linked with ship-building, as has already been shown in the evidence for the joiner William Culme's employment at Powderham.[1]

Contemporary advertisements in the local newspapers provide some evidence for activity in this field. For example, Nicholas Williams, joiner, advertises in *The Protestant Mercury: or The Exeter Post Boy*, for 18 May 1716:

Nicholas Williams, Joyner in Southgate-Street, EXON, sells all Sorts of Chests of Drawers Hanging-Presses Clock-Cases Cabinets Scrutoires Commode-Tables Desks Book-Cases and Looking Glasses, of the Newest Fashion and best Fineer'd Work in Walnut-Tree, also Japan'd work, with Variety of other Household-Furniture, by Wholesale or Retail. He has ROOMS to lett Furnish'd or Unfurnish'd.[2]

Links between the London and Exeter cabinet-makers' trades provide an interesting background to the work of Channon and his rivals. In 1725, Humphrey Wilcocks brought from London to stock his shop at the top of Fore Street Hill, Exeter, beds and hangings, 'chiney watered and damasked', painted linen for hangings, coach glasses, sconces, and for the new fashion of making tea 'tea tables and salvers'.[3] Judging from the recorded presence of an Otho Channon in London in 1725 (see p. 8), it seems probable that John Channon was not the first member of his family to set up business there. What other Exeter-trained craftsmen settled in London at this time? Certainly, London might be a market to aspire to, particularly for the higher-quality luxury goods such as silver and clocks. In 1739, the distinguished Exeter clockmaker Jacob Lovelace exhibited 'a Beautiful and Magnificent Musical Clock' at the 'Leg-Tavern in Fleet Street'. 'Never before exposed', it was 'valuable for its structure and the exact Performance of all its parts'. He also exhibited 'some other Machines by Clock-work; and the surprising power of the artificial Magnet' and claimed that he makes and sells 'all Sorts of Musical and other Clocks, Watches and Artificial magnets'.[4] Unfortunately the clock-case was destroyed by enemy action in the early 1940s when in the collection

14 CHANNON'S RIVALS AND THE LONDON MARKET

of the Liverpool Museum, but a lithograph of 1833 (Col. pl. 1) shows that it was contained in an elaborate case framed by Ionic pilasters supported by female caryatids. The broken pediment at the top supports reclining carved giltwood figures of Apollo and Diana. The case is veneered in an elaborate patterned wood which is adorned with what appear to be brass ornaments (although it is difficult to tell whether these are applied or inlaid and the character of the image is inevitably coloured by the date of its publication). The scrolls on the cresting look Regency in date rather than eighteenth century, and it is indeed possible that the case was further embellished in the early nineteenth century.

The lower section of the clock consists of cabinet doors which open out to reveal paintings of Exeter buildings on the interior, including a representation of the ruins of Rougemont Castle. It is certain that the clock-case was of a sophistication worthy of a London maker, and the suggestion that it may have been made by John Channon is plausible by comparison with the documented bookcases which he supplied in 1740 for William Courtenay at Powderham. The elaborate carved figures on the clock could have been supplied by one of Channon's neighbours in the St Martin's Lane area. It is known, for example, that the French sculptor L.F. Roubiliac (1702/5–62) made the bronze figures adorning a clock by the London maker Charles Clay known as the 'Temple of the Four Grand Monarchies' which was similarly advertised and exhibited in 1743.[5]

In London, although John Channon would have found the rivalry of his fellow craftsmen immensely challenging, if he was well organised he could have taken advantage of the wide range of skills on his doorstep. The description in *The Daily Advertiser* of Channon's premises as a 'Cabinet Warehouse'[6] suggests that he may have been acting as a retailer, and the advertisement earlier in the year in *The Craftsman* shows that he was supplying prints and picture frames in addition to furniture.[7]

The Westminster Poll Book of 1749 provides a useful record of the range of crafts practised by Channon's neighbours (Pl. 7).[8] By the early 1750s these included the leading cabinet-makers Thomas Chippendale (1718–79), William Hallett, senior

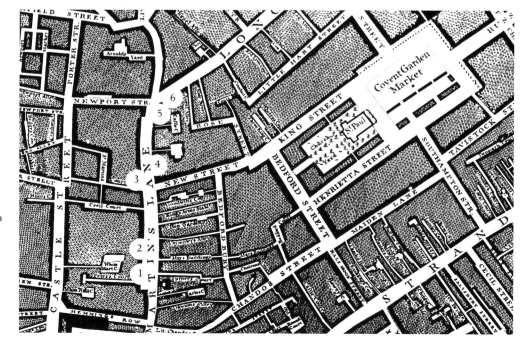

7. St Martin's Lane and the surrounding area from John Rocque's *Survey of London*, 1746, showing the location of John Channon's premises and those of earlier and rival cabinetmakers
1. John Channon from 1737 to 1779, then his widow until 1784
2. William Hubert until 1740, then his widow until 1751
3. Gerrit Jensen until 1715
4. Thomas Chippendale from 1753
5. William Vile and John Cobb from 1750
6. William Hallett from 1752
Museum of London

(1707–81), William Vile (d.1767) and John Cobb (c.1715–78). In order to establish a position in an extremely competitive environment, John Channon must have had a strong network of contacts and considerable financial backing to enable him to set up in St Martin's Lane, which was then emerging as the centre of the fashionable cabinet-making trade in London. It is understandable that in order to gain his reputation he would wish to develop a particular area of speciality. However, although the brass-inlaid furniture which may be attributed to Channon is often idiosyncratic in terms of taste and design, he must have been aware of the latest developments in style, for in 1754 both he and his former master Otho Channon subscribed to the first edition of Chippendale's *Director*.

The bookcases completed in 1740 for Sir William Courtenay's library at Powderham Castle, Devon, are Channon's only fully documented furniture (Col. Pl. XXIII and Pl. 4, 132–43). They combine carved giltwood decoration with engraved brass inlay and appear to herald a new phenomenon in terms of English furniture production, although closer study reveals that the production of brass-inlaid furniture was well established in London by the 1730s. The bookcase as a form of furniture developed during the late seventeenth century, and because of its scale and purpose tended to be architectural in character. The Powderham bookcases are no exception and the closest parallels in contemporary design are to be found in the work of architect-designers, for example, William Kent's design for an organ case published by John Vardy in 1744.[9] When John Channon first set up in London, designers of furniture were looking towards architectural pattern books for inspiration, such as James Gibbs' *A new book of Architecture*, which was first published in 1728 and reissued in parts in 1739.[10] The organisation of the interiors of contemporary bureau cabinets such as that at Kenwood (Pl. 61–4) and that at the Victoria and Albert Museum (Pl. 47–9) probably owes much to an increased awareness of architectural practice, although the end result is architectural fantasy. The closest parallel so far noted with the base of the Victoria and Albert Museum's cabinet on stand (Pl. 113–17) is the chest on stand included in Batty Langley's *City and Country Builders' and Workman's Treasury of Designs* published in 1740.[11]

For ornamentation a wealth of continental designs was published in London and easily available from the print shops in Great Newport Street and the Strand, adjacent to St Martin's Lane. It is probable that John Channon and his circle were familiar with the Bolognese Gaetano Brunetti's *Sixty Different Sorts of Ornaments*, published in London in 1736, or P. Babel's (referred to as Babel of Paris) *A New Book of Ornaments* published in 1752. Details such as ornamental mounts may have been inspired by B. Toro's *Masks and other Ornaments*, published in London in 1745.[12] Contemporary taste was not limited to the latest in continental design, for furniture by this group of cabinet-makers also draws on earlier sources of ornament (see Pl. 125 & 134) such as engravings by the French designer Jean Berain (1637–1711) and more unusually by the Dutch artist Hendrick Goltzius (1558–1617).

There was, however, a tradition of producing furniture with metal inlay in London, one which dated back to the late seventeenth century when it had centred, at least in part, on St Martin's Lane, in close proximity to the Court of St James's and London's expanding residential quarter. That tradition had been inspired by continental prototypes and it is not surprising to find that the earliest workshop associated with the production of furniture embellished with metal inlay was managed by a foreigner, Gerrit Jensen, who is thought to have been of Dutch origin. Jensen is first recorded in London in 1680 when he supplied furniture given by Charles II to the Emperor of Morocco. In 1694 he was paid by the royal household for 'A wrighting table with a cabinet to set over it and a large glass case upon a cabinet with Door finely Inlay'd with mettel for the closet of Whitehall' for £200, and in the following year he charged £70 'For a fine writing desk table inlaid with mettal'.[13] This is almost certainly the writing desk inlaid with pewter and brass which is still in the Royal Collection.[14] On the strength of this example, two similar writing commodes with crested mirrors *en suite*, originally supplied for Ralph, 1st Earl of Montagu, and now at Boughton House, Northamptonshire, are also attributed to Gerrit Jensen (Pl. 8). They are similarly inlaid with pewter, brass and copper.[15]

Gerrit Jensen died in 1715 and his will indicates that he had two houses and a warehouse in St Martin's Lane, premises which he had occupied since at least 1693 and which were situated on the west side of the street (Pl. 7). His business was evidently flourishing at the time of his death, for he also owned a country house at Brook Green, Hammersmith. He was survived by four children, two of whom were sons, Francis and Isaac.[16] Jensen's executors were Henry Lowman, John Hazard and Francis Vandenberghe. Furthermore his workshop included Edward Sloutt, later of Bolton Street, St Giles in the Fields, who 'came to live with Gerret Jenson as his apprentice' in July 1691 and continued as 'his apprentice & journeyman to January 1706'.[17] It is inconceivable that the Jensen workshop tradition was not continued after the master's death and further research in this area may uncover additional evidence.

Slightly later than the work of Gerrit Jensen, and possibly inspired by the productions of his workshop, furniture bearing the labels of G. Coxed and T. Woster, who worked in St Paul's Churchyard from about 1700 to 1736, is sometimes inlaid with stringing lines of pewter on a ground of burr wood stained to resemble tortoiseshell.[18]

8. Writing-commode veneered with ebony, kingwood, pewter, brass and copper, from Montagu House, Bloomsbury, attributed to Gerrit Jensen, c.1692. *The Duke of Buccleuch and Queensberry, Boughton House*

CHANNON'S RIVALS AND THE LONDON MARKET

The simplified use of arabesque patterns in furniture labelled by Coxed & Woster is closer to the furniture attributed to John Channon and makers of his circle than the dense and varied inlay from Jensen's workshop which is much nearer to the Parisian productions of André-Charles Boulle.[19]

Another intriguing London craftsman whose work is relevant in this context is Samuel Bennett, based at the sign of the Cabinet in Lothbury. He was responsible for a bureau-cabinet (*c*.1720) of walnut decorated with arabesque marquetry (Pl. 9 and 44) and surmounted by a broken pediment flanked with fluted pilasters and inlaid on the lower inside of the door with the inscription SAMUEL BENNETT LONDON FECIT.[20] The patterns executed in light wood marquetry on this piece are similar to those found inlaid in brass on some of the furniture that has been associated with John Channon, including the bureau-cabinet with Carlton Hobbs (Col. pl. IV & Pl. 45) and a card table which passed through the London salerooms in 1992 (Col. pl. XII).

The demand for brass-inlaid furniture was almost certainly stimulated by the presence of French 'Boulle' furniture in England, both in private collections and as part of the stock of London dealers. A Boulle writing-table dating from *c*.1700 is recorded at Erddig, Clwyd, in an inventory of 1726 (Pl. 10).[21] Amongst other early evidence for Boulle or brass-inlaid furniture in a private collection is the sale of the collection of Edgeley Hewer 'brought from his seat at Clapham to his house in Buckingham Street, York Buildings' in May 1729, six months after his death.[22] The parlour contained 'a tortoiseshel Buroe inlaid with brass', and the 'Drawing Room' and the 'Best Bedchamber' contained 'an ebony buroe inlaid with brass'. Four years later, the 'Rich Household Furniture' of Sir William Stanhope, Vice-Chamberlain of the King's household and Member of Parliament for Buckinghamshire, consisting of the contents of his house in Albemarle Street, St James's, were sold by the auctioneer Christopher Cock on 25 April 1733.[23] The 'Tapestry and fine Needlework Room' on the ground floor contained 'A French buroe inlaid with brass' which was valued at £4 4s. Another 'French Buroe inlaid with Tortoiseshell and brass' in the Drawing Room was worth six guineas. Perhaps more significant is the 'mahogany Desk and

9. Niche door on bureau-bookcase by Samuel Bennett (see Pl. 44). The marquetry is executed in boxwood set into burr walnut, *c*.1725. *The Trustees of the Victoria and Albert Museum*

10. Boulle writing-table with veneer of tortoiseshell and brass on a pine carcase, *c*.1695, in the collection at Erddig, Clwyd, by 1726. *The National Trust*

Book-case of the most curious Workmanship and ornamented with brass Work finely graved and glass Doors' which was estimated at the very high figure of £50. Judging by the description, this piece was likely to be of English manufacture although it was possibly made by an immigrant craftsman in London.

Two years later, the same auctioneer announced the sale of

The entire Collection of Mr. Wm Hubert, of St. Martin's Lane, (who is leaving off business)... Consisting of several valuable Pictures... with Great Variety of most Beautiful Florence and French Cabinets, inlaid with Oriental Agates, Mocos, Jaspers, Bloodstones and Lapis Lazuli etc., with Bookcases and Buroes richly inlaid, and ornamented with Bronze, finely chased and repaired and gilt with Gold. As likewise great Choice of very curious Bronze Lustres, Girandoles, Andirons, and Branches, gilt and repaired in the finest French Taste.[24]

The London Evening Post announced on 15 April 1740 his sudden death: 'Mr Hubert, a French Gentleman, a great Dealer in Pictures, curious Stones, etc.'[25] His will specifies that all his belongings were left to 'my very dear wife Marianne Gandron to disperse as she pleases'.[26] Early in 1741 a further sale of 'The entire Collection of Mr W. Hubert, late of St Martin's Lane, deceas'd' was held at Ford's auction house in the Haymarket, 'catalogues to be had Gratis at Mrs Hubert's on the Pavement in St Martin's Lane'.[27] Although the notice of this second sale does not specify brass-inlaid furniture, the widow Hubert evidently continued her husband's business for ten years after his death from the same premises in St Martin's Lane. In April 1751 the *General Advertiser* announced a further sale at Ford's auction house (known as 'Raphael's Academy') in the Haymarket which was occasioned by Mrs Hubert's return to France. The sale consisted of

A collection of Italian, French and Flemish Pictures, lately belonging to a Person of Distinction, deceas'd, together with some curious Bronzes, large Italian Cabinets, French Buroe Tables inlaid and ornamented with Brass etc: and likewise a large and capital Picture of the Judgement of Paris by Rubens and the well known cartoon of the Murder of the Innocents by Raphael, both formerly belonging to Mr. William Hubert of St. Martins Lane, deceased; which must now be sold without Reserve... and at the same time will be sold in one lot his curious cabinet of casts, pastes and impressions, containing upwards of 3,000 taken (by particular desire) from the most celebrated and valuable antique gems in the King of France's collection.[28]

Was this collection actually contained in a cabinet as the advertisement suggests, and if so, could it have provided the inspiration for the cabinets, described as medal cabinets, now at Bristol and in the Victoria and Albert Museum (Pl. 113 & Col. pl. XIX & XX)?

It is of course possible that John Channon himself had supplied Hubert with a cabinet to house his collection. Channon was a near neighbour of the Huberts in St Martin's Lane for fourteen years and would certainly have been familiar with their stock. Furthermore, surviving evidence points to Channon's having operated in a very similar capacity as a dealer in furniture, frames, paintings and prints. The inscription on the Powderham bookcases provides the only certain evidence for Channon's being personally responsible for the manufacture of furniture which he supplied. There is however substantial evidence to suggest that there were other London suppliers of brass-inlaid furniture. In February 1737, the year in which John Channon is first recorded in London, the *London Evening Post* announced that

John Renshaw, Cabinet-Maker, in Brook-Street, Holbourn, over-against Gravel-Street, having now finish'd a very curious Desk and Book-Case, which is allow'd by the Best and most impartial Judges, to far excel any Thing of the Kind that has ever been made, for its Beauty, Figure and Structure, which are very extraordinary. It chiefly consists of fine mahogany, embellished with Tortoiseshell, fine Brass Mouldings and Ornaments, with Palasters curiously wrought after the Corinthian Order. The Inside is compos'd in the most beautiful and convenient Manner; and it being Propos'd by Several Persons of Distinction to have it raffled for; Mr. Renshaw intends to dispose of it accordingly, at so easy a Rate as 2s 6d, each Chance, which doth purchase one 1699th Part of the said Desk and Book-Case, which is agreed to be raffled for by Mr. Foubert's Patent Mathematical Machine, it being impossible to use any Fraud or Deceit with it.

11. Advertisement print signed Potter. This may record furniture produced by a Thomas Potter who was in partnership with John Kelsey in the late 1730s.
The Trustees of the Victoria and Albert Museum

N.B. Notice will be given when and where it will be decided, so that everyone that pleases may be satisfy'd in the Disposition of their Fortune'.[29]

This description is very close to the bureau-cabinet acquired by the Victoria and Albert Museum in 1953 (Pl. 47), but is also strangely similar to the description of the desk and bookcase in Sir William Stanhope's sale four years earlier.[30] Was the design perhaps inspired by a knowledge of the latter?

In addition to the documentary evidence for brass-inlaid furniture cited above, there is also contemporary visual evidence. An advertisement print in the Victoria and Albert Museum which illustrates gaming-tables and commodes with sophisticated sprung mechanisms and a central cabinet on stand (Pl. 11) is signed Potter and may be linked with the Mr Potter recorded as a cabinet-maker in High Holborn in 1737.

20 CHANNON'S RIVALS AND THE LONDON MARKET

This may be Thomas Potter who is recorded as the partner of John Kelsey and who supplied furniture to Sir Richard Colt Hoare for Barn Elms House, London, in 1738. The fact that Kelsey's address was recorded in 1746 as 'over against the Bull and Gate in Holborn' adds credence to this suggestion.[31] In view of their close geographical proximity, was Thomas Potter perhaps connected with the John Renshaw cited above? It is worth remembering that Holborn was close to Clerkenwell, already an established centre of cabinet-making, but also renowned for its association with the watch trade, and its specialist craftsmen making brass watch parts including chains and cases. There may also be a connection with the William Potter who subscribed to John Furber's *Twelve Months of Flowers* in 1730, although Potter is a common name. The cabinet on stand is very similar in design to that acquired by the Victoria and Albert Museum in 1964 (Pl. 133).

The trade card (dating from about 1745) of Landall & Gordon, who describe themselves as 'Joyners, Cabinet & Chair-Makers at ye Griffin & Chair in Little Argyle Street by Swallow Street', illustrates (Pl. 12) a tea-chest on paw feet with a stylised bird-head escutcheon and bell-flower motifs in the corners. This is close to brass-inlaid examples in the Victoria and Albert Museum and in a London private collection (Pl. 162–3). A tea-chest with simple brass inlay, stamped T. LANDALL (Pl. 13), was

12. Trade card of Landall & Gordon, c.1745, which depicts their shop sign, and features a tea-chest suggesting that this may have been a special line. *The Trustees of the British Museum*

13. Tea-chest, mahogany with brass strings, c.1745, impressed along the top edge T. LANDALL. *Private collection*

recorded in a private collection, although its present whereabouts is unknown. Such tea-chests are recorded in contemporary collections: for example, the sale of the effects of the architect Nicholas Hawksmoor and the Hon. Colonel Mercer, Justice of the Peace for Middlesex who had died in November 1739, in 1740 included a 'neat mahogany tea chest with cannisters, ornamented with brass' valued at £9.[32] Thomas Landall, who was in partnership with John Gordon, also made 'Tables, Chairs, Setee-Beds, Looking-Glasses, Picture-frames, Window Blinds, & all sorts of Cabinet Work'. It is extremely likely, therefore, that this partnership was also producing other forms of brass-inlaid furniture.

Another source of brass-inlaid furniture in the 1730s was Frederick Hintz, who operated from the sign of The Porcupine, Newport Street, near Leicester Fields. In May 1738 the *Daily Post* announced the sale of 'A Choice Parcel of Desk and Book-Cases of Mahogany, Tea-Tables, Tea-Chests Tea-Boards, etc. all curiously made and inlaid with fine Figures of Brass and Mother of Pearl. They will be sold at a very reasonable Rate, the maker, FREDERICK HINTZ, designing soon to go abroad.'[33] This was John Frederick Hintz, of German birth, and a member of the Moravian brotherhood in London who died here in 1772 (see p. 28).[34] He has been identified as the Frederick Hintz of Ryders Court, Leicester Fields, whose label appears on stringed instruments dating between 1740 and 1776 and who was appointed 'Guitar-maker to her Majesty and the Royal Family' in 1763.[35]

Yet another possible source for the production of brass-inlaid furniture was a cabinet-maker in Soho called Trotter with whom the young Swiss-German George Michael Moser first worked when he came to London from Shaffhausen in 1726 'as a chaser for the brass decoration of cabinets, tables and such articles of furniture as required those species of ornaments, which at that time were in fashion'.[36] It is possible that this was the John Trotter recorded as an 'upholder' (or broker, see p. 46) and cabinet-maker who took out a Sun Insurance Policy in 1746/7 on the contents of his apartments and timber workshops over the sculptor Roubiliac's workshops on the east side of St Martin's Lane.[37]

J. Graveley is another name connected with this group of brass-inlaid furniture. The name is branded on the base of a bureau-cabinet of mahogany with rosewood cross-banding with engraved brass inlay which was sold at Sotheby's in 1963 (Pl. 50–2). No cabinet-maker of this name has yet come to light, but there was an upholsterer called Michael Graveley working in Davis Street between Grosvenor Square and Berkeley Square in 1749.[38] He may be identified with an apprentice of that name from Hatton in the county of York, who was apprenticed to the Huguenot upholsterer Remy George in London in April 1712.[39]

The likely producers of this type of furniture are recorded as operating in the 1730s and 1740s, but the market for brass-inlaid furniture was still flourishing in the 1760s and 1770s. There is evidence that one contemporary English designer was interested in French Boulle. A drawing in the Victoria and Albert Museum records a Boulle armoire (tall cupboard) and probably dates from the mid-1740s (Pl. 14). It has been attributed to John Vardy (d.1765) by comparison with his signed drawing of a *bureau plat* (flat-topped writing-table) then in Richard Arundale's collection at Allerton Park, Yorkshire. On the other hand, it is surprising that Thomas Chippendale's work, which is often French in character, reveals so little evidence of the use of inlaid brass as decoration, although such furniture passed through his hands. In 1759, he supplied a French tortoiseshell and brass commode to Dumfries House (Pl. 15).[40] The third edition of his *Director* included as plate CXXII 'Designs for Cabinets' in which the 'Ornaments may be of Brass or Silver, finely chased and put on; or they may be cut in Filigree-Work, in wood, Brass or Silver' (Pl. 90) and plate CXXXIV, a library-

14. Drawing of a boulle armoire, attributed to John Vardy, c.1746, on the strength of a comparison with the signed drawing of a *bureau plat* in the collection of Richard Arundale at Allerton Park. *The Trustees of the Victoria and Albert Museum*

15. Boulle writing table with veneer of tortoiseshell and brass supplied by Thomas Chippendale in 1759 for Dumfries House. *Private collection*

table with 'its Ends in a curve Shape' in which 'the Ornaments are intended for Brass-Work'.

The trade card of Pierre Langlois, who was operating from Tottenham Court Road in about 1760, advertised 'all Sorts of Fine Cabinets and Commodes made & inlaid in the Politest manner with Brass and Tortoishell'. One commode attributed to this maker bears a mount with a crowned C stamp, used on French bronzes between 1745 and 1749 as a duty mark. If this piece was of London manufacture, it provides intriguing evidence that contemporary French ornamental mounts were being imported (see p. 44).[41]

Evidence for the continuing popularity of French brass-inlaid furniture is gleaned partly from the wealth of sale catalogues which survive from the decade in which Mr Christie started his business as an auctioneer. In December 1766 'A Catalogue of the Genuine Houshold Furniture of a Noble Personage (deceas'd)' included a 'Variety of Cabinet Work in Mahogany, Rosewood, Japan, Tortoishell, inlaid with brass' and specifically 'a commode dressing table curiously inlaid with brass and tortoishell' and a 'tortoishell commode inlaid with brass', a 'set of dressing boxes, inlaid with brass tortoiseshell & a dressing glass' (which were bought by Sir Hugh Bailey), two very fine clocks and pedestals curiously inlaid with brass and tortoiseshell (one described as a fifteen-day clock by Daille) and a pair of stands inlaid with brass and tortoiseshell. The sale of the household furniture of Lord Bathurst at his house in St James's Square in May 1771 included 'a brass and tortoiseshell inlaid commode' which was bought by Lord Beecham for £25.[42]

Three years later Christie's sale of the effects of Richard Bateman included two 'neat tortoiseshell' commodes 'inlaid with brass' and a similar cabinet.[43] In 1777 the catalogue of 'Household Furniture of Sir Thomas Robinson at his late Residence adjoining Ranelagh House, Chelsea' provides more evidence for French Boulle, including in the Saloon 'an elegant *tortoiseshell commode* elaborately inlaid and ornamented with brass, lapis lazuli, pearl, etc and green coier [sic] ⟨cover⟩' which fetched £13 2s 6d and 'a French *Spring Clock*, the case elegantly design'd inlaid and embellish'd with brass or moulu' which fetched ten guineas. The Principal Dining Parlour contained '*a French commode* of distinguished elegance composed of brass, elaborately inlaid and magnificently embellished with or moulu, the top a high polished black yellow slab' which fetched £9 19s 6d; its pair, 'the embellishment varied but equally splended', fetched seven guineas.[44]

The evidence provided by sale catalogues in the 1720s and 1770s indicates that most of the second-hand brass-inlaid furniture on offer was French. This is reinforced by the occasional advertisement in the contemporary press. In May 1775 both the *Public Advertiser* and the *Morning Chronicle* announced the sale of the effects of 'a Lady deceased at her late Dwelling-house in Percy Street, Rathbone Place' which included 'a curious antique Tortoiseshell Commode inlaid with Brass'.[45] Is this the earliest recorded use of the term 'antique' in its modern sense? The epithet French remained highly fashionable and was used to market 'antique' as well as contemporary furniture. In August 1776 Kennet & Vernon, upholders, cabinet-makers, and undertakers, near Air Street, Piccadilly, assured their public that 'They have always on Sale a great Variety of fine Pin and other Glasses, Secretaires, elegant French inlaid and japanned Knife-cases, Pembroke Tables with rising Desks; Trou Madame, King and Queen, and Portobello Tables; Cylindrical Writing Tables, French inlaid Dressing Tables, Cabriole Chairs, Sophas, Confidants a la Pompadour, and inlaid Works of all kinds.'[46] The phenomenon of English eighteenth-century brass-inlaid furniture was certainly inspired by French prototypes, and this relationship is explored in greater detail in chapter 5.

4. The continental context: Germany

Helena Hayward and Sarah Medlam

The question of the relationship between the known brass-inlaid furniture, and in particular the Powderham bookcases and the other carcase furniture, and German furniture was raised by Symonds in 1956.[1] Since then the general feeling amongst writers on this group has been that the large scale of the pieces and the ambitious designs of the carcases, with curves often in two planes, must indicate influences from outside the sphere of standard English cabinet-making practice and in particular from Germany. Though the dish-topped tea tables might be seen as English pieces with a few exotic touches, the core group of cabinets and commodes are simply too flamboyant, too much in the continental tradition of *meubles d'apparat* not to be the result of some sort of collaboration or shared influence. This chapter seeks both to support some of those ideas and to demolish others. Some of the parallels between the more elaborate carcase furniture of the brass-inlaid group and the forms of furniture and the varieties of decoration found on pieces from Germany will be illustrated and discussed and suggestions made for the links between German and British practitioners of the technique. However, these parallels are not merely a question of Channon and his fellow users of brass absorbing new ideas and methods and motifs from what they saw of continental furniture. The flow of ideas clearly went in more than one direction and we must consider the factors which led cabinet-makers and patrons to look to other countries for ideas, and the routes of transmission of influences.

That John Channon himself should have been open to influences from the European mainland is unsurprising in terms both of his individual history and of his status as a London cabinet-maker of evident standing. From his childhood in Exeter he must have been conscious of the whole of continental Europe as a web of trading links. The sophisticated relationship of Exeter with its European trading partners in the wool trade has been mentioned in chapter 2. This contact clearly affected the architecture in local ports such as Topsham, which has many houses with Dutch gabling, and woodcarving in and around the city also reveals borrowings from Continental pattern books as early as the sixteenth century.[2] Contact was particularly close with Hamburg and Rotterdam, and the ships trading with those ports were each making as many journeys annually as those trading with London.[3] Barings were the most prominent of the German merchant families who settled in Exeter, but there were others from Bremen and Frankfurt as well as Hamburg,[4] while members of one Exeter family of merchants in the late eighteenth century had settled in Leghorn, Genoa and Nova Scotia as well as Topsham.[5] The idea of absorbing ideas and practice from overseas would have been well known to Channon from his earliest years.

When Channon moved to London in 1737, the German cabinet-maker Abraham Roentgen had already been working there as a journeyman from about 1733, having previously spent perhaps eighteen months in Holland.[6] A memoir written by Ludwig, the youngest son of David Roentgen, and Abraham's grandson, says that Abraham was particularly engaged while in London in 'engraving, making mosaics in wood and producing mechanical devices'[7] and that his work was sought after by 'the most expert masters', by whom he was richly rewarded.[8] Ludwig also states that his grandfather invented 'a mosaic in wood' and was able to work on his own account and market his skills profitably to other cabinet-makers.[9] It is known that he spent about five years in London and for some of this time worked with the firm of William Gomm at Newcastle House, St John's Square, Clerkenwell, but clearly that was not his only contact.[10] Beyond the general description of his specialities, nothing is known of the actual pieces he made while in England. However, two of the specialities attributed to him involved the use of metal, and the third may have done so: the 1730s were not a decade when marquetry was in high fashion and it is likely that the term 'mosaic' covered the use of inlays of brass and mother-of-pearl which are the subject of this study. Certainly when he was with Gomm, in Clerkenwell, Roentgen would have been in the centre of the metal-working trades, among the chasers and engravers, in a fine position to improve his techniques in working with metal. Greber believed that Abraham Roentgen learned the use of engraved brass in England and pointed out that in Germany until that time, engraved decoration on ivory had been more popular.[11] The undoubted implication of the description of his time in England is that he took back with him techniques which were already known in London and to the development of which he may himself have contributed.

Just as some of the English brass-inlaid furniture has frequently been described as having a Germanic appearance, so the early furniture produced by Roentgen in Germany is distinctly English in form. The tea table possibly supplied to the Landgraf of Hesse in 1741 (Pl. 16 & 17) could be taken for one of the English examples except for the fact that the brass is inlaid into fruitwood rather than mahogany, and a bureau illustrated by Hans Huth[12] shows the same combination of fruitwood and brass, on a very simple rectangular piece of the English type which often includes brass inlay. However, the width of this particular one would be unusual in an English example and the upper tier set with a cupboard between two banks of drawers is a distinctly

16. Tea table, by Abraham Roentgen, Herrnhag, possibly made for Landgraf Ludwig VIII von Hessen, c.1745. *Staatliche Kunstsammlungen, Kassel*

17. Detail of the top

German form. The cock beading on the edges of the drawers was an English feature adopted by Roentgen.[13] Interestingly, the main brass on this piece is engraved with a figure of Athene,[14] very close in feeling to the Roman Hero figures after Goltzius found on the Bristol cabinet (Pl. 122–5). Like other cabinet-makers, Abraham Roentgen regularly made use of Augsburg printed ornamental engravings for the decoration of his furniture.[15]

But what of the 'mechanical devices' in which Roentgen was also supposed to have specialised? To look at the forms of Abraham Roentgen's early pieces and then at the advertisement print associated with the obscure Mr Potter (Pl. 12) it is clear that two pieces, the harlequin gate-leg table (Pl. 18) and the adjustable reading stand (Pl. 20), relate directly to the engraved designs on the borders to the sheet (Pl. 19). A later type of drawing table made by Roentgen in some numbers is fitted with a double-hinged top. This makes use of the type of easel mechanism shown on a knee-hole form of base in the Potter advertisement print.[16] Hans Huth has pointed out that there were at that time no German precedents for the harlequin tables,[17] nor do there appear to be any earlier versions of these ingenious pieces in England. The care with which they are depicted may suggest that they were Potter's proud invention. Looking later, to the English brass-inlaid furniture of the 1750s and 1760s, there are similarities in form between the unfolding doors of the Murray cabinet (Col. pl. XVIII) with their two banks of small drawers in the thickness of the doors, and the similar construction on a smaller scale in the dressing tables and commodes made by the Roentgen firm in the 1760s.[18]

Channon may well have known Abraham Roentgen during the single year in which they were both in London (1737), and though this may seem a brief association at best, there is always the possibility that Channon had contact with him later. Certainly Abraham Roentgen valued his connections with England. When he was showing wares at the great Frankfurt Fair in 1754, and not for the first time, the Frankfurt *Intelligenzblatt* described his furniture as 'in the French and English taste'.[19] In later years Roentgen sent one of his best journeymen, Michael Rummer (1747–1812), to work with his old master[20] (perhaps in the Gomm workshops) to improve his skills, after which Rummer returned to Neuwied, where he specialised in the highest quality marquetry. In 1766 Abraham himself returned to England for a visit, at a time when he may have considered transplanting his workshop to London because of religious difficulties.[21] Casting aside this scheme, he nevertheless maintained his contact with England, taking as an apprentice an English-born fellow-Moravian called John Okeley who stayed at Neuwied until 1772.[22]

Abraham Roentgen's position as a member of the Moravian brotherhood is important in establishing a connection with the makers of brass-inlaid furniture in London, if not with Channon himself. One maker of brass-inlaid furniture already mentioned in chapter 3 was Frederick Hintz. The details of items to be sold by him in 1738 are listed in the advertisement quoted on p. 21 and the reason for the sale was given, that Frederick Hintz was 'designing soon to go abroad'.[23] The reason for his planned departure is explained by his recent attachment to the Moravian brotherhood in which he became interested in 1737.[24] The name 'Hinz' appears among the members of the ten-strong German Society set up by Count Zinzendorf in that year from among a group of interested Germans already settled in London.[25] The Moravian records[26] reveal evidence of constant travel between London and Marienborn, near Frankfurt, where the brotherhood first settled in 1736, and subsequently Herrnhag, where they moved in 1741. Indeed, after his sale, Hintz set off for Germany on 13 June 1738 in a group which included Abraham Roentgen and the famous preacher, John Wesley.[27] Hintz was settled in Herrnhag by 1742, as we shall see, but had evidently returned to

THE CONTINENTAL CONTEXT: GERMANY

18. Harlequin-action writing- and games table, by Abraham Roentgen, Herrnhag, c.1750. *The Trustees of the Victoria and Albert Museum*

20. Reading stand, by Abraham Roentgen, Neuwied, c.1750–60. *Schloss Pommersfelden*

19. Detail of the Potter advertisement print (Pl. 11), showing the designs relating to the furniture shown in Pl. 18 and 20. *The Trustees of the Victoria and Albert Museum*

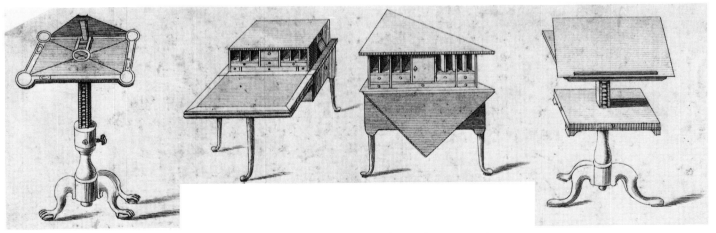

London by 1746.[28] As the community developed in England in the early 1740s, the new recruits included the future wife of Frederick Hintz. She was Ann (or Anna) Williams, born in Derbyshire in 1725, who was received into the congregation in London in 1744.[29] We know that Hintz himself was setting out again for Herrnhag on 22 November 1746, accompanying a distinguished Moravian evangelist (Cennick) and other illustrious leaders of the community.[30] Also in the group was a member by the name of Okeley who was, perhaps, the father of young John Okeley who went to Neuwied in 1766 as Roentgen's apprentice.[31] A week later Ann Williams followed with another group of Moravians[32] and the pair married in the chapel of Schloss Marienborn in April 1747.[33] They returned to London in July of that year as 'Labourers' (church workers)[34] evidently intending to devote their lives to the Moravians. They are described in the records of the Fetter Lane Chapel as being 'away' in 1748, presumably travelling for the community.[35] The chapel was then undergoing refurbishment and a harpsichord was needed which, it was hoped, Hintz would make.[36] This is the first evidence of Hintz's interest in musical instruments, which he may have made at an earlier date and on which he was later to concentrate. The couple's first child, Maria Theresa, was born in June 1751 and in her baptismal record her father is described as a cabinet-maker.[37] In 1752 it is known that they were sharing a house with a warden of the German congregation by the name of Senneff or Senft, who also had an English wife and was a shoe-maker by trade.[38] They were evidently closely-knit, supportive families, and Hintz is recorded in the same year as playing the guitar to soothe his friend on his deathbed.[39] Difficulties had arisen over their role in the Moravian brotherhood as Ann was criticised because she had 'too much of a worldly manner and took an unsuitable affectation of gentility',[40] and as a result of this her husband was advised to return to his trade, advice which, it is recorded, 'seemed heavy to them'.[41]

This return to a craft trade was, indeed, to prove difficult, not least because he soon chose to change his specialisation from that of cabinet-maker to that of musical-instrument maker.[42] He was also harassed by lack of money in 1752, which caused him to beg for help from the Moravians towards the cost of opening his new shop in Newport Street.[43] Yet by 1763 he was established and is recorded as guitar-maker to Her Majesty.[44] Despite this apparent success, Hintz's life at this time seemed to become increasingly gloomy. His wife died in 1763[45] and his relationship with the brotherhood waned. His burial in 1772 in the Moravian cemetry at Chelsea was allowed only as a result of his son's appeal. 'Poor Hintz', as he is referred to in the records, was finally buried near his wife.[46] A number of previous accounts refer to musical instruments by Frederick Hintz or Hinds dated between 1740 and 1776.[47] In view of the date of his death the latter date must be a misreading.

The connection of Abraham Roentgen and Johann Friedrich Hintz was closer than merely that of joint membership of the same religious community. Lack of cabinet-making facilities in Marienborn, where Roentgen arrived in 1738, led him to turn to a new life as a full-time worker for the church. Soon he was travelling again. In 1740 he set off from Germany to Carolina, to undertake, as Hintz was also to do, the role of church worker rather than cabinet-maker. But, as proved crucial for his future career, he suffered shipwreck in Ireland, and returned in June 1742 to settle in the new Moravian centre at Herrnhag,[48] after time spent in both Ireland and Holland. At that point, without house or workshop or tools, he was helped by his old associate, described as a 'professional colleague', Johann Friedrich Hintz, who had been received into the faith at Marienborn at about the same time as Roentgen.[49] Hintz was then already set up as a successful 'independent master' and the owner of a two-storey house. Knowing that Roentgen would like to earn 'as much as possible', Hintz offered him work, a workbench and the necessary tools. He was also ready to give Abraham a room in his house as temporary refuge, which was gladly accepted.[50] This generous offer and the description of them as 'professional colleagues' justifies the conclusion that they first collaborated in London in the making of brass-inlaid furniture.

Bearing in mind the sort of decoration found on some of the earlier furniture by Roentgen, could we attribute to Hintz's workshop some of the English tea tables decorated with detached brass plaques on which the decoration is entirely engraved

THE CONTINENTAL CONTEXT: GERMANY

and owes nothing to fine cutting or piercing (Col. pl. xxv)? Interestingly, this conclusion has been reached independently, by stylistic analysis of the furniture, in chapter 8. This raises the question of the precise relationship between the work of Hintz and Roentgen. Did Roentgen indeed invent brass and wood 'mosaic' (see p. 25), or was he developing a technique to which Hintz introduced him? Certainly he remained open to influences from England. In a printed circular which seems to have been sent out in 1772, his son David Roentgen described himself as an 'English cabinet-maker', and offered mahogany furniture with 'English locks and gilt ormolu'.[51] In that description he may have been making a general commendation of the goods, or he may have been giving an exact description. Nicholas Goodison[52] records the dramatic increase in the British overseas trade in brasswork after 1698, and quotes Defoe's comments of 1728 on the huge amounts sent to 'Holland, France, Italy, Venice, and to all Parts of Germany, Poland and Muscovy'. Defoe also records that some aspects of the metal trades had penetrated even the highest ranks of French interiors: 'Locks of all the fine Palaces of France, if narrowly inspected, will be found to be English'.[53]

But even leaving aside the question of specific links between Hintz and Roentgen, there are more general questions of relationship between Britain and Continental Europe which may have influenced the appearance of furniture particularly in the north German Protestant states of Hanover, Prussia and Saxony, whose princely and regal courts all provided a ready market for cabinet pieces displaying new forms and techniques from England and Holland as well as from France. The accession of George I in 1714 resulted in much coming and going between London and Hanover, and although the King himself preferred life in Hanover a constant exchange of ideas promoted in Germany an admiration for English craftsmanship. Hepplewhite's statement of 1788 that 'English taste and workmanship have, of late years, been much sought for'[54] is a casual reference to a highly important phenomenon which had been developing in European furniture design since the early eighteenth century.

The Prussian court archives contain many references to 'English cabinets' being made in Berlin. Queen Sophia Dorothea, wife of Frederick William I of Prussia, was a daughter of George I, and her cabinet-maker, Martin Böhme, is known to have supplied two 'English writing cabinets' in 1724/5.[55] A table supplied to her by him, using brass inlay on a ground of tortoiseshell, is shown in Pl. 22. Others working in Berlin in the English style in the first half of the eighteenth century included Franz Zurcher, who provided in 1728 a walnut writing-cabinet and a writing-table fitted with drawers.[56] A year previously, another Berlin cabinet-maker, whose name is not recorded, advertised his skills, acquired in London, Paris and Holland, in the use of brass, tortoiseshell, cedar and other woods for making 'French and English cabinets'.[57]

A number of 'English' pieces made by Böhme for his royal patron were subsequently given as gifts by Sophia Dorothea to her daughter, Fredericka Louisa, wife of the Margrave of Brandenburg-Ansbach; they survive today in the Ansbach Residenz. Like Berlin, Ansbach was also a Protestant court, and there were other dynastic connections with England as a result of the marriage of Caroline of Ansbach to the future George II in Hanover in 1705.

English influence was also strong in Saxony in the first half of the century and we find the Dresden cabinet-maker, Peter Hoese (1686–1761), who had worked in Italy and France and was experienced in the use of brass and tortoiseshell, providing 'English tables' in 1726 and 'English writing tables' in 1728.[58] In 1749, Michael Kümmel of Dresden (to whom has been attributed a splendid item of German cabinet-

30 THE CONTINENTAL CONTEXT: GERMANY

21. Bureau-cabinet, attributed to Michael Kümmel, Dresden, c.1750. *The Trustees of the Victoria and Albert Museum*

22. Top of a games table, by Martin Böhme, Berlin, c.1720, made for Queen Sophia Dorothea. *Schloss Charlottenburg, Berlin*

making, the cabinet made for Augustus the Strong (Augustus III), King of Poland and Elector of Saxony, now in the Victoria and Albert Museum (Pl. 21)) was described as 'a young man highly skilled in working brass and exotic woods and experienced in the decorative French and English designs'.[59]

In Mainz, from 1719, a writing-cabinet of architectural design, with columns, became one accepted form for the masterpiece required by the guild regulations,[60] and thus an English form of bureau which had developed in the late seventeenth century and which was still current, as we see from the many brass-inlaid versions, in the mid century in London, was given popular affirmation by its new status in northern Europe.

Not only were cabinet-makers describing themselves as English; the term extended to pieces of furniture, and aspects of their design. By about 1700 in Berlin a form known as an 'Englische Stuhl' was current. This was the high-backed caned chair which had been fashionable in Holland and Britain from about 1680.[61] Baltzer Sonneman, a chairmaker, delivered 'Englische Stuhle' to the court in 1726[62] and as late as 1733 a Johann Wunderlich also supplied eighteen 'Englische Stuhle'.[63] Somewhat earlier, in Dresden, in 1710 Augustus the Strong ordered twelve splat-back chairs 'in the English style'.[64] Further north, in Sweden the makers of cane-seated chairs called themselves 'English chair-makers'[65] and the use of the title 'English cabinet-maker' was a general term of self-advancement in Holland, Germany and Denmark by the mid century. Even at the other end of the continent, in Turin in the 1730s and 1740s, the value of 'English' as a recommendation for furniture is illustrated by the use of the term *scrivania all'inglese* to describe a bureau made by Pietro Piffetti for the Queen's apartments in Turin.[66] The continuation of the form is evidence of British

THE CONTINENTAL CONTEXT: GERMANY 31

design giving as well as taking inspiration from mainland Europe. English furniture also enjoyed popularity in Spain and Portugal. The use of the term 'English' for locally made pieces was often more a guarantee of quality rather than a description of the style of the pieces, and they may appear to English eyes to be somewhat exotic interpretations of English forms.

One of the reasons for this interest in the English style was the export trade in furniture from Britain, particularly to ports such as Hamburg[67] and Danzig (Gdansk), the figures for direct exports probably greatly increased by 'hidden' exports which travelled overland from Rotterdam and Amsterdam. The keenest and so far the only consistent scholar working on the export of furniture from Britain has been the late Edward Joy. In his unpublished thesis for the University of London in 1955,[68] in his subsequent working notes[69] and in a number of articles,[70] he discussed the considerable extent of this trade and gave figures which still remain the only accessible account. Though a few imported pieces surviving in Scandinavian collections have been published,[71] there is no similar record of imported pieces in Germany, but it must be from actual pieces that the forms of the knee-hole desk and the bureau were accepted into Germany, engraved designs for furniture not being commonly available until the second half of the eighteenth century. The dominance of German states in central Europe would also suggest that some of the British patterns were transmitted to Scandinavia in particular by the influence of cabinet-makers who had seen pieces in Germany. The rapidly developing export business of the Roentgen family may have been modelled on English firms. It was a very large scale undertaking, the first of its kind in Germany, but although it enjoyed courtly patronage it was never under the direction of any court.

The strong German tradition of *Wanderjahre*, the periods of travel which were part of the training of German craftsmen, was well established before the eighteenth century and provides another line for transmission of designs. The movement of craftsmen was determined partly by the religious or dynastic connections of their state, or by personal religious preference, though Paris, of course, remained the great magnet of fashion. During the eighteenth century the practice of craftsman migration is particularly well recorded for German cabinet-makers moving to Paris, either for periods of training or to establish themselves permanently. Although Huguenot immigration into Britain is well documented, little is known of Catholic French craftsmen or German craftsmen coming to England, although the idea of German immigrants providing new specialist skills was well instanced in the metalwork trades,[72] and was indeed recorded in the furniture trades in London as early as the sixteenth and seventeenth centuries.[73] In the later eighteenth century the contribution of a few highly skilled immigrants or visitors has been individually investigated (Pierre Langlois,[74] Christopher Fuhrlohg[75] etc.). A cursory reading of the *Dictionary of English Furniture Makers*[76] for foreign names is frustating, but yields some interesting points. French names dominate, particularly those of carvers and upholsterers. German names occur much less frequently, but their occurrence may be distorted, because so many names could be easily anglicised. In 1713–14 Henry Deickard (or Deckard) was recorded in the parish of St-Martin's-in-the-Fields as a cabinet-maker. Heinrich Steinfeldt (sometimes recorded as Steinfield) (1711–59) was a 'German cabinet-maker' in Warwick Street, Golden Square, and is known to have worked for Benjamin Mildmay, Earl Fitzwalter and in 1754 for the Earl of Ancaster,[77] while the upholder Nathaniel Spindler was active in Bread Street from 1703 to 1717. In 1727 Joachim Falck was recorded as a joiner in Southwark, and a tallboy by him is known. Donald Johnston recorded five other cabinet-makers whose deaths were listed in the German Church at the Savoy.[78] Such sporadic but solid evidence reveals a German cabinet-making presence, beside the metalworkers and the musical-instrument makers, another special grouping whose skills sometimes overlapped with those of the furniture makers and whose ranks Frederick Hintz joined in the latter part of his life. Visiting craftsmen are even more shadowy figures, and may well remain so, as this sort of travelling for experience inevitably took place before a craftsman had the money and training to establish himself.

Of British craftsmen travelling our ideas are similarly shadowy. There is early reference to a craftsman called Charles King employed as sculptor and carver to the Court at Berlin from 1703 until his death in 1751 and working in a version of the local style.[79] In London, Peter Hasert, before 1746, was excusing himself for late work by writing that he had a workman away, abroad.[80] He himself was a French immigrant and died in Paris while on a journey to Italy. Roentgen's dealings with the apprentice Okeley have been discussed earlier and Thomas Chippendale certainly visited Paris in 1768. These meagre examples of recorded instances however, should not lead us to conclude that travelling was unknown, and certainly the Moravian records contradict this view.

The claim of continental ancestry for some of the brass-inlaid pieces is based first on parallels of form and decoration. The scale of the Powderham bookcases relates to the large baroque armoires found in slightly different forms throughout northern Europe from the end of the seventeenth century, which continued to be produced until the middle of the eighteenth.[81] Pl. 23 illustrates an armoire, made in Brunswick between 1731 and 1735, with the monogram of Duke Ludwig Rudolf of Braunschweig-Wolfenbüttel and his Duchess, Christine Luise, which is now in the Kestner Museum, Hanover. It carries ivory and pewter marquetry, a reduced version of boulle, which

23. Large clothes-press, Brunswick, c.1731–5, made for Duke Ludwig Rudolf von Braunschweig und Wolfenbüttel, and his Duchess Christine Luise. *Kestner Museum, Hanover*

THE CONTINENTAL CONTEXT: GERMANY

24. Bookcase, by Johann Georg Nestfell, Wiesentheid, 1725, made for Count Rudolf Franz Erwein von Schönborn. *Schloss Pommersfelden*

relates its decoration as much as its form to the practices of John Channon. The confident curve of its cornice and the bold carved foot 'mounts' remind us of the Powderham pieces, as does the general 'low-waistedness' of the design. It is said to have been made for Schloss Salzahlum, near Brunswick.[82] Of almost the same date are the idiosyncratic series of collectors' cabinets made for the Graue Schloss in Brunswick in 1730–1, which carry the arms of the Dukedom of Brunswick, with large panels of pierced and engraved brass in Berainesque designs on both tiers.[83] An even closer parallel is the large bookcase now at Schloss Pommersfelden, made in 1725 by Johann Georg Nestfell, who was then cabinet-maker to Count Rudolf Franz Erwein von Schönborn at Schloss Wiesentheid (Pl. 24). This is the richest of a number of cabinets at Pommersfelden. The brasswork forms a pierced fret rather than an inlay, and is supplemented with carved giltwood details to set off the walnut. The pierced frets incorporate the initials of Count Rudolf. Like the Powderham bookcases in British furniture, these cabinets serve primarily as symbols of luxury and grandeur in German furniture.

The curving broken pediment on the Powderham bookcases finds some parallels in German furniture forms. There are similarities to a mirror-mounted bureau made in Dresden in 1725–30 attributed to Johann Gottfried Heinrich Grahl[84] (d.1734), and a cabinet of c.1730 from Brunswick[85] shows the same form in a piece with walnut marquetry, the ivory inlay incorporating figures below baldachinos, and plaques engraved with baskets of flowers and lily heads. Of particular interest in terms of the relationship between Hanoverian and English furniture of the mid-eighteenth century is the cabinet on stand made for George II in about 1750 (Pl. 25), now in the Herrenhausen-Museum, Hanover. This piece was illustrated in the 1970 edition of Kreisel,[86] with the identification 'English?'. In the 1983 edition (Kreisel and Himmelheber) it was dropped, presumably because its Englishness was by then undisputed. Yet to British eyes it looks no obvious native of London, and the use of walnut would no longer be in the highest fashion in London by the mid-century.

The rounded forms of some elements on furniture from the brass-inlaid group, in particular the low bombé forms of some of the bases of pillars or pilasters, as on the Powderham bookcases (Pl. 133) and the Carlton Hobbs bureau (Col. pl. IV), relate more to Dutch developments of the bureau or cabinet (it should be remembered that Roentgen worked in Holland as well as in London during his years away, and the unknown German maker quoted on page 29 was said to have worked also in Holland) or to the bombé bases so regularly used on Dutch clocks of the eighteenth century. Where these elements occurred on German furniture, they were related to Dutch influences, as they were when they occurred in England. A very large armoire of this form, with bombé bases to the columns dividing the front and with a towering broken-scrolled pediment is illustrated in Kreisel and Himmelheber.[87] This piece is attributed to the workshops of Johann Köster in Tønder, Schleswig-Holstein, and dated to the 1750s.[88] Bearing in mind the date, it is less easy to talk of direct continental influences on Channon, reaching him with a significant time-lag, than to talk of him as a cabinet-maker with a marked awareness of foreign possibilities. Certainly the states of the north-western seaboard of Europe, in particular Schleswig-Holstein, produced some of the furniture most superficially similar to pieces in the brass-inlaid group. In particular some of the bureaux produced in the Altona region in the 1740s to 1770s maintain the rococo forms throughout and show adventurous profiles and an opulent contrast of veneers and giltwood reminiscent of the Powderham bookcases and of the metal mounts on the commodes.[89] They seem to be the last occurrence of the Channon taste.

The concave curvatures which make the Channon library commodes so unusual as forms in British furniture, and so challenging to the cabinet-maker, certainly make one think first of German furniture and in particular that of Saxony. The Augustus Rex cabinet in the Victoria and Albert Museum (Pl. 21) shows perhaps the most elaborate curving of marquetry ever attempted, but a cabinet made for the royal castle of Rosenborg in 1755 (Pl. 26) by Christian Friedrich Lehmann, the German-born cabinet-maker to the court in Copenhagen, follows its spirit quite closely. If we look at the lower sections of both these cabinets, we can see close similarities with some of Chippendale's designs. In plate CXXII of the 1762 edition of the *Director* (Pl. 90), we see a very similar shape, elevated on a stand to form a cabinet.

To turn from form to decoration, there are scattered examples of brass inlay in

German furniture, in every grade of complexity, but the technique was clearly a speciality (as in Britain). The use of brass for lining flutes was well known in France and Holland by the early eighteenth century, and this was a practice also followed in Germany. But among the furniture using inlay of brass stringing and plaques there are small, defined groups. Two bookcases made in Potsdam between 1733 and 1740 for Queen Elizabeth Christina, wife of Frederick the Great, demonstrate both an English form and a use of exotic woods with brass that relates to the English pieces. The bookcases are veneered in cedar, walnut and padouk, on oak and lime, with brass inlay and brass handles to the mirrored doors.[90] The use of padouk is particularly interesting in relation to the recent identification of this wood in several of the English brass-inlaid pieces (see chapter 4). At Schloss Charlottenburg, Berlin, there are a number of pieces showing brass marquetry, and more using applied mouldings in brass to outline panels, to edge drawers, or as mountings to the edge of furniture. These pieces mostly date from the 1750s. There is also a pair of low corner cabinets of heavily figured walnut with brass stringing,[91] dating from the 1730s, and an early

25. Medal cabinet, Hanover or London, c.1740–50, made for George II. *Herrenhausen Museum, Hanover*

26. Cabinet, by Christian Friederich Lehmann, Copenhagen, 1755, made for Frederick V of Denmark. *Royal Collections at Rosenborg Castle, Copenhagen*

27. Detail of brass inlay on a corner cupboard, c.1750 *Schloss Charlottenburg*

rococo double-height corner cupboard with brass mouldings, but also with marquetry of flowing scrolls on the top, outlined with brass stringing (Pl. 27).[92]

The tradition of simplifying boulle marquetry into a single marquetry of one metal with a wood veneer established itself almost as soon as the taste for the more elaborate version became widespread. In the Low Countries and in south German centres such as Augsburg there are many desks and cabinets which are decorated with pewter against a ground of amaranth or other exotic wood and sometimes this technique is combined with boulle. In such pieces the designs are often confined by the shape of drawer front or frieze and show groups of figures engraved on plaques of pewter which are not pierced and are not cut out in shapes except along the top edge. The Berainesque plaques on the Powderham bookcases (Pl. 135–8) are cut in this way, with all decoration carried out on the surface of the metal, and with no piercing. A Brunswick armoire in the Kunstmuseum, Düsseldorf,[93] illustrates a development of this into pierced and delicately cut panels of pewter marquetry which are more important for their filigree effect. These relate to the pierced scrolled designs on the British pieces, which reach their greatest sophistication in the Murray cabinet (Col. pl. XVII).

It is the cabinets which are at the heart of this exploration of the Anglo-German connections. Their form and decoration both illustrate a taste which may, for good commercial reasons, have been represented as 'French' in the 1740s and 1750s, but which owes quite as much to the transmutation of French designs and techniques in the work of the best German cabinet-makers of the early eighteenth century. The cabinets are the most ambitious English creations in their use of brass inlay and mounts, and the display of such a cabinet in the centre of the Potter advertisement print (Pl. 11) is surely a firm declaration of their importance in the eyes of their maker. This engraving, and the two cabinets on stands, of which it appears to be a conflated illustration (Pl. 113 & Col. pl. XIX), suggest a wish by Potter to identify himself with the market for furniture of the most dramatic European baroque form and decoration, a market which developed from the modest brass-inlaid pieces made in London by the German, Frederick Hintz and to which John Channon made outstanding contributions. Such a lavishness was not to re-appear again until the demonstrably French boulle work supplied by Daguerre to the Prince Regent and his coterie at the end of the century.

5. The continental context: France
Carolyn Sargentson

By the mid-eighteenth century, the French manner had become the dominant high style in England. While full-scale interior decorative schemes 'à la française' were rare, French furniture and other items were acquired in Britain for collections and furnishing projects, and domestic design and manufacture also played a critical role in the history of design and taste at this period.[1] The advertisements cited in chapter 3 show that French furniture was accessible on the London market, and this included brass-inlaid furniture evocative of the furniture produced in the workshops of André-Charles Boulle, cabinet-maker to Louis XIV. During the late-seventeenth and eighteenth centuries this furniture became the canon for French taste, and many workshops in Paris, London, Holland and Germany produced imitations and interpretations of the work of 'le célèbre Boulle'.

The extent to which English patrons would have understood the design and manufacture of French furniture in the eighteenth century is unclear. While we know that the francophile Lord Chesterfield had a clear understanding of French taste when he wrote 'I am at present in the process of ruining myself by building a fine house here, which will be finished in the French style with abundance of sculpture and gilding',[2] it is also worth noting that when John Loveday visited Erddig in 1732 he wrote in his journal that he saw Henry VIII's writing desk.[3] This comment offers a rare and extraordinary insight into the way in which an unsophisticated eye might perceive a rather standard piece of French boulle marquetry furniture at this date.

The extent to which imported French furniture was a real commercial threat to the British is unclear – very little information on this subject has been published, and it is difficult to get even an impression of the quantity of imports involved. A print of 1757 entitled 'The Imports of Great Britain from France', a satire on French taste, shows French foods and luxury goods on the quayside in London.[4] Customs duties were payable on French imports, and it is clear that this generated a certain amount of fraud. Edward Joy writes about Chippendale's trouble with the customs in 1769, when he underestimated the value of five dozen French chairs which had arrived on the Calais packet (the chairs were unfinished, destined for completion in his London workshops).[5]

The group of London-made furniture under consideration in this book represents one thread within a much larger history of design in Britain 'in the French manner'. This history is well documented in the exhibition catalogue *Rococo Art and Design in Hogarth's England*. It is clear that British views of the French and their design and taste were somewhat ambiguous, even conflicting – while designers and makers were producing rococo schemes for enthusiastic clients, by the mid-century a francophobic polemic was being generated by the Anti-Gallican Society (founded in 1745). Linda Colley suggests that the apparent conflict over the expression of French high style in Britain at this period can be explained in terms of a concerted attempt by the British to compete commercially with the French within the luxury market – 'by

38 THE CONTINENTAL CONTEXT: FRANCE

catering for the public's taste for the French fashions, they reduced the demand for French imports and thus advanced England's own fine art and decorative industries'.[6]

The brass-inlaid furniture made in London during the reign of George II evokes French high style in a number of ways, through the combination of specific materials, the copying of specific models of French mounts, and the relationship between such mounts and exotic veneers. French sources for the design of the brass-inlaid furniture under consideration in this book fall into two categories. On the one hand, the overall relationship between the gilt-bronze mounts and exotic veneers of the London group relates very closely to the French Régence aesthetic of the early part of the eighteenth century, and in particular to the combination of bronze mounts, ebony and engraved-metal inlay associated with the products of the Boulle workshops and its many imitators in France and wider Europe. On the other, Channon used a specific French design by Berain for the Powderham bookcases, and other specific sources can be traced for some of the gilt-bronze mounts used on the commodes and cabinets.

However, some of the forms used by the London workshops are distinctly British and were not part of the French repertoire. Typically French forms used by Parisian workshops were the commode (chest of drawers with two or more drawers), bureau or *bureau plat* (flat-topped writing-table) and armoire. In this respect, while the library table and Southwick Park commode followed the French fashion for commodes veneered with exotic woods and embellished with gilt-bronze mounts, the Bristol and Victoria and Albert Museum cabinets on stands were quite different from French prototypes. Most importantly, the French styles and design sources used by London workshops were, by the 1740s and 1750s, somewhat outmoded in Paris. In many ways, therefore, although these pieces represent stylistic innovation in British furniture, they appear rather backward-looking in a broader continental context.

Specific elements of the London-made group can be related to the French furniture

28. Parquet from Royal Swedish coach, Oppenordt, 1696. *Royal Palace, Stockholm*

29. Powderham bookcase, detail of column. *The Trustees of the Victoria and Albert Museum*

aesthetic and particular design and supply sources. In particular, the Powerham bookcases have been ornamented with several engraved brass plates (see Pl. 135–7). The single source for all these plates is a print after Jean Berain, Pl. 134, the first plate of a set of five panels of ornament, mainly used for tapestries in the eighteenth century France and Germany.[7] In the centre of the Berain panel appear Venus and Love on a shell supported by four winged sirens. Above them is a canopy with drapery held up by two putti – this configuration appears on the front of the pedestals beneath the columns on the bookcases (see Pl. 135). The Berain panel shows a triton holding a nymph at the lower left, and to the right a siren is astride a dolphin – these correspond to the sides of the bookcase pedestals (Pl. 136 & 137). Either side of the canopy, two caryatids hold up a vase from which water is pouring over their heads, and above this motif, separated by a plinth or strapwork band, a fountain – these can be seen on the two lockplates of the main doors of the bookcases, the vase replaced by the opening for the key (see Pl. 138).

The Bristol cabinet is aesthetically analogous to the ebony, tortoiseshell, engraved metal inlay and gilt-bronze mounts traditionally found in the design of Boulle furniture of the Régence period. The only piece within the group to incorporate real tortoiseshell is the Victoria and Albert Museum cabinet (Pl. 36 & 47). The maker of the Bristol cabinet cleverly exploits the visual effect of a veneer of burr wood (yew) to imitate tortoiseshell (see Col. pl. XIX–XX). The shell motif at the centre of the upper section is made up of ebony, brass and burr-wood sections in a manner which directly recalls the boulle aesthetic manifest in furniture such as the parquetry design illustrated in Pl. 33. The effect of this combination is striking, though the overall form of the piece is overwhelmingly English and a Paris-trained eye would be unlikely to mistake it for the product of a French workshop.

The Boulle aesthetic of engraved brass ornament on tortoiseshell or ebony is evoked in other English pieces by a mastic infill, such as the brass-inlaid sections on the Powderham bookcases (Pl. 135), or wood, as used for the roundels of dark veneer and brass on the top of the Victoria and Albert Museum library table (Pl. 107). The Southwick Park commode appears to have a mastic infill in the frieze (Pl. 37). A cabinet assumed to be of German manufacture is also inlaid with some kind of mastic substance to achieve a similar effect.[8]

Several of the London pieces are embellished with gilt-bronze mounts which are copied or adapted from French models. The cockerel-heads key escutcheon at the centre of the Bristol cabinet is extremely close to a model used regularly by the Boulle workshops (see Pl. 30 & 31). The Bristol mount appears to be an adaptation rather than a specific copy in that it is shorter at the base than the French examples, which tend to finish below the keyhole with a single or double twist. The keyhole on the

30. Bristol cabinet (Col. pl. XIX), detail of escutcheon. *Bristol Museums and Art Gallery*

31. Commode, André-Charles Boulle, 1708–9, detail of escutcheon. *Musée de Versailles*

English model is rounded at the base in a typically English manner, rather than straight as was the French tradition. The claw feet terminating in acanthus leaves are also close to the type used by the Boulle workshops, notably for desks and commodes. The mount with the bearded head and wings (Pl. 118) could be inspired by one of Oppenordt's models.[9]

The gilt-bronze mounts which surmount the Bristol cabinet are most unusual – the central, elongated section seems to be inspired by the underside of a carved footplank of a carriage. Such large vases executed in bronze are rarely found on cabinets, though a French exception is the large armoire (Pl. 34), which is surmounted with a range of gilt bronze, including two large vases, two figures and a pair of musical trophies. Alternatively, the vases might have been modelled after those from a carriage, or a vase from a stairway, such as that of *c*.1750 by Caffieri now in the Musée de la Sérrurerie, Paris.[10]

The library table, the Murray writing-cabinet (Col. pl. XVII) and other pieces in the 'nymph and satyr' group share an interesting repertoire of gilt-bronze mounts which have their design sources in Paris some decades earlier. The central pair of London mounts recalls the conventional arrangement of caryatids each side of a fireplace, and the origin of this model may lie in such a design.[11] Several chimney-pieces at Versailles bear female heads cast in bronze at each corner,[12] and a design for a chimney-piece originally at Versailles but later moved to the Château of Compiègne (now destroyed) shows flanking male figures very close to the male corner mounts on the Victoria and Albert Museum library table and the Murray cabinet.[13]

Certainly female mounts (*espagnolettes*) are very characteristic of the French Régence, used in their many forms particularly on commodes.[14] Their disposition, flanking the centre section of drawers on the Victoria and Albert Museum library table, also has some French precedent. Among the ornate bronzes on Louis XV's medal cabinet, delivered to Versailles in 1739 by Gaudreaux (cabinet-maker to the King) and the Slodtz brothers (sculptors), is a central female figure with face and a chute of ornament (Pl. 32). A design survives for this piece by the Slodtz brothers, who are also likely to have modelled the bronzes.[15] Cressent ornaments a pair of bookcases with terms representing the four seasons, though the bust of each term is angled slightly.[16] The model for each of these terms would have been different, whereas the London maker has had two identical mounts cast from a single model, thereby greatly reducing the cost of the embellishment of the veneered carcase.

The design for the dolphin mounts may have their origin in a set of French mounts for a pair of armoires, one of which was formerly in the collection of Machault d'Arnouville, now at Versailles, and the other, in *contrepartie*, in a private collection (see Pl. 34). The eight dolphin mounts flanking each of the five larger dragons on the *armoires* are close to those on the library table. In particular, the left mount at the base of the central pilaster and plinth of the *armoire* is very close to the London model (Pl. 109) in that it has a tail with three fins rather than four, as has its opposite. However, the London and Paris mounts were certainly cast from a different model – close examination shows that they differ in both form and detail.[17] Another possible source for the dolphins is a print published in London by J. Nicholls, supposedly after Jean Berain and engraved by Mersonau, which comprises a side view of a dolphin with a twist in its raised tail.[18]

The knee mounts on the Victoria and Albert Museum medal cabinet, Pl. 117, also follow a French model of the Régence period.[19] Several commodes, made by different makers in Paris around 1715–30, bear corner mounts of almost identical design. These French commodes exemplify the Régence style, which combines a figured veneer, often of only one wood, with dominant gilt-bronze mounts, elaborately worked, at the

32. Medal cabinet, Gaudreaux, 1739. *Musée de Versailles*

I. Musical clock made by Jacob Lovelace (d.1766) and exhibited in London in 1739, lithograph, 1833. *Devon and Exeter Institution*

II. Pedestal, detail, attributed to André-Charles Boulle, c.1700. *Christie's*

III. Commode, stamped F.L. *Maurice Segoura*

IV. Bureau-cabinet, probably by John Channon, c.1740, padouk with brass mouldings and inlay. *Carlton Hobbs*

v. Bureau-cabinet, probably by John Channon, *c.*1740–5, mahogany; brass inlay on the writing slope based on a design by Nicholas Pineau (Pl. 65). *Sotheby's*

VI. Detail of the prospect of the bureau cabinet illustrated in Pl. 70 with a brass rosette, chequered strings and stellar ornament in light and dark woods.

VII. The prospect of the padouk cabinet (Col. pl. IV) showing a pair of engraved harlequin figures and the central spindle mechanism.
Carlton Hobbs

VIII. Harlequin games table, possibly by Potter & Kelsey, *c.*1745, mahogany with brass plates on the knees and feet. *Christie's*

IX. The harlequin games table with the till raised. *Christie's*

x. Anglo-Oriental card-table, padouk, with concertina under-frame and a small frieze drawer, c.1735–40. *Christie's*

xi. The card-table shown extended. *Sotheby's Inc., New York.*

xii. Top of the card-table shown closed, inlaid with engraved brass foliate roundels (compare Pl. 45). *Christie's*

xiii. Top of the card-table shown open, padouk with mother-of-pearl inlay. *Christie's*

xiv. Sideboard table, padouk with brass mouldings and inlay, c.1740–50. Formerly at Vale Royal, Cheshire. *Carlton Hobbs*

xv. Detail of carved mask on apron

xvi. Detail of fronded foot with brass inlay

XVII. The Murray writing-cabinet, probably by John Channon, *c*.1750, mahogany with profuse gilt brass mounts and inlay; formerly at Ochtertyre, Scotland. *Leeds City Art Galleries*

XVIII. The Murray writing-cabinet with the doors and desk drawer shown open

xix. Cabinet on stand, veneered in burr yew with brass mounts, mouldings and inlay, attributed to John Channon, c.1740. *Bristol Museums and Art Gallery*

xx. The cabinet on stand shown open, the hinged flaps inside the doors open to reveal shallow velvet-lined spaces, possibly for the display of miniatures

XXI. Companion half of the back-to-back library table probably by John Channon: the missing mounts have since been replicated. The other half is illustrated Pl. 106–9. *Private collection*

XXII. Commode, probably by John Channon, *c*.1750, mahogany with brass mounts and inlay, the fretwork border around the base and top is filled with black wax; formerly at Southwick Park, Hampshire. *Leeds City Art Galleries*

XXIII. One of the pair of Powderham bookcases by John Channon, 1740, padouk with carved and gilt decoration and brass inlays based on an engraving by Berain (see Pl. 134–8). *The Trustees of the Victoria and Albert Museum*

XXIV. Tea table, possibly by Frederick Hintz, *c.*1745, mahogany, with engraved brass and mother-of-pearl inlay on the top and tripod. *Sotheby's*

xxv. Tea table, mahogany, inlaid with engraved brass plaques and strings, c.1750. *Norman Adams Ltd*

XXVI. Tea table, mahogany, the top inlaid with a simple system of brass strings, centres on a plaque engraved JEG, c.1755. *Sotheby's*

XXVII. Tea table, mahogany, raised on a triquetra support, the top with high-quality brass and mother-of-pearl inlay, c.1750. *Sotheby's*

XXVIII. Pair of tea-chests, burr elm with walnut cross-banding and brass stringing, c.1740–50. *Sotheby's*

corners, feet, and often the *cul-de-lampe* and on the drawers. In this, the Parisian and London commodes are very close – the London workshops were imitating the French fashion of the 1710s–1730s.

However, the disposition of the female mounts differs slightly between the Paris and London versions – while the French commodes are decorated with the mounts on the front corners only, each of the corners on the base of the London cabinet was allocated a mount. Col. pl. III shows a commode stamped F.L., presumed to be by François Lieutaud, of kingwood veneer with female heads at each of the two front corners.[20] A commode veneered with palisander stamped by François Mondon bears the same mount but within a different configuration of gilt-bronze motifs.[21] Another example, a commode stamped by Louis Simon Painsun, bears the same mounts at the front corners.[22] (An early-eighteenth-century commode of sarcophagus form at François Léage, Paris, is also decorated with very similar corner mounts, though they are not identical.) The same model is also used on two *bureaux plats*, one in the Bayerisches Nationalmuseum, Munich, and the other formerly with Galerie Aveline, Paris.[23] Pradère attributes the stamp to the cabinet-maker and dealer (*marchand mercier*) Noel Gérard. Finally, the Musée des Arts Décoratifs have a version of this mount, currently forming part of the display of bronze mounts in the eighteenth-century galleries.

The model was not, therefore, uncommon. The versions differ slightly in their design and execution – on the Victoria and Albert Museum mounts the cresting is finished rather coarsely, and the uppermost scroll is much thicker at the top than those on the commode stamped F.L. (compare Pl. 117 & Col. pl. III). The Mondon and F.L. mounts appear to be more finely chased than those on the London cabinet (indeed, there seems to be very little chasing on the London mounts[24]). In particular, the pattern chased on the winged areas at the side of the female head on the London and Mondon mounts differs, which clearly shows that different chasers, if not founders, were involved.[25] Each set of mounts has been fitted to a veneered carcase of different form and profile, which does not necessarily exclude the possibility that they were cast from the same mould. It is possible that a two-dimensional design was the source – however, none has yet come to light.

The metal composition of the bronzes on the London-made library desk were tested and found to be of the same alloy. This indicates that the mounts were produced by the same founder, in London or Paris. Certainly the quality of this set of mounts is of a high standard (see detail, Pl. 108), and it is tempting to deduce from this that they might be of French manufacture. However, so little is known of the London trade at this time that this is far from conclusive. It is, however, interesting that, with the exception of the dolphin mounts, each of the mounts is cast in pairs. While this is a satisfactory design for the two caryatid mounts, and the corner-foot mounts, the identical male corner mounts do not fit the carcase to the same degree on each side. Whereas the mount on the right corner fits the curving profile of the corner of the commode, that on the left corner fits much less closely. Ideally, a matching pair of corner mounts should have been used, which would have required two moulds. It is possible that the mounts were bought from a London or Paris supplier, rather than designed specifically for this piece, and that the cabinet-maker accepted the compromise in the lack of correspondence between the mounts and the veneered carcase.

In the case of the dolphins, however, mounts cast from the same mould would have been unacceptable. The dolphin mounts on the library table are a matching pair, each cast from a separate mould. However, a detailed examination of each mount shows that they are not identical opposites – the section above the head of the dolphin to the left is flatter and wider than its counterpart. The raised spine of the latter is crisper than the other's. The quality and crispness of the chasing, and perhaps the casting, is greater on the right-hand mount. It is possible that the mould for the first mount was copied in order to produce an identical opposite, but that the form and quality of its design was slightly altered in the two intermediary impressions which would have been produced in its making.

Possible sources for the London workshop producing these mounts include the acquisition of the lead model (from London or Paris) for the mount which would itself be produced in London, the making of a mould which copied the French mounts, either in Paris or London, or the purchase of a mount cast in Paris from the same mould as the mounts on the French commodes.

The design and manufacture of bronze mounts in Paris is a complex and under-researched subject, not least because the bronzes are rarely marked and archival sources difficult to identify. Although cabinet-makers were not, in theory, permitted to produce their own mounts we know that the cabinet-maker Charles Cressent produced gilt-bronze mounts in contravention of his corporate statutes (the Parisian equivalent to guild regulations). The Boulle workshops, through royal privilege, produced mounts for furniture, and these include the best-documented designs for gilt-bronze mounts in the early-eighteenth century,[26] widely copied by Parisian founders for cabinet-makers, dealers and clients. While the Boulle workshop tended to retain control over its gilt-bronze mounts designs, it seems that models for mounts, and copies of mounts, were circulated within the Parisian market-place for embellishments for furnishings.[27] A group of Régence cabinet-makers seem to have shared a repertoire of bronze mounts – this included Lieutaud, Gérard and Poitou, whose known inventories list models for bronze mounts. Gérard and Poitou stocked bronze mounts cast and ready for chasing, which shows their role in the co-ordination of the production and finishing of such mounts.[28] When he was prosecuted by the corporation, Cressent's stock was sold by auction,[29] as were models from the Boulle workshop on the death of André-Charles in 1732. The dealers (*marchands merciers*), too, held their own models for mounts and co-ordinated their production. Indeed, it is interesting that Noel Gérard, a *marchand mercier* with at least one English client,[30] seems to have been involved with at least two of the pieces which relate to the London group. The commode (Pl. 33) is convincingly attributed to him, and the pair of armoires (Pl. 34) may well have been those described in his inventory of 1736.[31] His inventory lists cast models and cast bronze, listing specifically mounts for commodes in ungilded bronze. Unfortunately, no evidence survives to suggest that he was involved in the commerce in bronze models and

33. *Bureau plat*, attributed to Noel Gérard. Bayerisches Nationalmuseum, Munich

THE CONTINENTAL CONTEXT: FRANCE

34. Armoire, boulle marquetry. *Christie's*

mounts, but here may lie the key to understanding the distribution of mounts between different cabinet-makers in Paris and beyond.

Very little is known of the trade and market mechanisms in Paris which would have made the mounts or their design available to a London cabinet-maker. The mounts with crowned C used on the commode made by Langlois in London provide somewhat rare evidence of a Paris-made mount stamped by the corporation of founders for 1745–9. However, copies and imitations of Parisian mounts might have been made in London or Paris. Cressent stated in 1733 that the reason cabinet-makers kept their own models and contravened corporate regulations by having bronze mounts gilded in his workshop was 'because they fear that their models will be stolen'.[32] Svend Eriksen reproduced and translated a document on the safeguarding of bronze models in Paris.[33] The document, drawn up by the *bronziers* in 1766, concerned 'the theft and plagiary which are made daily of their models':

Learning of a fine model they buy or get someone to buy for them the first cast taken from that model and give it to a founder or to an outside workman, and get him to make after-casts which they then have chased either by a master-founder or by an outside workman. The master or outside workman to whom the merchant gives the piece to be copied and to have a cast taken therefrom is well aware that it is a stolen piece and also takes copies for himself to take casts therefrom, and by this means a piece whose inventor has as yet sold only one or very few copies becomes so common that he has no more sale for it.

The outcome of this petition was a series of regulations ordering that designs and models for bronzes be registered with the Office of the Corporation, and forbidding members of the Corporation and others from plagiarising the models.

An early-eighteenth-century dispute over models for bronze mounts documents a specific example, and demonstrates that this issue was current much earlier than the 1760s. On 25 October 1719 François Roussel, *ébéniste du roy*, arbitrated in an argument over money between the cabinet-maker François Lieutaud and his client Sieur Vaultier.[34] Lieutaud had supplied Vaultier with a long-case clock. It was agreed that the value of the components of the clock were as follows: for the cabinetwork 90 *livres*, for the bronzes 90 *livres* and for the models made especially for this clock, 200 *livres*. Roussel decreed that the client should pay for half of the latter, and Lieutaud the other half. Roussel remarks, however, that Lieutaud was convinced that Vaultier had allowed another cabinet-maker to remove the bronzes and take an impression of them. Roussel examined the clock and observed that Lietaud was right, and that there was evidence that the bronzes had been removed from their original position. He continued 'Lieutaud told me that he knew precisely which cabinet-maker was working on them at this moment.' It was agreed that if this could be proved, Vaultier would be obliged to pay the full value of 200 *livres* for the models for the bronzes.

Michael Sturmer cites Campbell's *Description of all Trades* in which he defines the profession of founder in London:

The founder is the man most employed in a brazier's shop: his Business is to cast all Works that are made of brass. He has models generally of the Work designed, to which he fits the mould to cast his metal in: he seldom designs anything himself, and his chief skill lies in melting the brass and running it into the Mould evenly. There are various Sorts of Founders: Founders who cast only for the Coach-Makers; and those who cast Buckles, Studs and Bars for the Saddlers; and Several other sorts of Founders.[35]

The London-based designers and suppliers of models for bronze mounts are little documented. Charles Magniac, who worked for James Cox, was described as a chaser in 1754.[36] Goodison states that Dominique Jean was 'an important supplier of fine mounts to the fashionable furniture-makers'.[37] He married Pierre Langlois' daughter and may well have supplied his father-in-law with gilt-bronze mounts. Other bronze-workers involved in the design, casting and chasing of mounts for furniture at the mid-century include Diederich Nicolaus Anderson, Pyke, William Bent and Brimingham (or Bermingham). The Harache family, too, are intriguing – Thomas was 'a jeweller and dealer in toys, china and ornaments', who had a shop in Pall Mall where Boulton bought some vases in 1768.[38] Pierre Harache of St Martin's Lane was a Huguenot silversmith, whose premises were taken over by William Vile, cabinet-maker, in 1751.[39]

These potential explanations of the relationship between the London brass-inlaid furniture group and the Parisian furniture and bronze trades should be read with some caution. Although it is difficult to imagine the back-to-back library table, the Southwick Park commode and the Murray writing-cabinet without their mounts, or indeed with different mounts, it is important to recognise that there has been since the eighteenth century a considerable trade in gilt-bronze mounts, and it is possible that the examples cited may have originally been fitted with different mounts. However, since the furniture by Channon and his circle has not until recently received much acclaim, it may be safe to assume that pieces are unlikely to have been embellished since their original manufacture.

6. Furniture manufacture and workshop organisation

Josephine Darrah, Sarah Medlam, Anthony North and Kevin Rogers

Trade practices

In the thirty years since the last detailed examination of mid-eighteenth-century English brass-inlaid furniture, which since then has been loosely referred to as by John Channon, eighteenth-century production techniques and materials have undergone a major re-examination. The concept of the master craftsman, executing a large body of commissioned work independent of a labour force, specialist skills or an economically managed business, is now seen as a romantic view of the eighteenth-century furniture trade. Likewise, the notion that mahogany was almost the universal wood used for fashionable eighteenth-century furniture is now recognised as an over-simplification. In fact, by the mid-eighteenth century a wide variety of exotic tropical timbers was available on the London market.

Examination of the construction and materials of some of the brass-inlaid furniture produced in Britain between 1730 and 1765 raises many questions concerning the skills and techniques employed. Our understanding of standard workshop practices needs fuller discussion in relation to the idea of the master craftsman.

Certainly, unsubstantiated Channon attributions should be re-examined. Only the bookcases, each bearing a plaque marked John Channon and dated 1740, can be accepted as indisputably his. A study of construction and levels of technical skill shows that a number of other workshops were producing this ostentatiously decorated furniture; suggestions are made as to the products of these workshops (see chapter 8).

By the 1740s methods of manufacture among a variety of trades had reached a new level of organisation.[1] The change in production techniques of the mid-eighteenth century relied not on the development of labour-saving machinery but on the re-organisation of labour and sub-division of tasks in the manufacturing process. Workers became increasingly specialised and skilled in one particular part of the train of manufacture. When R. Campbell published *The London Tradesman* in 1747, the manner in which goods were manufactured had become highly ordered, with many craftsmen specialising in the production of parts for another trade. The mid-eighteenth-century London workshop was not an independent, self-sufficient entity. Campbell describes the organisation of the 'upholder'[2] or broker, who might employ the skills of 'Cabinet Makers, Glass-Grinders, Looking-Glass Frame-Carvers, Carvers of Chairs, Testers and Posts of Bed[s], the Woolen draper, the Mercer, the Linen-Draper, Several Species of Smiths, and a vast many Tradesmen of the other mechanic Branches'.[3]

The organisation of a cabinet-maker's workshop was equally complex. A cabinet-maker might work under the direction of an upholder but the more successful businesses, in terms both of profit and of innovative design, functioned independently of such a director. The shop would almost certainly sub-contract specialist work, because it would not be economic to employ highly specialised tradesmen full-time.

The most frequently used of the contracted services would be those of the carver.[4]

The brass-inlaid furniture under discussion features many skills and techniques which would not have been within the competence of one craftsman, possibly not even within the remit of a single workshop, and would have been drawn from the wider pool of London trades. The creation of many of these pieces required metalworkers, brass and mother-of-pearl engravers and other craftsmen to carry out complex inlay and veneering, carvers, turners, gilders and joiners. For example, Channon's Powderham bookcases (Pl. 132–43) are decorated with boldly carved and gilt swags of fruit and incorporate engraved brass plates, mastic, and carefully matched veneers (Pl. 35).

The amount of brass-inlaid furniture surviving from this period suggests that it was a minor, though grand, specialism of workshops producing a wider range. The production of such furniture would be split up into separate tasks, each workman being responsible for a certain type of job. This by no means implies that an apprentice was not fully trained in the skills necessary to produce a complete piece of furniture, but rather that the demands of production would compel journeymen, once trained, to specialise in one skill, and masters to employ them in that capacity. It is most unlikely that the master craftsman completed any of those processes himself; his role was that of manager, overseeing the various steps of production, organising the supply of materials and dealing with matters such as design, marketing and book-keeping.

The size of workshops varied. As only three apprentices are recorded in John Channon's shop, his own facilities may have been limited. The inventory of Paul Saunders' stock-in-trade, which Samuel Norman purchased in 1760, lists '32 Benches One with Another', which implies that there were at least as many employees. The layout of this shop is alluded to also in the inventory, with a lower and upper shop, tapestry room, two sheds for the storage of woods and two other storage rooms. The Linnell operation was larger still, with forty to fifty employees by the early 1760s. The inventory taken in 1763 begins in the garrets, moving down through the shop. There were separate spaces for beating and drying feathers, a carving shop, a gilding shop, cabinet shop, chair room, glass shop, an upholsterers' shop (which was highly organised in itself) and a joiners' shop.

The range of skills required within a workshop depended on how parts were assembled for manufacture. Some or many of the components listed in the Linnell and Saunders shops may have been ordered from specialist suppliers. Even the production of much simpler turned chairs involved sophisticated organisation.[5] Chairmakers

35. Book-matched veneers on plinth of the Powderham bookcase (Col. pl. XXIII).
The Trustees of the Victoria and Albert Museum

bought in parts from turners who worked as independent craftsmen, and cabinet-makers (like goldsmiths, tailors or coach-makers) either purchased ready-made parts, or had them made up in batches in their own workshops.

Craftsmen in the employ of Linnell and Saunders were capable of cutting and shaping legs for chairs, tables and many other furniture parts. However, they were shrewd businessmen, working on carefully calculated profit margins. The surviving inventories of contemporary furniture-makers record enormous stocks of furniture elements. The inventories of Saunders, 1760,[6] and William Linnell, 1763,[7] list parts for tables, beds, cabinets and chairs. Paul Saunders had '10 Setts of Mahogany Feet $2\frac{1}{2}$', '61 Sides for Beds', '102 End for Do [beds]', and '30 Mahogany Feet for Breakfast Tables'.[8] In the Linnells' shop, the compiler of the inventory listed '38 setts of claws for pillar and claw tables', '79 pair of mahogany arms for chairs', '122 pair of mahogany arms for chairs', '200 top ribs Do [chairs]', '222 Marlborough feet for tables and chairs Do', '35 table legs with turned toes', '21 pair of O G legs for chairs Do'. Parts intended specifically for cabinets included 'some turned astrigalls for doors', 'a parcel mahogany fronted doors,' and '5 mahogany fronted drawers with partitions'.[9] Interestingly, Samuel Norman's inventory lists 'Brass Wire Work for Dressing Table' and 'Brass wire'.[10]

It is known that certain firms marketed their wares and skills by means of illustration. The Potter advertisement print (Pl. 11) records the wares of an apparently important workshop.[11] It depicts the variety of furniture forms available to the consumer; the large cabinet on stand in the centre may represent a piece of speculative furniture available for purchase, or may have been made to order. Certainly it indicates that the firm (possibly Kelsey & Potter) was capable of producing highly specialised furniture, in this case a collector's cabinet, and that the workshop could either execute or orchestrate the various skills displayed or suggested by the illustration, such as inlay, metalwork, carving and gilding, and possessed the ability to produce ambitious designs. The cabinet on stand (Pl. 113) bears a striking resemblance to the collector's cabinet on the Potter advertisement; the relationship between the two, and the exact status of the cabinet as a speculative or commissioned piece, remain among the mysteries of this study.

Contemporary London newspaper advertisements provide evidence of the speculative production of furniture as opposed to commissioned pieces. Whereas commissioned work was ordered to the customer's specification and the risk of losing revenue lay only in the ability of the cabinet-maker to collect payment, the speculative furniture trade involved a much higher risk – the investment of a substantial amount of capital in specialist labour, exotic woods and mounts – in a market which was stirred continually by the winds of fashion.

Speculatively designed and produced pieces served as a means of showing off the capabilities of a cabinet-maker's shop. Such furniture might incorporate parts imported from the continent, or be made in emulation of the latest continental styles. An example of such a piece was listed for sale in the *Daily Advertiser* in 1744,

> To be sold, at Mr. Evan's, a Cabinet Maker, in St. Paul's Churchyard, a Small and very Curious inlaid Cabinet, on a Frame, a proper Piece of Furniture for any elegant House, containing above One Hundred and Fifty Drawers contrived in the most useful Way, many of which are secret, fit for a Medallist or a Virtuoso, This Cabinet has many fine Italian Stone Landscapes; and must be pleasing to any curious Eye for the Inspection only.[12]

Likewise John Renshaw, a cabinet-maker in Brook Street, Holborn, in 1737 wished to 'acquaint the Publick' with a newly finished speculative piece of furniture which incorporated exotic materials.[13]

Woods: the selection of exotic timbers and the interest in natural philosophy

Many pieces of eighteenth-century furniture are loosely described as 'mahogany' – the dominant wood used by British cabinet-makers from about 1730 to 1770 for fashionable pieces.[14] Much of the surviving furniture of this period now has a uniform appearance, delicate variations of hue and texture produced by the careful selection of woods when first used having been lost as a result of repeated polishing, bleaching, and natural darkening. It is important to ascertain by scientific analysis which varieties of mahogany or other exotic timbers were used during the mid-eighteenth century.

Contemporary inventories, surviving pieces of furniture and architectural fittings confirm that although mahogany was used in Spain in the sixteenth century, it was probably introduced into the English timber market only during the mid-seventeenth century.[15] A significant but highly idiosyncratic early example of its use is a chair dated 1661 in Aberdeen.[16] The second earliest documented use is found in a written description of the wainscotting and floors installed at Nottingham Castle in 1680; again, this example is probably atypical. The statistics for imports to Britain from Christmas 1699 to Christmas 1700 include the first known record for the trade in mahogany from Jamaica,[17] while the earliest newspaper advertisement for the wood is in the *London Gazette* in 1702:[18] 'On Wednesday the 3d of March next, at 9 in the morning, will be exposed to public Sale by the Candle, at Salters-Hall in St Swithern's Lane, London' the contents of two prize ships. These included 'lackered Tea-Tables' and a variety of wood, including 'Nicaragua and Mahogany Wood, West India Box etc' and 'Brazelletto, Mohogany, Ebbone'.

By the 1730s, the London timber trade in tropical woods was well under way. Contemporary newspaper advertisements of London merchants and inventories of the stock-in-trade of cabinet-makers list a wide variety of imported timbers which were available. Woods commonly advertised by the timber trade included angola, amboyna, campeachy, guiney wood, manchineel and nicarogo.[19] Many woods were colloquially referred to by the place-name of the sea port or colony from which they were exported; for example, Porto Bello, Nicorago, Angola, Campeachy and Guiney Wood. Exotic timbers were also mentioned in advertisements for second-hand or ready-made furniture in similar newspapers.[20] Available from London merchants between 1730 and 1760 were rosewood chairs and cabinets, grenoble clock cases,[21] 'curious Pieces of Furniture, highly finished, in Walnut Tree, Mahogany, Amboyna and other Woods'[22] and 'a great Quantity of Chairs made of Walnut-Tree, Mahogany, Rosewood, Angola or Guiney wood'.[23]

For the purposes of this study, wood analysis has been undertaken on eleven pieces in the collections at Temple Newsam and at the Victoria and Albert Museum.[24] All are likely to have been manufactured between 1730 to 1765 and are ornamented with brass inlay. Of this small sample, ten pieces employ padouk veneers. All ten probably use exactly the same species of padouk, *Pterocarpus indicus*.[25] Depending on the conditions of growth, the colouration of *P. indicus* varies from purple to yellow and is characterised by pink and purple stripes. It is best known in Europe as amboyna, its burr form. The selection of padouk as opposed to mahogany for this group of furniture is likely to have been made purely for reasons of prestige, as there are no obvious physical characteristics which make padouk more suitable than mahogany to take brass inlay. The only surviving fully documented pieces of furniture by John Channon, the Powderham bookcases, are veneered in padouk (described in an inventory of 1762 as 'manchineel').

Scientific analysis of the veneers on this group of furniture also reveals subsequent alterations. For example, the cabinet on stand (Pl. 113) is veneered on the exterior with padouk on a carcase of Cuban mahogany (*Swietenia mahogani*) and native oak (*Quercus sp.*). This piece retains three carved gilt-wood pilasters which were replaced in the 1960s with plainer fluted pilasters. Recent examination suggested on stylistic grounds that the earlier pilasters were nineteenth-century replacements, but scientific analysis indicates that they are made of the same wood as the carcase, suggesting that they may be original to the piece.[26] The twentieth-century replacements are of a wood of the *Leguminosae* family which in its colour and appearance bears a superficial resemblance to mahogany.

Cuban mahogany was used also both for the exterior veneer and for the drawer linings of the secretaire (Pl. 47). As a veneer wood, mahogany would have been an expensive option for drawer linings. The padouk surface of the writing-table (Pl. 80–1) benefits from the contrast provided by an outer band of partridge wood (*Caesalpinia granadillo*), also known as Grenadillo or Red Ebony, although this has been disfigured by a later dark coating or stain. The library table (Pl. 106–9) is also veneered in Cuban mahogany, with the exception of the brass key pattern which is set into a padouk veneer with ebony in the pierced brass roundels (Pl. 107). A similar contrast of Cuban mahogany and padouk is found on the tea-chest (Pl. 162).

The exotic timbers used in the Channon group of furniture came from both the West and the East Indies. What we now call Cuban mahogany was first imported to England from Jamaica, although by 1748 much of the Jamaican wood had been cut, and later supplies came from Santo Domingo and Cuba. *Pterocarpus indicus* (padouk) is native of India, Ceylon, Malaya, the Moluccas, Java and the Phillipines and would have been imported through the East India Company. Partridge wood is a south American timber from Venezuela.

These pieces of eighteenth-century furniture, although a chance grouping, emphasise the importance given to the choice of grain patterns, the arrangement of veneers and the extent to which the exotic nature of veneer woods was appreciated. On many pieces, it is the figuring of the veneers which enhances the furniture forms. The Kenwood bureau-cabinet (Pl. 61–4), the Carlton Hobbs bureau-bookcase (Col. pl. IV) and the Murray cabinet (Col. pl. XVII–XVIII) are the three outstanding examples of matched veneer work. This process involves the careful slicing of a single block of figured wood for use on all the large drawer fronts of the cabinets. On the Murray cabinet, the four long drawer fronts are all faced with veneers taken from the same piece of wood, each repeating a pattern of burr and plain grain. To achieve this effect, the veneers had to be cut as thin as possible. The lively figure of the wood grain poses a high degree of technical difficulty in this task, because the very figuring which is admired causes the veneer wood to be more than usually brittle and liable to break when cut in fine sheets. On the Kenwood bureau, in addition to the 'matched' veneer drawer fronts, the frieze of the cabinet's pediment uses repetitive 'book-matched' veneers of crotched (flame) mahogany. This book-matching is used on several pieces in the brass-inlaid group and is shown to great effect on the column plinths of the Powderham bookcases (Pl. 35). These two methods of arranging veneers were not new to the cabinet-making trade during the mid-eighteenth century but were a means by which the high quality and flamboyant figure of woods could be shown to the maximum effect.

The presence of exotic woods in the furniture commissioned for affluent households was not only an indicator of wealth and fashion. The value of the woods to the patron was perhaps associated with the ability of the client to distinguish types of woods and his intellectual appreciation of both the aesthetic and the scientific interest of exotic timbers (although the extent of knowledge of tropical woods amongst amateurs is not a subject which has been studied). Exotic woods offered a variety of colours and figured grain for cabinet-makers to exploit for decorative purposes. Within this group of furniture some pieces use several different types of imported woods. The two most striking examples of the use of contrasting woods in this group of brass-inlaid furniture are the bureau-cabinets of about 1745 at Kenwood (Pl. 66) and a secretaire of about 1740 owned by Carlton Hobbs (Col. pl. IV). The latter example[27] features a padouk[28] front with walnut sides, but relies also on at least two other woods, one of which may be mahogany, to complement the engraved brass. William Linnell's inventory lists, aside from the typical mahogany and walnut tree, 'rosewood, ebony, fustick,[29] red wood,[30] and medeira wood'.[31] Samuel Norman had in stock 'Violette Veniers,[32] Rose wood, Black Ebony, Virginea Walnut Tree, Cherry' and 'Odds and Ends of Several Sorts of Wood'. The inventory of the contents of Powderham Castle, dated 1762, describes the primary wood of John Channon's brass-inlaid bookcases as 'Manchineel'.[33] In fact, many items in the Powderham inventory specify types of wood: 'an allagazante Table' valued at £3.0.0, 'a Manchineel Table £1.1.0,' 'Rosewood Side Table £1.1.0' and 'an Eight Day Time Piece in an Ebony Case £5.5.0' are described in addition to the many mahogany pieces.

Whether any relationship existed between the choice of woods used in certain fine cabinets and the growing amateur interest in the study of natural history is uncertain, but undeniably during the eighteenth century the availability of 'new' woods provided full scope to patrons with such an interest. By the end of the seventeenth century nearly 130 hardy trees and shrubs had been introduced to this country.[34] Collecting botanical specimens had become a recognised interest for gentlemen. In the early 1760s a shift in collecting interest had taken place: systematic scientific inquiry and analysis began to take the place of collecting curiosities.[35] A significant number of cabinets for collections of curios and scientific specimens survive from the second half of the century; one in particular, dating from about 1760, now in the Lady Lever Collection,[36] constructed of rosewood and amboyna and using a variety of exotic timbers for the veneers facing the fronts of the myriad drawers, seems quite deliberately to unite the scientific, the aesthetic and the practical aspects of the new discoveries in timber. When these attitudes to the use of wood first became current is not known, but it is significant that several of the cabinets decorated with brass inlay house narrow specimen-drawers (Pl. 133).

Other materials

Several of the decorative techniques employed on these cabinets are intended to imitate other materials. Only one piece, the bureau-bookcase at the Victoria and Albert Museum[37] (Pl. 36) is ornamented with a deep cavetto moulding in the cornice of the pediment, overlaid with red tortoiseshell. The signed bookcases at Powderham Castle demonstrate a probable attempt to imitate tortoiseshell in the plaques on the pedestals (Pl. 135). This effect is achieved by chiselling out a section of the brass and scoring and in-filling it with a dark translucent mastic which allows the golden qualities of the brass to shine faintly through. The use of mastic seems to differ from piece to piece. It has been suggested (see p. 39) that its use on the Powderham pieces is intended merely to imitate the colour of the wood ground, without the need for piercing the plate; but the mastic must always have been significantly darker than even the unfaded wood, and represented a contrast either of ebony or of tortoiseshell. In considering this, it is interesting to remember that the Berain-derived design of the main Powderham panels (Pl. 135) is more than once found as the centrepiece to boulle panels,[38] and this original use may well have provided the inspiration for the use of mastic in imitation of tortoiseshell. Mastic is found also in the pierced fretwork (Pl. 37)

52 FURNITURE MANUFACTURE

36. Detail of tortoiseshell on the cornice of bureau cabinet illustrated in Pl. 47. *The Trustees of the Victoria and Albert Museum*

37. Detail of brass fretwork on base of the Southwick Park commode (Col. pl. XXII). *Leeds City Art Galleries*

of the Southwick commode, where it provides a contrast to the brass. A red pigment is used to highlight the engraved brasses on several pieces. The pigment used in conjunction with padouk gives the impression of pierced brass work in-filled with wood. On the Murray writing-cabinet the particularly successful combination of the red pigment and mahogany (Pl. 102) is heightened by the fine quality of the engraving on the brasswork. A further interesting use of 'substitute' materials is found in the interior writing compartment drawers of the Kenwood bureau-bookcase, where a light-coloured wood, possibly box, maple or holly, has been used to imitate the brass stringing found on the exterior drawers (Pl. 62). The use of a pliable wood rather than the thin strips of rigid brass on these curving drawer fronts has proved to be much more stable and enduring.

Other minor materials such as engraved mother-of-pearl or ivory inlays are used for their own worth (Pl. 56, 152 & 180). The use of pearl shell on one card table (Col. pl. XIII) may relate to oriental practice,[39] but in most cases the derivation seems to be from the Boulle technique, either directly or through the simplified versions of multi-material marquetry (see pp. 15–16) which had their origins in the late seventeenth century.

Joints and construction

Through the apprenticeship system, individual workshop traditions of construction were transmitted with minor alteration to each new generation. It is this consistency of workshop practice which allows us to compare and group furniture by characteristics other than those of style and ornament. Cabinet-makers rely on two basic types of joint which either slide or lock to unite the members of a piece of furniture.[40] The focus of this subsection is the use of one form of locking joint, the dovetail, and a type of sliding joint, the rebate (Pl. 38).

The group of cabinets with which we are concerned relies on the same basic joints as furniture produced around 1700. For example, the types of joint found in the drawers and carcase of a bureau-desk *circa* 1710[41] are virtually identical to those employed in the production of a brass-inlaid bureau-bookcase (Pl. 47)[42] which is thought to date from about 1740. The selection of oak and deal as secondary woods and the use of rare or expensive timbers both for the main-drawer veneers and as solid timber for the linings of smaller desk drawers is found in both the mid-century brass-inlaid group and pieces made thirty years earlier.[43] However, the cabinet-making skills displayed in the earlier piece are by no means comparable to those displayed throughout the brass-inlaid group of furniture, the construction of which differs by its high degree of finish on interior surfaces and the precision of standard joints.

Pieces of carcase furniture within this group all display finely worked interiors. There are several types of internal drawers (Pl. 39 & 93). Such miniature drawers provided an opportunity for a workshop to display to best advantage several different feats of cabinet-making such as rebate and dovetail joints on a minute scale. The construction of small drawers is carried out with finely cut boards, ranging from two to four millimetres in thickness and demonstrating the ability both to cut slender boards and to create delicate joints. The drawers range from those with complex partitions for

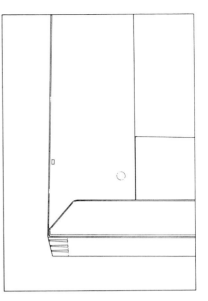

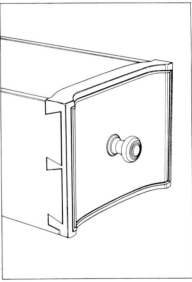

38. Diagrams of joint construction showing dovetails and rebate joints *drawn by Andrew Green*

39. Interior drawer from the cabinet in Pl. 47 showing thinness of timber and setting of base. *The Trustees of the Victoria and Albert Museum*

special use (Pl. 107) to plain banks (Pl. 113). A workshop's abilities also were manifested in the complexity of drawer shapes. From examination of these three qualities of construction, the distribution and type of joints, drawer shapes, and thinness of timbers, it becomes clear that several workshops were involved in the production of brass-inlaid furniture and that pieces can be tentatively attributed to workshop groups on the basis of cabinet-making techniques. Earlier pieces such as the Samuel Bennett bureau-bookcase *c*.1725 (Pl. 44) are not of the same standard of construction as those dating from the 1740s and 1750s. There is a steady progression from the neat workmanship used by Bennett to the highly finished interior spaces of pieces made in the mid-century. A major difference lies in the finishing of drawer sides and the polishing of concealed compartments, trays and drawers. The level of skills needed to produce the elaborately shaped drawers of the later pieces was far greater (Pl. 49). Another unusual feature of the later pieces of furniture is the use of figured mahogany for the smaller drawer and tray bottoms and the use of mahogany even for the larger drawer linings on pieces such as the library table and the Murray writing-cabinet.[44]

Continental links in design are clear but the link with continental construction is, as yet, obscure. However, one possible link in construction technique is seen when comparing the dust-boards of a Bernard van Risem Burgh commode[45] and the drawer construction of the Southwick Park commode. The floating panels used for the dust-boards of the BVRB commode and the flush-framed panels in the drawer bottoms of the Southwick commode (Pl. 40) may provide evidence of continental influences on this group of furniture though the detailed handling of these differs, the BVRB piece showing fielded panels where the commode drawer bases are painstakingly flush-panelled. Neither construction feature is typical of London or Paris workshop traditions. Similarly, the parallels between the carcase work and veneering of the curved niche sections of the library tables (Pl. 106) and the management of similar forms on German high-fashion furniture of the period has been mentioned elsewhere (see p. 34). Though the exact links remain uncertain, it is likely that European techniques of construction interested top London cabinet-makers as much as decorative techniques.

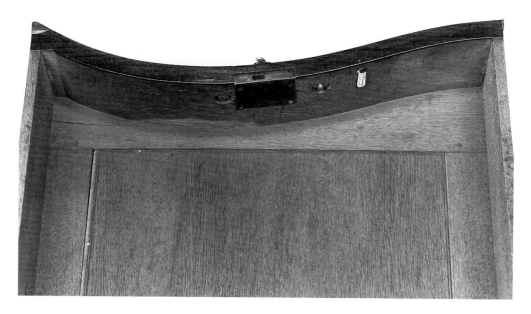

40. Detail of the base of a drawer from the Southwick Park commode (Col. pl. XXII). *Leeds City Art Galleries*

Inlaid brass and brass mounts

Two features especially define the furniture associated with John Channon and his circle: the use of brass-inlaid work and elaborate cast-brass mounts. The simplest inlays consist of stringing arranged as rectangular frames for other ornament. An elaboration of this form of ornament can be seen on top of the library table which is inset with a Greek key pattern (Pl. 107). The most sophisticated inlaid work, such as that to be found on the Murray writing-cabinet, consists of large figurative elements carefully cut out, the surfaces engraved and hatched, set flush into the wood (Pl. 101–2). The Powderham bookcases are also inlaid with large brass bell flowers, scrolling foliage, shell work and the Courtenay arms.

The tea-chest (Pl. 162) has inlaid work similar in character to that found on the Powderham bookcases in the form of large flowers, framing the lock-plate. The cabinet on stand (Pl. 114) has inlays of rather different form with tightly scrolling foliage arranged around masks and cast mounts (Pl. 42). The engraving of the hinge plates on this cabinet is markedly superior to that found on other brass inlays. It depicts a hung fleece with entwined serpents and scrolling foliage. The quality of the engraving is exceptional and suggests that it must be the work of an heraldic engraver (Pl. 115). These craftsmen specialised in engraving coats of arms on metalwork and produced the fine book-plates so characteristic of the period. As these plates are separate elements applied to the carcase, it seems reasonable to assume that they were specially commissioned. Another brass which differs in style and character is the plate on the Powderham bookcases engraved with Channon's name and the date 1740

41. Detail of Corinthian capital from the cabinet on stand illustrated in Pl. 113 showing two-piece casting held together by rivets. *The Trustees of the Victoria and Albert Museum*

42. Detail of engraved brass inlays on lower section of the cabinet on stand illustrated in Pl. 113. *The Trustees of the Victoria and Albert Museum*

(Pl. 6). The lettering is reminiscent of engraved work found on contemporary English commemorative brasses.[46] The felicitous choice of Gothic lettering strongly suggests that an engraver specialising in monumental brasses was commissioned to execute these tablets.

A prominent feature of the library table attributed to Channon is the lavish cast-bronze mounts. On the upper section of each corner are satyr masks crowned with leaves incorporating at the base, ribbons, foliage and shell motifs (Pl. 109). Above the drawers in the centre are two female heads in classical style set above volutes, shells and cast foliage (Pl. 108). Mounted at the sides and on the drawers are a series of handles and escutcheons, also of bronze cast in relief. The edges of the desk are outlined with narrow cast beading following the profile. The quality of both the casting and the finishing of these mounts is very high: where appropriate, the surfaces have been matted with a fine punch to add contrasting texture to the surface, and the mounts are gilt. In order to fit the dolphin mounts to the concave central section, the fins have had to be sharply bent. The mounts on the drawers are in high rococo style of the 1740s and 50s, whereas the figurative mounts at the corners reflect an earlier period and are in a style more commonly found around 1720. It has been pointed out that the mounts have much in common with those on contemporary French furniture and there seems no doubt that high-quality French mounts were their inspiration (see pp. 40–1).[47]

The problem of attributing fine-quality bronze work of the 1740s and 1750s is frequently solved by immediately ascribing it to French craftsmen. However, so little is known about what was produced in England under French influence at this period that it is worth considering the possibilities of the mounts having been made in England. Although virtually nothing is known about English bronze work at the date when the back-to-back library table was made, more is known about English craftsmen using other materials. English silversmiths, for example, were using virtually identical techniques to make candlesticks to those a 'bronzier' would employ to make bronze mounts.[48] The required form was first produced in wax or wood, then cast in a sand mould, afterwards being finished off with a variety of tools such as chisels and matting punches. English silversmiths of the 1740s were producing cast candlesticks in advanced rococo style virtually identical to those made in contemporary Paris. A candlestick of 1744 by the London goldsmith Thomas Gilpin, for example, with its cast shell-work and rococo swirls, could well pass as French, and the fine sculptural and figurative silver wares produced in London in the 1740s to the designs of G.M. Moser bears comparison with the best continental work of the period.[49] It is also worth recalling in this context that only thirty years after the Powderham bookcases were made, Matthew Boulton was producing his mounted wares at the Soho Manufactory in Birmingham, using, as far as is known, English craftsmen.[50] The ormolu mounts produced by Boulton were of outstanding quality and imply a long tradition of skilled apprentices and craftsmen working on similar wares in England. The problem of trying to establish where the mounts on John Channon's furniture were produced is exacerbated by the all-pervasive continental influence on ormolu at the period. The mounts on the cabinet on stand (Pl. 113), for example, are virtually identical to those on the three French commodes of the 1720s (see p. 40). Some of the mounts display curious features; for instance, the capitals on the columns are of unusual construction (Pl. 41): instead of being cast as one solid element, they are made in two, then pegged together – an unnecessarily complicated construction. It seems extraordinary that a workshop did not have either a deep enough mould or the means of making one for this comparatively simple element. A feature of the tea-chest (Pl. 162) is the use of lion's-paw feet cast in bronze. The handle is also a fine casting. The brass-inlaid

INLAID BRASS AND BRASS MOUNTS

43. Detail of cast-brass inlays from the stock of a gun by Griffin, English, about 1740. *The Trustees of the Victoria and Albert Museum*

elements are rather large for the surfaces into which they are set, and there seems a possibility that they were intended originally for a larger piece of furniture.

The engraved brass inlays vary considerably both in design and quality. On the upper surface of the library table, for example, the inlay consists of a plain key pattern with pierced roundels at the corners. The Powderham bookcases feature bell flowers, key patterns, figurative designs and scrolling foliage, while the plates on the pedestals below the columns are directly copied from one of Jean Berain's engravings (Pl. 134–8). There is none of the intensity of decoration that typifies Boulle's work, with the use of scrolling foliage, interlaced strapwork, birds and vase forms, all carried out in very small brass elements. By comparison, the inlays on the bookcases are large and rather clumsy. It is as if the central theme of French inlay, the figures and architectural motifs, have been taken from the design and set within a simple frame. In Channon's work the veneered ground is as important as the brass inlays. The cutting and engraving of the figures is particularly naive and it seems apparent that the engraver who worked on the Powderham bookcases was more at home with floral scrolls and larger ornament.

An examination of engraved brass produced in England in the second quarter of the eighteenth century shows that the quality varied considerably. Some work, such as the engraved back-plates and dials of the best clocks, are almost invariably very well done; the same can be said also about heraldic engraving on brasswork. The engraved work on English firearms is also worth noting in this context. English firearms of the 1730s and 1740s provide an interesting parallel for the inlaid work on furniture. Engraved brass sheets are used to decorate gunstocks; plain linear forms are frequently used, the ornament designed to contrast with a stock of figured walnut. Brass was also used on high-quality specially commissioned firearms such as the gun made for the Earl of Hyndford (1701–67) by the London gunmaker Griffin, supplied in about 1740 (Pl. 43). This has very-high-quality cast and engraved brass equal to the best of contemporary silversmiths' work.

Engraver's work on brass and steel is almost invariably anonymous. Occasionally the survival of a work-book can briefly lift the veil. Fortunately the work-book of an English engraver named William Palmer (1737–1812) has survived and gives an insight into this particular craft.[51] Although Palmer was active at a period much later than the engraver who worked on the Channon pieces, a glance at the various pulls and designs contained in the book gives a good idea of the range of jobs such a craftsman would undertake. His chief work was done on London-made firearms but he also engraved boxes, book-plates and plates that could well have been set into furniture. The designs could all be done in brass, steel and silver. Palmer was apprenticed to the London master engraver and goldsmith, John Pine, and then to Richard Searle, a stationery engraver. Both would have been working in the 1730s and 1740s. It is thus clear that Channon and his rivals would have had no difficulty in finding skilled engravers in London able to produce engraved brass inlays for their furniture.

In conclusion, it seems probable that the brass-inlaid work on Channon's furniture was executed in England. It is likely that the elaborate bronze mounts such as appear on the 'nymph and satyr' group are also English, although the debt to continental craftsmen is considerable. A lack of documentation or signatures means that the craftsmen who produced this metalwork must at present remain anonymous.

7. Furniture survey

Bureau-cabinets

Bureau-cabinets, together with dish-topped pillar and claw tables, were the most popular forms of brass-inlaid furniture. Gerrit Jensen (fl. 1680–1715) was the first London cabinet-maker to use metal inlay on furniture in imitation of the French technique. Although he had no true followers, a number of early-eighteenth-century bureau-cabinets are recorded, veneered with figured walnut, burr elm or mulberry, cross-banded with kingwood and inlaid with modest pewter stringing lines. Several bear the trade label of Coxed & Woster, 'At the White Swan . . . St Paul's Churchyard, London' (fl. 1690–1726).[1] These makers seem never to have developed the decorative potential of metal inlay, and their successors in business at the White Swan, Henry and Philip Bell, are not known to have employed the technique. Therefore, while interesting forerunners of brass-inlaid cabinet furniture, Coxed & Woster are marginal to the main tradition.

It is no easy task to date the repertoire of brass-inlaid cabinets or even to decide whether examples were made before or after the Powderham bookcases of 1740. However, the evidence of Sir William Stanhope's sale in 1733 (see pp. 17–18), the Hintz advertisement of 1738, a walnut barometer-case with brass inlay housing an instrument by Charles Orme dated 1736[2] and other strands of evidence indicate that the fashion for brass inlay started in the 1730s – a little earlier than previously thought.

R.W. Symonds first drew attention to certain common features of design between a lavish padouk bureau cabinet copiously inlaid with engraved brass, which H. Blairman & Sons had purchased at Christie's[3] (Col. pl. IV) and a veneered walnut writing-cabinet in the Victoria and Albert Museum decorated with panels of intricate boxwood arabesque marquetry and inlaid on the back of the door with the maker's name 'SAMUEL BENNETT / FECIT LONDON' (Pl. 44).[4] An oval brass plate with the cypher J E P is set into the back of the door of the padouk cabinet; these initials might refer to a member of the Pott family, since it was sold at Christie's by Lady Pott, Clifton Hampden, Abington, Berkshire.

The similarities between these two pieces of furniture include an upper stage enclosed by a single mirror-fronted door, flanked by pilasters resting on bulbous bases; arabesque marquetry centring on a mask on the bottom rail of the door (Pl. 45–6); the presence of lifting handles and design of the entablature. In the absence of a maker's name for the refined padouk scrutoire, it is tempting to suggest that Samuel Bennett (fl. 1723–41) was the author of both, the difference in quality being accounted for by the superior technical finish possible when using tropical hardwoods. As one would expect, oak and deal have been used in the carcase of both pieces, and while the signed walnut cabinet betrays a distinctly old-fashioned character, it is conceivable that they were produced in the same workshop at widely separated dates, c.1720 and c.1740. Symonds rejected this idea but the similarities allow for the possibility of a common authorship.

44. Bureau cabinet by Samuel Bennett, London c.1725, walnut with arabesque marquetry (see Pl. 9). *The Trustees of the Victoria and Albert Museum*

45. Detail of brass marquetry above the desk slope on the padouk cabinet (Col. pl. IV). *Sotheby's*

46. Detail of marquetry in light wood above the desk slope on the walnut cabinet illustrated in Pl. 44. *The Trustees of the Victoria and Albert Museum*

The later padouk version has, of course, been updated with innovative brass inlay, cockbeads, case mouldings, solid mahogany drawer linings, keyhole covers, a modern desk interior and other refinements. A highly distinctive feature is the quality of the brass-cased locks which, as Symonds pointed out, resemble the work of a gunsmith rather than a locksmith; the keyholes are covered by spring flaps released by a spiked instrument and various extremely ingenious secret catches open concealed document compartments, while a central brass spindle can be adjusted to prevent four drawers at the rear opening with the suction when the close-fitting central unit housing a monogrammed pigeon-hole is pulled forward (Col. pl. VII). Two brass tablets either side of the middle writing-drawer are engraved with harlequins holding clubs, which interestingly link this piece to the Bristol medal cabinet (Pl. 120) and so provide encouragement for scholars who favour a Channon attribution. It might be significant that the spandrels of the inner central niche of Bennett's cabinet are inlaid with royal crowns (Pl. 9), a device that is prominently engraved on a bureau (Pl. 79) and a tea table (Pl. 150). These scrutoires usefully serve to introduce a magnificent series of bureau-cabinets (or desks and bookcases as they would have been known at the time) enriched with brass which are among the finest achievements of English cabinet-making.

In 1953, the Victoria and Albert Museum purchased a bureau-cabinet that had formerly been in the collection of Alan Good, Glympton Park, Oxfordshire (Pl. 47). The upper stage, enclosed by mirror-fronted double doors faced with three Corinthian pilasters, is headed by a segmental pediment with side arches, but the present finials are not original. The slope centres on a brass shield flanked by cornucopia and eagles (Pl. 48) and is outlined with a string panel, having corner ornaments and interlace round the keyhole, a pattern of inlay that is repeated on the drawer fronts, which have handle plates finely engraved with double eagle heads, creating a unified effect of great richness. The front is veneered with book-matched figured mahogany, cross-banded in

BUREAU-CABINETS 61

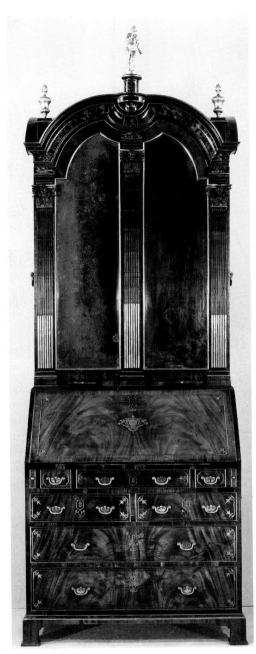

padouk, but the really striking feature is the use of red stained tortoiseshell to line the cavetto moulding of the arched pediments (Pl. 36). The typically English carcase construction makes the introduction of a decorative technique associated with Continental Boulle work even more exceptional. The square bracket feet with ground-level mouldings and semi-concealed pilaster compartments create links with other secretaires, while the very curvaceous prospect centring on a half-round stepped plinth is Germanic in character (Pl. 49).

By chance, a letter, apparently documenting this cabinet, has survived (slightly shortened in quotation):[5]

47. Bureau-cabinet, mahogany with padouk cross-banding, brass inlay and red tortoiseshell lining the cornice, c.1740. Formerly at Glympton Park, Oxon. *The Trustees of the Victoria and Albert Museum*

48. Brass inlay on the writing slope with paired birds and cornucopia

49. The shaped prospect with a central stepped drawer

50. Bureau-cabinet, by J. Graveley, padouk with partridge wood crossbanding and brass inlay, c.1740–5. *Pelham Galleries*

51. Detail of J. GRAVELEY brand on underside of the carcase. *The Trustees of the Victoria and Albert Museum*

52. Detail of perching bird amid scrolls on a door of the Graveley cabinet. *Pelham Galleries*

BUREAU-CABINETS

Heckington 16 May 1772

Dear Sir

I take this opportunity of sending the Desk and Bookcase, you seemed desireous of Having – It cost me in London (Tho' then Second-Hand) Twenty Guineas – But, (tho' it has been very well used in my Custody) as it must be necessarily worse for wear in my Possession, I do not desire more than Eighteen Guineas for it of you, & as you was so genteel to offer me ye full price it cost me, I hope you will not disapprove of it with this abatement. ...

Your very sincere Friend   John Noble Taylor

A bureau-cabinet of capital importance, which in 1963 passed through Sotheby's into the London trade and was known to John Hayward, but has since disappeared, had the name 'J. GRAVELEY' branded underneath the base (Pl. 50–1). This method of a maker identifying his work is rare but not unknown on English furniture of the period. Sadly, no master cabinet-maker named J. Graveley has so far been recorded, which suggests that the name may be that of a journeyman, possibly a repairer, conceivably the owner. It is disappointing that after the discovery of a signature the individual should prove so elusive. Photographs show a well-proportioned, typically English cabinet, veneered in padouk with partridge-wood cross-banding raised on lion's paws, the base-moulding carved with scrolling foliage and centring on a shell. The mirror-fronted double doors are bordered with panels of engraved brass arabesque inlay inhabited by birds (Pl. 52), while the bureau slope and drawer fronts display stringing and interlace. Two sophisticated writing-tables (Pl. 80–3) and a secretaire (Pl. 54) can be firmly attributed on grounds of stylistic analogy to the same workshop.

A related example, formerly in the R. Cookson collection, veneered in sabicu (Pl. 53), stands on square bracket feet and is generally much plainer. The doors in the upper stage are rather sparingly inlaid with narrow brass frets, but the slope is richly laid out with fronded corner shells and a rococo key escutcheon.

Another fine brass-inlaid bureau-cabinet, now known only from photographs (Pl. 54), displays intriguing affinities with a handsome but plain walnut example bearing

53. Bureau-cabinet, possibly by J. Graveley, sabicu with brass inlay, *c.*1745. *Apter Fredericks*

54. Bureau-cabinet, probably by J. Graveley, *c.*1740, mahogany with brass inlay closely similar to Pl. 50. *The Trustees of the Victoria and Albert Museum*

the trade label of John Belchier which Partridge (Fine Art) Ltd had in stock in 1988.[6] The similarities hardly justify grooming Belchier as belonging to the coterie of makers producing brass-inlaid cabinet furniture, but it is worth bearing his name in mind. Both pieces have a flattened segmental cornice, a single mirror-fronted door, candle-slides, three frieze drawers and square bracket feet; but it is the carefully studied proportions that might imply a common authorship. The later mahogany version has shells and narrow fretwork arabesques on the doorframe, including perched-bird motifs on the shoulders. The slope and drawer fronts are inlaid with a familiar system of string panels and interlace accented by husk-like leaf motifs. These patterns are exactly repeated on the Graveley secretaire (Pl. 50).

A tall and dignified, but not very elaborately fitted, desk and bookcase inlaid with brass and mother-of-pearl once belonged to the Rev. R.L. Parker, whose grand-daughter, Mrs V.M. Brooks, consigned it to Sotheby's.[7] It is now owned by a private American collector (Pl. 55–60). The cabinet, veneered in well-figured book-matched mahogany, is headed by an open architectural pediment with dentil enrichments and a turned wrythen finial. The solid double doors are each inlaid in brass with a single, beautifully engraved carnation and a tulip (Pl. 57) within elegant borders featuring urns of flowers, shells, fleur-de-lys, butterflies, snails (Pl. 58) and rococo lockplates accented by mother-of-pearl tassels. The slope is enriched with a squirrel eating an apple from a basket of fruit, flanked by snails (Pl. 60) – motifs that occasionally appear on Boulle furniture. This picturesque detail creates an interesting link between the cabinet and a 'dish-top' pillar and claw table on which is found (in separate compartments) a bushy-tailed squirrel and a bowl of fruit (Pl. 150). The desk is simply fitted with letter-holes and small drawers centring on a shaped mirror-faced door with a drawer below fronted by steps – not an unusual arrangement (Pl. 55). In common with other bureau-cabinets, this example has candle-slides, despite the solid mahogany door panels.

There is a possibility that this masterpiece has a Channon connection, because his brother, Otho, subscribed to Robert Furber's *Twelve Months of Flowers*, while John helped to market them from his shop in St Martin's Lane. An advertisement in the *Craftsman* on 24 July 1742 naming Channon as a supplier is quoted in full on p. 5. Furber's monthly *Flowers* are botanical prints portraying vases of flowers. The tulips for March and in the floral border to the list of subscribers (Pl. 1) have a very similar quality, especially in the hatched and cross-hatched areas, to the specimen tulip on the door of the cabinet. Both could be the work of Henry Fletcher, who engraved the designs. It is well worth knowing that at this early stage in his career John Channon was dealing in art prints, since he used engravings as a source for his brass inlay and later traded in Old Masters, presumably as a branch of his business as a frame-

56. Bureau-cabinet, possibly by Frederick Hintz, mahogany with brass and mother-of-pearl inlay. *Private collection*

55 (*opposite*). The prospect centring on a stepped drawer

57. Detail of engraved brass tulip, possibly inspired by Furber's *Twelve Months of Flowers*

58. Detail of vase of flowers and snail

59. Inlay on the bureau writing slope

60. Detail of squirrel eating from a basket of fruit, motifs which occur also on Pl. 150

maker.[8] An alternative candidate is Frederick Hintz, who in 1738 advertised for sale mahogany desks and bookcases 'inlaid with Fine figures of Brass and Mother of Pearl'.

In 1959, the Iveagh Bequest, Kenwood, purchased from Malletts a Palladian desk and bookcase designed in the highest style of elegance, its richly figured mahogany surfaces profusely inlaid with engraved brass and mother-of-pearl details (Pl. 61). It is comparable to an architectural bureau-cabinet having mirror doors formerly in the Percival Griffiths collection,[9] but, in a typically English fashion, the decorative brasswork is in the rococo taste. A very interesting feature, strongly suggesting a special commission, is the antiquarian flavour of the ornament on the prospect or desk interior which centres on a small door inlaid with a warrior figure (Pl. 62) akin to the Roman heroes (copied from a sixteenth-century source) on the lock-plates of the Bristol cabinet (Pl. 122–5). The spandrels of the arched letter-holes are inset with a series of eighteen strangely primitive mother-of-pearl motifs, including a monk, a Turk, various heads, a chicken, pigeon, fish, etc. (Pl. 62). This diminutive pearl-shell ornament appears curiously eccentric on a such a majestic piece, although it is of course visible only when the desk section is opened up.

The timber and cabinet-work are of outstanding quality; the mahogany-lined main drawers and the lopers have brass cockbeads, the base and slope are cased in brass mouldings and the pilasters have brass flutes. The flap is embellished with four rococo cartouches delicately engraved with flowers and a foliate lock-plate with keyhole cover released by activating a spring at the bottom of the slope (Pl. 63). Panelled doors in the upper stage, enriched with a design of acanthus fronds and serpentine lines, open to reveal the pleasant conceit of a Georgian doorway with pilasters and fan-light neatly detailed in brass and surrounded by an elaborate arrangement of small drawers, folio partitions and letter-holes (Pl. 64). Behind the little door lies a nest of concealed compartments released by secret catches. It is sad that so little is known about the provenance of this great piece of furniture, although luckily the handles link it to Channon's œuvre.

Another splendid desk and bookcase (in private hands) displays the hallmarks of the same workshop – profuse brass inlay, brass mouldings and cockbeads, mahogany drawer linings, a spring-loaded escutcheon cover on the fall and a well-fitted shaped desk interior (Col. pl. v). It has replacement handles and restored bracket feet but is of enormous interest because the ornament on the slope provides a precise date *post quem*, having been copied from a design for a console table in Nicholas Pineau's *Nouveau Dessins de Tables* (published in Paris in 1737 and reissued in a pirated form by Batty & Thomas Langley in their *City and Country Builder's and Workman's Treasury of Designs*, 1740, pl. CXLIII) (Pl. 65).[10] The inlay is not an exact translation of the engraving, certain details being omitted such as the table top; however, the carved apron is cleverly retained as a keyhole escutcheon. The fact that Pineau's progressive design was plagiarised by the Langleys and exploited by the maker or patron who commissioned this cabinet tells us something of value about English attitudes to the French rococo at this period.

A distinguished but somehow less memorable final group of four desks and bookcases remains to be discussed: all are of standard form, originally with shaped, gilt-edged, single or double mirror-lined doors, although in one case the looking-glass and in another the gilt border is now missing. The inlaid brass escutcheons on the falls are identical, consisting of a cartouche set between stylised leafy bird-heads linked by strapwork, and the locks incorporate spring-loaded keyhole covers. Furthermore, the design of the string border and engraved brass palmette corner ornaments is precisely the same on three of the slopes. This uniformity of treatment indicates that these pieces were produced in the same workshop. The distinctive escutcheon design interestingly

61. Bureau-cabinet, possibly by John Channon, c.1745–50, mahogany with brass mouldings, engraved brass and mother-of-pearl inlay. *English Heritage (The Iveagh Bequest, Kenwood)*

62. Detail of brass inlay on central prospect door with quaint mother-of-pearl figures in the spandrels, and white wood strings

63. Detail of rococo brass inlay engraved with floral motifs on the writing slope

64. Bureau cabinet shown open

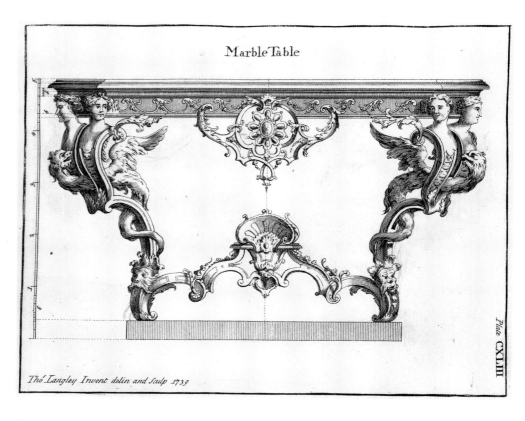

65. Design for a table (pirated from Nicholas Pineau) published in Batty Langley's *City and Country Builder's and Workman's Treasury of Designs*, 1740, and used as a source for the inlay on the bureau-cabinet illustrated in Col. pl. v. *Leeds City Libraries*

links them to a group of brass-inlaid tea-chests (Pl. 165) and dressing-boxes (Pl. 170–2) which display this feature as well, and it occurs also on a tea-chest depicted on Landall & Gordon's trade card of *c*.1745 (Pl. 161). Little is known of Thomas Landall, but John Gordon's surviving bills and furniture prove he was well able to supply cabinet-work of this high quality in the 1750s after the partnership ended.[11] He certainly provided mahogany desks and bookcases to the Dukes of Atholl and Gordon, although brass inlay is not specifically mentioned.

A bureau-cabinet sold by Phillips on 14 June 1988 had descended in the Palling family of Brownshill Court, Painswick, Gloucestershire (Pl. 66); its most unusual feature is the desk interior fitted with drawers and letter-holes centring on a mirrored recess, flanked by secret compartments and fronted by a chequer-inlaid stairway with gilt bannister and a boxwood and ebony star on the writing-bed (Pl. 67). The closely similar desk and bookcase which Partridge (Fine Art) Ltd acquired in 1988 (Pl. 70) was published by them as having been made for Henry Hobhouse, Queen's Square, Bristol.[12] The desk interior is more elaborately shaped and fitted than the Palling family example; it too centres on a mirror-faced door (fronted by steps) which opens to reveal simulated columns and a chequer-board floor (Col. pl. VI). The small drawers, pilasters that pull forward to reveal secret compartments and the bed are inlaid with chequered strings, pointed stars and a rosette, while the shaped apron has a traditional sunburst.

A third cabinet, with the same pattern of brass inlay on the slope, is known only from a trade advertisement of 1953 (Pl. 68). The single upper door is now clear-glazed and flanked by a heavy pair of carved and gilt swags of fruit and flowers applied to the pilasters. The festoons may not be original, but they are certainly a snug fit and can be compared to the cresting on the Powderham bookcases. Finally, another cabinet with the bird-head key-plate and a single mirror-lined upper door was sold at Sotheby's, New York, on 16 September 1988 (Pl. 69). The pilasters are fluted with brass and

66. Bureau-cabinet, possibly by Landall & Gordon, *c.*1745, mahogany with brass inlay (including a fronded bird-head escutcheon). Formerly owned by the Palling family of Painswick, Glos. *Jonathan Harris*

67. Detail of the prospect of Pl. 66 with fluted pilaster secret compartments

68. Bureau-cabinet, possibly by Landall & Gordon, c.1745, mahogany with fronded bird-head brass inlay and carved gilt-wood festoons on the pilasters. The door originally fronted by a mirror. *Ronald A. Lee*

69. Bureau-cabinet, possibly by Landall & Gordon, c.1745, mahogany with fronded bird-head brass inlay. *Sotheby's Inc., New York*

70. Bureau-cabinet, possibly by Landall & Gordon, c.1745, mahogany with brass inlay (including fronded bird-head escutcheon). Col. pl. VI shows a detail of the prospect. Formerly owned by Henry Hobhouse, Bristol. *Partridge (Fine Arts) plc*

headed by Trophies of War for which an engraved source may well exist. There are one or two other fringe desks and bookcases which deserve a note,[13] but we have now considered the core members of this group.

Tables and desks

The attractive walnut slab table (Pl. 71) earns itself a lonely place at the head of this chapter because the frieze centres on a brass oval embellished with a conventional shell, while the cabriole front legs are also mounted on the knees with shell motifs. Although small, it is a stylish table of c.1725, when one would have expected such finely detailed decoration to be parcel gilt rather than thin-gauge repoussé brass; it appears to be an early, possibly Dutch inspired, instance of the taste for applied brass ornament. Two burr walnut side tables at Antony, Cornwall, the cabriole legs carved with gesso-gilt satyr heads, female masks with tall plumed headdresses and fronded toes serve as a vivid reminder of the lavishness of parcel gilding before cast-brass mounts became fashionable.

The tables and desks discussed in this section have been arranged into loose anthologies. Firstly, there are pieces of orthodox design, except for the fact that they are enlivened with decorative brass mounts or inlay – the slab table, walnut chamber-table, silver table from Haddo, a routine mahogany bureau-table and standard oval gateleg table fall into this category. A second group of tables combines exotic hard-woods with brass inlay to produce lavish effects sometimes reminiscent of Oriental workmanship. Lastly, a small number of multi-purpose mechanical gaming, breakfast and architects' tables and related designs on the Potter advertisement sheet (Pl. 11) are discussed.

The walnut chamber-table, fronted by a single frieze drawer, and supported on cabriole legs with deep lapettes and pad feet, is of crucial importance because the top centres on a flowing rosette inlaid in brass bordered by a string panel with re-entrant corners (Pl. 72–3). It must date from very near the start of the tradition for inlaying furniture with linear brass patterns. The design is not especially ambitious, neither is it primitive – restrained best describes the personality of this table with its shaped aprons, neatly cut mouldings and well-matched veneers. It has a solid walnut top and

71. Slab table, walnut with brass mounts, c.1725. *Ronald A. Lee*

TABLES AND DESKS 75

72. Top of walnut chamber table

73. Chamber table, walnut with brass inlay, c.1735–40. *M.A. Pilkington*

legs, a veneered oak carcase and oak drawer-linings; the end-lifting handles are unlikely to be original.

A table of almost identical form but with a shallow tray-top was found in a ruinous condition in the basement of Haddo House, Scotland, and painstakingly restored (Pl. 74). The use of mahogany suggests it is slightly later than the walnut example; the darker timber acts as a superior foil for the elaborately curvilinear brass rosette and the hardwood permits a higher technical finish, although both are of London quality and attributable to the same workshop. Contemporary conversation pictures confirm that such tables were intended to hold the tea service.[14]

The tops of scalloped pillar and claw tables also provided a fine field for flowing designs (Pl. 158), but incomparably the most spectacular systems of brass stringing are inlaid directly into the top of a large oval mahogany gateleg table (Pl. 75–6). It is an excitingly original creation in which the scale and general impressiveness of the brass patterns makes a powerful artistic statement. The flaps are bordered by strings with neat shells in the corners and a central tendril-and-leaf design, while the fixed top centres on a rose motif with more curiously abstract plant forms at each end. The uncluttered, almost classical purity of the ornament is highly distinctive and a challenge to source hunters.

A mahogany writing-desk of unusual design with two short and two long drawers, plus a slide at either end, the front with blind drawers and a cupboard in the kneehole is finely inlaid with brass pilasters combined with brass mouldings and cockbeads (Pl. 77). The desk is supported on six cabriole legs ending in 'podgy' ball and claw feet which are similar in character to those on a comparable writing-table with parcel-gilt and brass enrichments at Holkham Hall, Norfolk. A little lady's writing-bureau is much more domestic in scale (Pl. 78); its use of rosewood emphasises how richly-figured tropical hardwoods became increasingly a feature of this adventurous tradition of cabinet-making. The brass inlay is confined to string panels on the drawers, a simple border with vivid, rather unEnglish looking, corner ornaments on the desk

74. Tea table, mahogany, the top inlaid with brass stringing, *c.*1740. From Haddo House, Aberdeen. *The National Trust for Scotland*

TABLES AND DESKS 77

75. Top of oval gateleg table. *Jeremy Ltd*

76. Oval gateleg table, mahogany with brass inlay, c.1750. *Ronald A. Lee*

77. Writing desk, mahogany with brass inlay and mouldings, c.1750. *Malletts*

78. Lady's bureau, possibly by Frederick Hintz, rosewood with brass inlay and a marquetry star motif, c.1740–5. *Ronald A. Lee*

slope and a distinctive escutcheon engraved with the Royal Crown, a plumed mask and slug-like supporters – the plate incorporates a spring-action key-hole cover released by a pressure point (Pl. 79). Although hardly a major masterpiece, this desk helps in a small way to define the essential character of the prodigy furniture that followed, and is firmly linked by the Crown and escutcheon to the main tradition of brass-inlaid furniture.[15]

79. Detail of lock escutcheon on Pl. 78 engraved with a Royal Crown and plumed mask

Two most luxurious tables with identical tops demonstrate the sophisticated decorative effects achieved by combining tropical veneers and engraved brass inlay. One table was acquired by the Victoria and Albert Museum in 1944 (Pl. 80–1), its companion by the Fine Arts Museums of San Francisco in 1978 (Pl. 82–3). They are not quite a pair, the former lacking brass enrichment on the pad feet and having a full-length slide and drawer in the frieze (suggesting use as a writing-table). The frame of the other example (once in the Hochschild collection), is of even higher quality, the central cartouche being elegantly engraved with the crest of the Marsh family of Langden and Denton in Kent. The field of both tables is confidently laid out with an inner, elaborately lobed panel of light mahogany outlined by cross-banded partridge-wood borders and an outer field of dark figured mahogany; the banding is edged with brass strings and punctuated by engraved bell husks and dot clusters. The shield on the Victoria and Albert Museum table is blank, but the Marsh crest and mantling is superbly engraved; they feature respectively a tiny satyr mask and a helmeted head. Both tables are sumptuous. The layout of the tops is very similar in plan and decorative detail to the slope of the Graveley bureau (Pl. 50) suggesting a common authorship. It has been pointed out that the unusual angled-leg joints reflect Oriental structural techniques.[16]

The exotic padouk-wood concertina-action card-table decorated with inlaid brass arabesque marquetry roundels and stringing lines is, by any standards, a thrilling piece of furniture (Col. pl. X–XIII). The baize-lined interior centres on a lobed panel bordered and inlaid with engraved mother-of-pearl floral sprays with similar dished circles for candlesticks and oval counter-wells. The shimmering effect created by candlelight must have been ravishing. The frieze is inlaid with brass ovals and contains a small central drawer with hardwood linings. The cushion-moulded apron and plain cabriole legs are similar to the two tables just discussed and the Ince Blundell architect's table (Pl. 89) while the late baroque marquetry inlay is related to the Carlton Hobbs bureau-cabinet (Col. pl. IV). Despite these analogies, the mother-of-pearl flowers look distinctly Oriental, while the lock that secures the top and the hooks that brace the concertina frame are sophisticated for an English card-table of this date. The possibility exists that this is an imported Oriental card-table which was inlaid with brass by Hintz, Channon, Landall or some other London firm specialising in this decorative technique. It so happens that on 18 November 1983 Sotheby's sold a pair of padouk card-tables of identical pattern to the example we are considering, including all the mother-of-pearl features, but lacking any brass inlay. Accordingly, 'blanks' could have been available for enriching with brass. Also, Hyde Park Antiques of Broadway, New York, recently had in stock a padouk card-table combining Oriental inflections and candle-wells enriched with floral inlay executed in pearl shell. In his article 'Furniture in the Soane Museum'[17] R.W. Symonds published one of eight rosewood chairs of English design but Chinese workmanship, elaborately decorated with mother-of-pearl, including the arms of Sir Gregory Page, Bt, inlaid on the splat, c.1725. Symonds pointed out that at this time large quantities of chairs, tables and scrutoires were imported from the East Indies, the majority of this furniture being plain rosewood; but in 1726 '24 No Chairs of rosewood inlaid with Mother-of-Pearl £12' were listed in the records.[18]

80. Top of writing-table veneered in padouk, cross-banded with partridge wood, the brass inlay closely similar to that on the slope of the Graveley bureau (Pl. 50)

81. Writing table, probably by J. Graveley, *c.*1740–5, padouk with brass inlay and a slide above the frieze drawer.
The Trustees of the Victoria and Albert Museum

TABLES AND DESKS 81

82. Top of writing-table, centring on a cartouche engraved with the crest of the Marsh family of Langden and Denton in Kent

83. Writing-table, probably by J. Graveley, c.1740–5, padouk with partridge wood cross-banding and brass inlay. *The Fine Arts Museums of San Francisco*

Little reliable information has been published on furniture made in Asia in the English style, although trade seems to have been brisk during the second quarter of the eighteenth century.[19] Officers and the crew of ships were allowed to bring back private venture goods, of which furniture was popular because it could be dismantled. An important documented group of pieces exported from Canton to Denmark in 1735, 1737 and 1738 has been identified, while Vilhelm Slomann[20] quotes a contract from an account book of private trade conducted by the Dane Christian Lintrup and Assam Goa of Canton in 1741:

Agreed about the following assortments which shall be ready at the arrival of the ship Dronningen (to Canton) every sort of the prices quoted as follows: Two big bureau of rosewood of which the nether part shall consist of two pieces; the upper measure $3\frac{1}{2}$ cobis on the two sides and 4 cobis in the centre, the doors shall on the innersides have looking glasses and on the outersides all covered with flowers and leaf work engraved in relief. For the salary to work on and for white copper locks, keys, hinges and all other metal fittings is agreed . . . 150.

Other entries show that Assam Goa received models from which he could make two tables and four gueridons as well as an English chair to be made in a set of twelve.

After a glance at some admittedly patchy evidence, a case can be made for believing that this exotic card-table was made in the East Indies in the English taste, the brass inlay added in London. Clearly, the firms involved in producing brass-inlaid furniture had access to exceptional stocks of tropical hardwood, so they or their suppliers could well have imported furniture or even repertoires of components from time to time.

A massive padouk sideboard table, formerly owned by the Lords Delamere, Vale Royal, Cheshire, can best be described as an example of prodigy furniture (Col. pl. XIV–XVI). The towering Powderham bookcases also made to a gigantic scale, employing an amazing quantity of prized tropical hardwood and inlaid with brass, are among the few comparable structures. The Delamere sideboard, over ten feet long, centres on a rather French-looking carved female mask with headdress, the end and side friezes display stylised fronded shells, and the knees of the cabriole legs are ornamented with coffee beans and acanthus. The corner mouldings, borders and legs are inlaid and faced with brass. The lavish effect is so overpowering that one can hardly avoid wondering if the table was perhaps originally made for some Colonial banqueting-hall, which might account for its stupendous showiness. During the last century this inconveniently huge table was dismantled and re-assembled as two console tables. After a period of separation both were sold by Diana, Lady Delamere, at Christie's, on 25 September 1980, and eventually passed to Carlton Hobbs, who restored the table to its original form, giving it a new marble top.[21] While the concept of an exotic commission is probably far-fetched, the use of padouk on such a spectacular scale, certain broad similarities with French *bureau-plats*, and the very strung-out character of the design make this a highly enigmatic example of London furniture.

Two very smart side-tables discovered in dealers' photographic archives are of capital interest because both are closely related to the richly styled Bristol collector's cabinet; the hipped cabriole legs of this group are ornamented with large gilt-brass helmeted and winged warrior's head with fronded lion's-paw feet (Pl. 84). The smaller of the side-tables (46 inches wide) is of padouk and the decoration has all been expertly carved, exactly reproducing the intricate details of the bronze casting on the supports of the illustrious Bristol cabinet (Pl. 85 & 118). If it was originally parcel gilt no traces of gold remain. The second table, once owned by Leonard Knight, has a drawer in the frieze, while the legs feature precisely the same vigorous gilt-metal mounts of a warrior and leafy lion's paws (Pl. 86). It is satisfying to be able to bring into the core group a piece of furniture devoid of brass enrichment and a handsome side-table, both almost certainly from the Channon workshop.

84. Centre table, possibly by John Channon, padouk, c.1740–5, the carved ornament inspired by metal mounts. *Ronald A. Lee*

85. Detail of carved winged and helmeted warrior mask replicating mounts found on a side table (Pl. 86) and the Bristol cabinet (Pl. 118). *Jonathan Harris*

86. Side table, possibly by John Channon, padouk, c.1740–5, with a frieze drawer; identical leg mounts are found on the Bristol cabinet (Pl. 118). *Ronald A. Lee*

A remarkable sheet of furniture designs has recently created a wave of academic interest (Pl. 11).[22] It features an ostentatious medal cabinet on stand, its apron inscribed 'Potter London' and displays every appearance of being a free portrait of the celebrated example attributed to Channon now in the Victoria and Albert Museum (Pl. 113). This masterpiece is surrounded by fifteen lesser specimens of ingenious mechanical tables and stands, mainly for eating, writing and gaming. Potter may be identified as Thomas Potter of Holborn, recorded in partnership with John Kelsey in a 1738 account at Stourhead which itemises a (presumably hinged and ratcheted) bed-table. Here we have visually linked a highly spectacular brass-embellished cabinet and an eccentric repertoire of multi-purpose harlequin tables and stands. On 15 November 1990 the executors of the late Colonel William Stirling Keir sold at Christie's a mahogany brass-inlaid triple-flap harlequin games-table; the top flap enclosed a backgammon and chess board, the central flap was baize-lined and provided with counter-wells, and the rising till had an open partitioned tray top and pigeon-holes above small drawers (Col. pl. VIII–IX). In overall design, it is not unlike some of Potter's engravings and even closer in inspiration to a triple-flap rosewood harlequin table brought back from Canton in 1737 by Captain Allewelt and now at Fredensborg Castle, Denmark.[23] Accordingly, the possibility that Potter stocked some Oriental imports cannot be lightly dismissed. Interesting parallels exist with Roentgen's first period mechanical furniture.

A most inventive mahogany breakfast-table (Pl. 88), lacking brass inlay but corresponding exactly to a Potter design (Pl. 87), was acquired at Christie's by Temple

87. Engraving for a breakfast table from the Potter design sheet, *c.*1745. *The Trustees of the Victoria and Albert Museum*

88. Breakfast table, probably by Potter & Kelsey, *c.*1745, mahogany fitted with a tray which lowers into the deep framing and flaps designed as hinged slides. *Leeds City Art Galleries*

Newsam on 16 July 1992. It is rectangular with cabriole legs and the interior is fitted with a loose tray to hold the breakfast things. When the meal is finished, by the release of two catches, the tray lowers into the deep framing and the two 'Pembroke'-type flaps can then be raised and slide across the top so that the table is available for reading, writing or work. It is an elegantly functional arrangement which neatly avoided the alternative practice of clearing the table-top by placing left-over food in a lattice cupboard below.[24]

The Ince Blundell architect's table, entirely veneered in rosewood with solid cabriole legs, also belongs to the family of brass-inlaid and mounted furniture, although the low-relief mounts with their intricate masks, shells and foliage stand slightly apart (Pl. 89). The top of the table is hinged to form a slope and has a second set of hinges to enable the top to fold right back to reveal an elaborately fitted interior, which houses a second adjustable slope, a pair of candle sconces, lidded compartments and frieze drawers at each end containing a snuffer and two more adjustable candle branches. This important provenanced architect's table was almost certainly a special commission, since nothing else quite like it has ever been recorded; its uniqueness inevitably encourages speculation about a possible exotic origin.

89. Architect's table, rosewood with brass mounts, strings and candle-arms, c.1740–5; from Ince Blundell Hall, Liverpool. *National Museums and Galleries on Merseyside*

The 'nymph and satyr' group

Most English patrons when commissioning case furniture preferred sober Palladian ideals of taste. Accordingly cabinet-makers were encouraged to invest their designs with a formal architectural character, perhaps enlivened by an overlay of rococo detail. The repertoire of bureau-cabinets with brass inlay reflects these conventional ideas of genteel elegance. Carved looking-glass frames, stands, wall-brackets, table-frames and chairs captured the flowing lines and festive spirit of rococo ornament earlier than cabinet furniture, which was never so susceptible to florid curvilinear styling.

Thomas Chippendale first applied rococo attributes to a full range of English household furniture in his *Director*, 1754. He exploited decorative motifs taken from naturalistic plant and animal life and delightful details borrowed from the worlds of Pan and Venus, together with reeds, waves, rocks, shells, waterfalls and flames embraced by a balanced system of frilly curves and fronded scrolls. However, few of the more audacious rococo show cabinets in the *Director* were ever executed, while many others had their rich details severely pruned on the work-bench. That Chippendale was aware of the fashion for brass-inlaid furniture is clear from pl. CXXII in the third edition of his *Director* (Pl. 90) illustrating two ambitious cabinets on stands in which, according to a prefatory note, the 'Ornaments may be Brass, or Silver, finely chased and put on; or they may be cut in Filigree-Work, in Wood, Brass, or Silver'. The range of ornamental motifs featured in these two designs include nymphs and satyrs, a Bacchus mask, putto, dolphins, vases of flowers, garlands, flame work, shells, falling water, acanthus and husk chains. Although no cabinet based on either engraving has been traced, the upper stage of the right-hand design is almost a sketch for the great back-to-back library table (Pl. 106). There is in fact an extraordinary constellation of full-blooded rococo brass-mounted and -inlaid cabinet furniture that combines the same decorative vocabulary with vigorous all-embracing curvilinear forms. This elite group, here attributed to John Channon, unquestionably represents the most grandiloquent rococo cabinet furniture made in any English workshop.

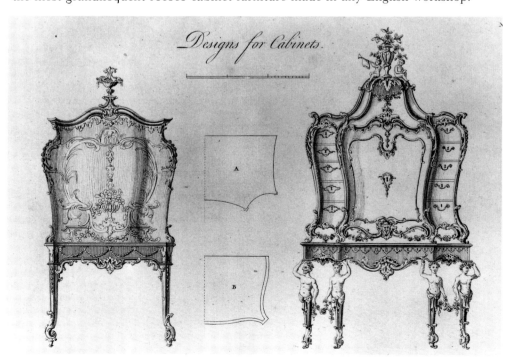

90. Thomas Chippendale, *The Director*, 1762, pl. CXXII; a prefatory note states the 'Ornaments may be cut in Filigree-Work, in Wood, Brass, or Silver'. The cabinet on the right is not unlike the design of the library table (Pl. 106). *The Chippendale Society*

The Murray writing-cabinet deserves to be one of the few named pieces of English furniture (Col. pl. XVII–XVIII & Pl. 91–102). It passed by descent to Sir William Keith Murray of Ochtertyre, Perthshire, Scotland, who sold it at Christie's in 1949. After being refused an export licence, it was purchased by Major Arthur Bull and acquired from the beneficiaries of his estate for Temple Newsam, in 1985. Unfortunately no relevant documentation in the form of letters, inventories, or bills has been found among the Ochtertyre papers at the National Library of Scotland. A metal tab attached to the key ring is lettered 'GILT CABINET' (Pl. 91), which aptly describes the profusion of ormolu mounts and brass inlay. The firm responsible for this masterpiece must have deliberately set out to make the most luxurious furniture in London. It is, as Symonds claimed, 'a *tour de force* of the English cabinet maker's craft', of exceptionally elaborate design and very richly ornamented.

The cabinet is constructed in three parts, held together by robust wrought-iron hooks and eyes at the back (Pl. 98) – a method of fixing sometimes found on earlier walnut desks and bookcases. The lower stage, in the form of a serpentine commode, has a fitted desk-drawer with slide which pulls forward on divided corner trusses. The serpentine-fronted upper stage is enclosed by two massive doors hinged half-way back on the sides so that when opened they form deep wings housing banks of small drawers, pigeon-holes and folio partitions (Col. pl. XVIII). Only one other cabinet with comparable storage capacity in the doors is known (Pl. 103). The inner façade of compartments and drawers centres on a cupboard containing a total of no fewer than seventeen secret drawers gradually revealed by releasing hidden catches and operating ingenious sliding panels (Pl. 92). The separate cornice, faced with a spectacular rococo waterfall mount (Pl. 96), is decorated at the corners with gilt brass figures freely copied from the famous *Venus de Medici* (Pl. 93) and the *Faun in Rosso Antico* excavated only in 1736. Small versions of these were frequently sold to Grand Tourists.

Most English cabinet-makers of the rococo period used brass mounts modestly to give a smart but not ostentatious appearance to their furniture. However, the creator of the Murray writing-cabinet displayed a far more positive attitude towards the role of mounts, employing an exuberant repertoire that included winged satyr heads (Pl. 94), nereid masks (Pl. 95), cascading water (Pl. 96), rock work, clusters of sea-shells, tied ribbons and fronded scrolls, all exquisitely chased and brilliantly fire gilt. The elaborately rocaille drawer handles (Pl. 97) echo the flamboyant cornice mount: their superb quality suggests the work of a goldsmith rather than a bronzier. They have in the past been attributed to Paris,[25] but are quite unlike the mounts on French furniture – so their authorship remains a gripping mystery. The arcadian character of the cabinet is enhanced by the engraved brass inlay on the doors, which are ornamented with seated figures of Ceres and Mercury (Pl. 101), an entwined pair of dragons and a Bacchus mask with vine trail (Pl. 102), one leaf concealing a keyhole cover (Pl. 99–100). No source has yet been traced for these ornaments, but they are reminiscent of the designs of Paul van Somer and Cuvilliés' early work.[26] The drawer-fronts and

91. Key-ring and tab from the Murray cabinet; the spiked instruments are for releasing hidden spring catches

92. The Murray writing-cabinet: detail showing some of the 17 secret compartments in the central niche cupboard

93. Gilt bronze finial figure based on the *Venus de Medici*

94. Satyr corner mount with waterfall, tied ribbons and a laurel spray

95. Nereid corner mount with rockwork, shells and falling water

THE 'NYMPH AND SATYR' GROUP

96. Detail of rococo cresting mount

97. Winged handle escutcheon found on many pieces on the so called 'nymph and satyr' group

98. The Murray writing-cabinet: one of the massive iron hooks and eyes that hold the separate stages together

borders are enriched by arabesques inspired by Berain; even the sides are outlined with brass strings and the internal divisions edged with fine brass lines. The discrepancy between the progressive rococo mounts and the rather retarded character of the inlay (which is however of superlative quality) has often been commented on.

90 FURNITURE SURVEY

99. The Murray writing-cabinet: keyhole escutcheon with spring flap, released by activating a pressure point

100. Back of keyhole escutcheon showing the spring mechanism and flap open

101. Engraved brass inlay of Mercury and Ceres with fronded strap work, an eagle displayed and diaper patterns

102. Engraved brass inlay of dragons and a satyr mask, presumably based on a printed source

A second mahogany writing-cabinet of closely similar design to the Murray cabinet was sent by a Mrs Matthews of Ealing to Christie's in 1919 and acquired by Lord Leverhulme, whose executors sold it again at the Anderson Galleries, New York, in 1926. It re-appeared on the London art market in 1948, was bought by a Portuguese collector and is now in a Lisbon museum (Pl. 103–5). Although highly ambitious with fully serpentine front and ends inlaid with brass arabesque and trellis work, the same unusual fold-back doors (each containing a small cupboard, twelve drawers and a slide), and including a fitted desk-drawer which pulls forward on corner supports, the overall effects is somewhat less rich. This is because, apart from providing lively rococo key-hole and handle escutcheons, the cabinet-maker has not used gilt-metal mounts. Instead, the canted corners of the upper stage are fluently carved with caryatids representing Diana with a crescent on her brow (Pl. 105) and the helmeted head of either Minerva or Mars. The carving of the figures, emerging from leafy sheaths with pendants of fruit and flowers below, is of the highest order and may be compared to the sharply detailed warrior masks on a table (Pl. 85) related to the Bristol cabinet. Although the drawers are all constructed of mahogany and edged with brass cock-beads, showing that no expense was spared, the interior is slightly disappointing, being merely fitted with adjustable shelves, and the solid plinth gives a rather heavy appearance. The Murray writing-cabinet and this example must have been made a few years apart in the same workshop.

Back-to-back writing-tables first came into fashion during the reign of George II. Both halves were of identical knee-hole and pedestal form and when placed back-to-back formed a large centre-table for a room such as a library.[27] Of course they could also be used separately (as, for example, a writing-desk and dressing-table) and many pairs must have parted company. This has unfortunately been the fate of a sumptuous pair from the same workshop as the Murray writing-cabinet. According to a family tradition, they came from Alderman Beckford's house, Fonthill Splendens in Wiltshire (they may be mentioned in John Britton's description of an unnamed house that matches Fonthill), one standing in the principal bed-chamber a 'Superb dressing table with brass carved ornaments', its companion in another bedroom. However, in 1801, the year of the first Fonthill sale, a report in the *Gentleman's Magazine* refers to 'Two library tables ... of the most elegant construction and exquisite workmanship'.[28] One table re-appeared on the London market in 1956 and was purchased by the Victoria and Albert Museum (Pl. 106); its companion was sold at Phillips by Sir George Holford in 1928, and after five changes of ownership was bought by an American collector at Christie's on 6 July 1989 for £1,100,000 – a world auction record for English furniture (Col. pl. XXI).

The two halves are of identical exaggerated serpentine and bombe form with lancet-shaped niches at each end and canted corners used as 'display' areas, but the façades, as one would expect on a library writing-table of the period, are each differently fitted for the convenience of the user. The section now at the Victoria and Albert Museum has, like the Murray cabinet, a long, well-fitted desk drawer with writing-slide which pulls forward on corner-truss supports (Pl. 107). There are four drawers in each pedestal and the ogee knee-hole accommodates a further nest of five small drawers. The opposite façade, while of virtually identical design, in fact houses a single narrow central drawer above the knee-hole which contains a concave cupboard, while the pedestals, styled as false drawers, form doors to cupboards. There is evidence of major reconstruction of the interior and several missing mounts have recently been replaced by replicas.

The complex curvature of the front demanded, as Symonds wrote 'craftsmanship of almost unbelievable skill and ingenuity',[29] not only in the carcase work; the veneer for

92 FURNITURE SURVEY

103 (*above*). Detail of corner truss: the carved head with a crescent represents Diana. *Photograph courtesy The Winterthur Library*

104. Writing-cabinet, probably by John Channon, *c.*1740–5, mahogany with brass inlay. *Fundacao Madieros, Lisbon; Photograph courtesy The Winterthur Library*

105. Writing-cabinet, the doors shown open, each incorporating banks of drawers around a niche-cupboard and a slide. *Photograph courtesy The Winterthur Library*

each drawer-front and the canopy over the knee-hole had to be laid on in several pieces because of the shaping in two planes. The drawers are outlined with brass strings and cockbeads and the top is inset on three sides with a Greek-key border spaced with ebony paterae inlaid into a band of padouk (Pl. 107). However, the most imposing feature of the tables is the extravagant display of cast, chased and gilt brass mounts (Pl. 109). Most are from the same moulds as those on the Murray cabinet – with the lively addition of a pair of winged dolphins (attributes of Venus) and a cartouche at the foot of one knee-hole, plus a superb lock-mount headed by shell clusters and rock work above the other knee-hole (Pl. 108). The confident handling of rococo design and

106. Half of a back-to-back library table, probably by John Channon, c.1750–5, mahogany with gilt-brass mounts and inlay; possibly commissioned by Alderman Beckford for Fonthill Splendens or his London house. *The Trustees of the Victoria and Albert Museum*

107. Desk drawer with writing-slide: the brass key-pattern border is inlaid into padouk and punctuated by ebony roundels

THE 'NYMPH AND SATYR' GROUP

108. Detail of nereid mounts and rockwork with shells above a superb rococo lock-plate

109. Detail showing nymph and satyr mounts, dolphins, handles and brass cockbeading

absence of any baroque motifs suggests this masterpiece dates from about 1760. It is certainly extravagant, although hardly more so than the distorted contours in some of Chippendale's *Director* designs (Pl. 90).[30] There is no compelling reason on the evidence of craftsmanship or style to suppose that either the Murray cabinet or this amazing library table are the work of immigrant tradesmen.

In 1956 (the year that the library table was acquired by the Victoria and Albert Museum) an exceedingly grand serpentine commode with the same distinctive nereid console mounts and winged handle escutcheons appeared in Harrod's saleroom (Col. pl. XXII). It came originally from Southwick Park, Hampshire, home of the Thistlethwayte family (who had subscribed to Chippendale's *Director*), and passed by descent to Eva Borthwick-Norton, who consigned it for auction. A small ivory tab fixed inside one drawer is inscribed 'Old Drawers/SE Bedroom'. This mahogany commode, which was purchased for Temple Newsam, displays a love of curved surfaces, for not only is the front of serpentine form, but most unusually the sides have been fully shaped as well. The edge of the top and plinth are banded with brass Gothic-pattern frets in-filled with black wax, while the top is outlined with a brass string. The rich ormolu mounts are of the same pattern as those on the Murray cabinet and the library table. The secondary timbers (oak, pine) and construction are typically English, apart from the drawers which have unlaminated white oak fronts and oak bottoms of framed, flush-beaded panel construction (Pl. 41) – a refinement encountered in no other group of London furniture.

In 1960, Louis Clarke bequeathed to the Fitzwilliam Museum, Cambridge, a more modest version of the Southwick commode which he had probably acquired from Partridge (Pl. 110). It is serpentine-fronted but has straight ends and lacks fretted bands around the top and plinth. However, all the mounts (with the addition of carrying handles) correspond to those on the Temple Newsam commode and both are of identical construction, even down to the drawer linings and wooden stops being attached to the sides of the commode rather than the dustboards.

A third commode, known only from two photographs, is of rectangular design with a ribbon and rosette moulding round the top, short lion-paw feet and carved aprons (Pl. 111). According to Percy Macquoid, the timber is 'light-coloured rosewood',[31] which provides a link with brass-inlaid furniture, but the most striking feature is the elaborate rococo handle-plates which match those on the other two commodes, the Murray cabinet and the library table. The box-like form and carved enrichments have more in common with a group of case furniture tentatively attributed to William Hallett,[32] rather than the design attitudes of the Channon workshop.

A more impressive piece, again known only from a photograph (taken when Moss Harris had it in stock in about 1924), is a small cabinet on stand with the familiar nymph and satyr head and lower console mounts, some of which have been cut down to fit the narrower spaces (Pl. 112). The high-relief carving of the cabriole legs and knee-hole flanks is of excellent quality and may one day assist in making an attribution. The drawers interestingly are not cockbeaded, but the handle-plates correspond to those on the magnificent Kenwood secretaire. The serpentine contours of the stand contrast strangely with the severe cornice and broken pediment, resulting in something of an artistic failure, while the vacant-looking cupboard door must surely originally have been panelled. Finally, a photograph in the Victoria and Albert Museum archive[33] of an antique shop at Woodchester shows the lower stage of a very similar cabinet on stand which combines parcel-gilt carved enrichments with the usual repertoire of brass mounts.

THE 'NYMPH AND SATYR' GROUP 97

110. Commode, probably by John Channon, c.1750, mahogany with the familiar repertoire of chased brass mounts. *The Fitzwilliam Museum*

111. Commode, probably by John Channon, c.1740–5, rosewood with typical handle-plates. *Lewis Hinckley*

112. Cabinet on stand, probably by John Channon, c.1750, mahogany with brass mounts; the glazing not original. *The Henry Francis du Pont Winterthur Library*

Cabinets on stands

The bureau-cabinets decorated with brass inlay on the whole display the characteristic restraint of English furniture made during the first half of the eighteenth century and fall within the normal range of London cabinet-making. However, two cabinets on stands, one at Bristol (Col. pl. xix–xx), the other owned by the Victoria and Albert Museum (Pl. 113–17), represent the baroque tradition in which sumptuous cabinets were valued as spectacular status symbols, formed the focal points of rooms, and were regarded as the summit of artistic achievement. The Victoria and Albert Museum cabinet was assigned to Sotheby's of London by Mrs Amy Guest of New York and auctioned on 2 February 1962. The illustration in the sale catalogue shows it prior to restoration by the dealer, J.A. Lewis. When offered in the sale-room the cabinet was fronted by clear-glazed doors and three pilasters of nineteenth-century date, carved with gilt Regence ornament interspersed with Roman medallion heads. The interior was adapted so that it could serve as a display cabinet. The general design has many features in common with the Louis XV style medal cabinet depicted on the Potter design sheet (Pl. 11), although there is little doubt that it was originally fitted with tiers of shallow shelves, rather than a bank of drawers.

Before selling it to the Victoria and Albert Museum in 1964, J.A. Lewis re-silvered the bevelled glass doors and backed them with mahogany, taken from the rear of the cabinet. The design of the new brass inlay inside the doors was copied from that on the sides. Another back was made to replace the mahogany original. The carved pilasters were removed and replaced by the present fluted and stopped columns copied from a brass-inlaid bureau cabinet in the national collection (Pl. 47).

This heavily restored but, because of its high quality and ambitious design, immensely significant cabinet has a semi-circular broken pediment at the front and segmental pediments at the sides which resemble the bureau-cabinet decorated with tortoiseshell and brass inlay (Pl. 50). The cresting is headed by gilt-metal portrait busts inscribed with the names of three Roman emperors: Caesar Augustus, Vespasian and Vitellus (according to Malcom Baker they are Italian eighteenth-century and of mediocre quality). These finials are unlikely to be original, because faint marks on the pediment indicate that the cabinet may have been surmounted by recumbent figures similar to Justice and Britannia shown on the Potter design sheet (Pl. 11). The stand contains two mahogany-lined drawers; the upper one, with a slide, was originally partitioned for writing materials and had a pull-out ink-well on the right-hand side. Springs behind the drawers provided a release mechanism. An exceptional feature is the massive sculptural mount on the knee of each cabriole leg cast in the form of a plumed female mask with pendant flowers and foliage (Pl. 117). They are of the same design but those on the rear legs are from different moulds. Mounts of identical pattern have been recorded on several Parisian commodes (see pp. 40–1), which indicates a French origin, although the casting could have been undertaken in London.

While some elements of the engraved brass inlay relate to the decoration found on other pieces, this cabinet has its own distinctive repertoire of ornament. For instance, the drawer fronts are panelled with standard interlaced strings, but enriched also with a complex diaper pattern derived from Boulle marquetry and have finely chased handles (Pl. 42 & 117). The lock-plates on the door are engraved with putti blowing flutes (Pl. 116) and a plaque beneath the central finial bust features two more putti. The door spandrels centre on lion masks amid arabesques (Pl. 114), while elsewhere there are female masks, shells and at the foot of the central pilaster a basket of fruit flanked by a pair of putti. The most enigmatic decorative detail is the emblem of a ram pendant from entwined serpents engraved on each central pair of hinge-plates (Pl.

100 FURNITURE SURVEY

113. Cabinet on stand, mahogany and padouk with brass mounts, mouldings and inlay, attributed to John Channon, c.1740: the mirror plates and pilasters are not original. *The Trustees of the Victoria and Albert Museum*

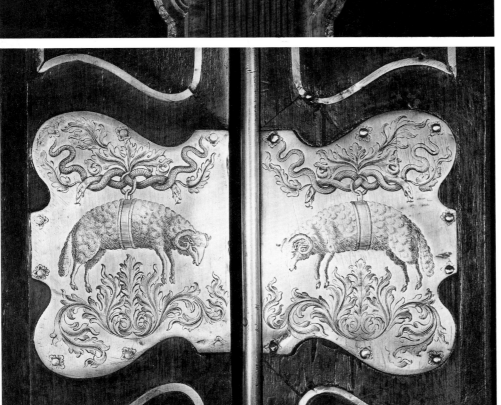

114. Door spandrels inlaid with engraved lion's heads amid scrolling foliage; cast-brass capital

115. One of four sets of hinge plates engraved with a ram pendant from entwined snakes – possibly a maker's emblem

116. One of two lock-plates, each engraved with a putto playing a wind instrument

115). They are of course visible only when the doors stand fully open. J.F. Hayward rejected the idea that the device represented the badge of the Order of the Golden Fleece because their fleece was suspended from a fire-steel not snakes.[34] He then considered whether it might be a maker's emblem: the cabinet-maker William Master traded 'at the Golden Fleece, Coventry Street, Piccadilly', but the device on his printed bill-head at Blair Castle dated 1746 does not include snakes. Phineas Evans of St Paul's Church Yard used the same sign, and tantalisingly one tradesman 'upon the pavement' in St Martin's Lane, part of the street where Channon lived, is known to have employed the Golden Fleece as a shop sign.[35]

If the Victoria and Albert Museum medal cabinet leaves something to be desired on the grounds of extensive restoration, the same cannot be said of a smaller but even more sumptuous cabinet on stand in almost mint condition, acquired by Bristol Art Gallery from Gerald Kerin Ltd in 1966 (Col. pl. XIX–XX & Pl. 118–27). It is exceptional for the profusion of gilt-metal mounts and case mouldings, combined with brass inlay to create an effect of ostentatious splendour rarely encountered in English furniture. The hipped cabriole legs are mounted with winged and helmeted warrior masks (Pl. 118) and fronded lion's-paw feet. An identical set of mounts has been recorded on a side table (Pl. 86) and the same motifs, carved from solid padouk, occur on another table (Pl. 85). The upper of two frieze drawers is fitted for writing; both have ornamental lock mounts, the lower escutcheon being flanked by French cockerel heads – a detail found on Parisian furniture (Pl. 30) – see pp. 39–40.

The cabinet is fronted by double doors, each faced with an arched panel of richly figured burr wood which has in the past been identified as thuya and amboyna but

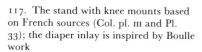

117. The stand with knee mounts based on French sources (Col. pl. III and Pl. 33); the diaper inlay is inspired by Boulle work

looks more like native yew, and may have been chosen for a fancied resemblance to tortoiseshell. The spandrels are decorated with scrolling arabesque marquetry inhabited by birds on a veneered ebony ground (Pl. 119), and there are similar small panels at the base. The doors open to reveal a bank of 46 shallow specimen drawers with a small central cupboard containing seven more drawers. The door to this niche has a mount formed of a single casting similar to those used on Régence clocks; it features a bust of Mars flanked by putti holding a bow and a pipe between satyr and female terms (Pl. 121), and a central cartouche is left blank. The lock-plate of the inner door is engraved with a *commedia del'arte* figure holding a club (Pl. 120) which provides an important decorative link to the embellishment of a distinguished padouk secretaire (Pl. 122–5). The main doors are fitted inside with an unusual arrangement of veneered flaps, which hinge open to reveal narrow velvet-lined compartments which could be used to display miniatures. Further refinements include flush bolts operated by levers cast as a helmeted head, and the two lock-plates which are boldly engraved with warriors copied from a suite of prints portraying *The Roman Heroes* by H. Goltzius published in 1586 (Pl. 122–5). The numerous martial figures give this cabinet a strongly masculine character. It is perhaps worth pausing to remember that John Channon's elder brother, Otho, named his sons after Roman emperors – Titus Vespasian, Tiberius and Caligula.[36] The family was apparently devoted to Roman history.

The pediment is a triumph of curvilinear complexity and ornamental elaboration (Pl. 126). At the top is a blank shield amid a baroque confection of shells, animal and human masks, monster heads, floral festoons and swirling acanthus in cast brass. The tympanum, veneered like the rest of the cabinet in burr yew, centres on a large inlaid shell flanked by three-dimensional foliate volutes and prominent vase finials (Pl. 127). For sheer virtuosity the Bristol cabinet approaches the quality of French Boulle work more nearly than any other piece of English brass-inlaid furniture, although it must be acknowledged that the mounts are an amalgam rather than suggesting specific design.

118. Winged and helmeted warrior mask (see Col. pl. XIX), also found on two tables (Pl. 85–6); possibly inspired by one of Bernard Toro's prints

119. Door spandrel inlaid with scrolling foliage inhabited by a bird on an ebony ground (see Col. pl. XIX)

120. The Bristol cabinet, Col. pl. XIX: detail of cast and chased brass mounts on the niche door

121. Lock-plate inside the niche door engraved with a harlequin holding a club; the same figure occurs on the bureau in Col. pl. VII

122. Right-hand lock-plate

123. Publis Horatus, from *The Roman Heroes*, by H. Goltzius, 1586. *The Trustees of the Victoria and Albert Museum*

CABINETS ON STANDS 105

124. The Bristol cabinet, Col. pl. XIX: left-hand lock-plate

125. Mucius Scaevola, from *The Roman Heroes*, by H. Goltzius, 1586. *The Trustees of the Victoria and Albert Museum*

126. Detail of inlaid brass shell and mounts on the cresting

127. Detail of cast-brass corner finial, possibly taken from a carriage

There are two very different cabinets on stands in the collection of the National Museums and Galleries on Merseyside, both of which stand apart from the mainstream tradition of brass-inlaid furniture. The earliest is a monumental cabinet raised on a chest of drawers with massive parcel-gilt corner trusses carved with Homeric heads (Pl. 128). The four corner pilasters, the frieze and the door panels are outlined with brass stringing and corner mouldings. The brass inlay is not at all showy but gives the façade a surface richness in tune with the parcel-gilt cornice and stand. The veneered ground is a type of mahogany, possibly sabicu. Fortunately, Lord Leverhulme recorded the provenance of this memorable cabinet, which came originally from Kirtlington Park, Oxfordshire. Sir James Dashwood's account at Hoare's Bank includes four payments between 1747 and 1752 totalling over £500 to William Hallett, a fashionable London cabinet-maker who is currently regarded as the most likely author.[37] Hallett's name (and that of John Boson) is sometimes associated with a group of Kentian mahogany lion-mask furniture, so it may be worth recording that an important commode belonging to this group, displayed by the National Trust at Beningbrough Hall, has very fine engraved brass escutcheon plates set into the drawer fronts (Pl. 129).

The second Merseyside piece, shown at Sudley Art Gallery, is a very sophisticated chinoiserie china-cabinet on stand of about 1760, the doors inlaid with delicate brass arabesques (Pl. 130). It came from the Beausire family of Liverpool merchants (a provenance not likely to be old), but interestingly a manuscript design for this cabinet has been found at the Victoria and Albert Museum.[38] It is not signed but displays some resemblance to a small collection of drawings, including a 'Chinese Cabinet' attributed to William Gomm in the John Downs collection at Winterthur Museum, Delaware.[39] (Gomm was one of the masters under whom Abraham Roentgen worked when he came to London in or after 1736.) The Beausire cabinet does not appear to belong to a coherent sub-group of brass-inlaid furniture, although a 'companion' example has an inlaid lattice-work key-plate.[40] The maker seems merely to have chosen a decorative option that was normally practised only by a few specialist firms. An otherwise routine secretaire bookcase[41] has little inlaid brass fleur-de-lys corner ornaments on the doors, while the Henry Huntington collection in Los Angeles contains a pair of colossal mahogany presses with carved female heads and a little brass inlay – they are certainly on an heroic 'Channon' scale.[42] A census of George II period furniture shows several well-defined mainstream traditions for the use of brass inlay with a scatter of fringe pieces.

The fashion had passed by about 1765 and was not revived until the Regency period when refugee French ebenistes reintroduced Boulle techniques into London workshops. During the early nineteenth century this method of decorating furniture became vastly more popular than it had been in the reign of George II, although once again it was mainly confined to tradesmen based in the capital. Virtually the only impressive example of early Neo-classical furniture enriched with brass inlay is an exquisite, possibly architect-designed, cabinet of c.1770 combining highly elaborate panels of engraved brass marquetry with pilasters veneered in red tortoiseshell (Pl. 131).

The Powderham bookcases

Although John Hayward was not the first scholar to notice that the Powderham bookcases each display a plaque inscribed '17 J Channon Fecit 40'[43] it was following his article about them in 1966[44] that they became the most talked-about pieces of English furniture (Col. pl. XXIII and Pl. 132). Twenty years later, they were accepted by the Government in lieu of inheritance tax and acquired by the Victoria and Albert

128. Cabinet on chest-of-drawers, attributed to William Hallett, c.1747, probably sabicu, with Homeric heads and parcel-gilt carving, the upper stage inlaid with brass strings. *National Museums and Galleries on Merseyside*

129. Engraved brass handle escutcheon on a mahogany lion-mask commode, c.1750; at Beningbrough Hall, Yorkshire. *The National Trust*

130. China cabinet, mahogany, parcelgilt with brass inlay at the corners of the door frames, c.1755–60. *National Museums and Galleries on Merseyside*

131. Collector's cabinet, mahogany, tulipwood and kingwood with engraved brass inlay, the pilasters veneered with red tortoiseshell, c.1770–5; later rosewood stand. *Pelham Galleries*

132. The Powderham bookcase, no. II, one of a pair bearing brass tablets engraved '17 J. CHANNON 40' (Pl. 141). Veneered in padouk, the main brass plates copied directly from a design published by Jean Berain, *c*.1700. *The Trustees of the Victoria and Albert Museum*

133. Powderham bookcase: detail of carved and gilt decoration on the pediment

Museum on condition that they remain in situ. In view of their importance as a 'Rosetta stone' for Channon furniture, the time is long overdue for making available a detailed pictorial record of the decorative brass inlays.

The bookcases are believed to be the earliest examples of English furniture signed by the maker on an engraved brass plate (Pl. 141) – a practice only generally adopted in the late eighteenth century by several firms producing patent furniture. In addition to the inscribed tablets, the account books of Sir William Courtenay of Powderham record under 29 April 1741 the payment 'part on account' to John Channon of £50, which presumably refers to the bookcases.[45] They were originally commissioned for the library on the first floor, which still contains a very elaborate carved and gilt architectural chimney-piece with overmantel (Pl. 5) echoed by the surround of two door-cases on the west wall.[46] This fixed woodwork may be the work of Otho Channon, who in March 1743 was paid £27 13s 'in full of all demands' and further sums in 1748 and 1751. An inventory taken on the death of Sir William Courtenay in 1762 lists in the library 'Two Manchineel Book Cases carv'd gilded & inlaid with Brass';[47] they were still there when the 1789 inventory was compiled, but shortly afterwards the library became a bedroom and both bookcases were moved to the ante-room downstairs.[48] Manchineel (known later as padouk) was a fine ornamental tropical wood growing principally in the West Indies.[49] The original ensemble must have created a spectacle of baroque magnificence.

The bookcases are built on a towering scale, being over twelve feet high with two tiers of double doors fronted by brass wire mesh; the massive broken swan-neck pediment with leaf blocks is festooned with carved and gilt fruit and flowers (Pl. 133) while the frieze centres on a bracket for a bust. The upper stage is flanked by very grand Corinthian columns which swing back with the doors on 'Parliament hinges',

134. Design by Jean Berain, *c.*1700, which provided the source for the main brass plaques on the Powderham bookcases. *The Trustees of the Victoria and Albert Museum*

135. Powderham bookcase: Venus and Love on a shell supported by four winged sirens, copied from Berain; small areas of black mastic simulating ebony banding survive.

136. Siren seated on a dolphin on plinth, copied from Berain

137. Triton holding a nymph in his arms on plinth, copied from Berain

138. Caryatid lock plates copied from Berain's engraving

139. Powderham bookcase: engraved brass putti heading the columns

140. The Courtenay family coat of arms and dolphin crest on a bracket for a bust

141. Inscribed tablet with finely engraved shell and arabesque inlay

142. Detail of inlay on door frame

143. Detail of inlay on door frame

and the plinths rest on block bases, each ornamented with a pair of gilt-wood dolphins (Pl. 35), an attribute of Venus and also of the Courtenay family crest. In view of their size, it is remarkable that the bookcases are veneered in a rare and exotic timber (padouk, on a mainly oak and pine carcase) – the original unfaded colour can be seen beneath the column bases where the surface has been protected from light. The darker complexion must have provided a splendid foil for the profuse brass inlay which is the most striking feature of these masterpieces.

The plinths are faced with a mythological scene showing Venus and Cupid standing on a shell upheld by four winged mermaids emerging from leafy stems; a baldachin above is supported by two swans and a pair of putti (Pl. 135). On each of the inner sides of the plinths a siren appears seated on a dolphin amid waves (Pl. 136), while the outer sides feature a triton holding a nymph (Pl. 137). These vignettes, together with the lock-plates of demi-cherubs with arms held aloft, headed by shells and fountains (Pl. 138), are all copied directly from one of Berain's engravings (Pl. 134).[50] Areas of banding are cross-hatched and filled with black wax or mastic in imitation of ebony. The columns, richly inlaid with brass fluting and bell flowers, are headed by blocks inlaid with pairs of winged putti (Pl. 139); the intricate key-pattern frieze centres on a bracket for a bust bearing the Courtenay coat of arms and crest (a dolphin) executed in engraved brass (Pl. 140). This leaves the narrow door surrounds, which are embellished with stylised foliage, masks and shells. It is in fact the brass marquetry on the doors that provides the closest stylistic analogies with other brass-inlaid furniture (Pl. 141–3).

The heraldic content of the decorative programme celebrates the Courtenay family, but other elements refer to the theme of love, an appropriate allusion because the bookcases were presumably ordered by William Courtenay in anticipation of his marriage to Lady Aylesford in 1741. The quality of the engraved brass inlay is very uneven, being particularly coarse on the bracket (although viewed from ground level it appears luxurious); the main figure panels are also lacking in finesse. The plates seem to have suffered rather cavalier treatment over the years. There is no reason to doubt that the name-tablets are contemporary. At this period, few leading London firms identified their work and those few who used a trade label seem to have employed it sparingly. John Channon was, presumably because of his local connection, moved by a sense of pride to advertise this prestigious commission.

Pillar and claw tables

One of the most popular types of table in use between about 1725 and 1775 was of tripod form with a circular tip-up top. Perhaps because they were so common, Chippendale did not feature them in his *Director*; however, Ince & Mayhew illustrated three not entirely typical examples described as 'claw tables' in their *Universal System of Houshold Furniture*, 1762, pl. XIII, and probably contributed three similar designs to the second edition of *Genteel Houshold Furniture*, 1764 or 1765, pl. 38. In Yorkshire they were called 'screen' tables and in Lancashire 'snap' tables; many are described in contemporary accounts as 'pillar and claw tables' or 'tea tables' – the word preferred today.

The different design types and their various social uses repay study. Many examples have a plain circular top supported on a simple pillar and claw (the latter term referring to tripod legs, not ball-and-claw feet); they were intended to be covered by a cloth (hence a lack of enrichment) and served as a supper table, although this appears not to be a period term. A perspective design published by Thomas Malton in 1783 (Pl. 144)[51] shows one set for a meal, but confusingly lacking a tablecloth. The 'little oak Stand which I usually dine upon' noted in the will of Anne Metcalfe, a widowed gentlewoman of Hawes, Yorkshire (1770), may well have been of this kind.[52]

Another large family of circular tables had dished tops; these were more expensive – the Gillow price list of c.1746 records that snap tables with a 'plain top' cost 1s per foot to work while those with a 'sunk top' cost 2s per foot.[53] More stylish models might have a carved 'scollop' border, known today as a 'pie-crust' edge, derived from silver salvers. These functioned as tea tables, the raised rim preventing the china service from sliding or being swept off. Some were provided with open 'fret-work' or 'banister' (spindle) galleries to prevent accidents. Flat-topped pillar and claw tables were of course multi-purpose and could be used for reading, writing, work or as occasional tables. In 1764 Chippendale sold Sir Lawrence Dundas 'a very neat work Table with a Hexagon top and a Carv'd pillar and Claws £3 13s 6d' which survives[54] – it is small, the segmental veneered top measuring only 25 inches across, and usefully allows us to identify this fairly common design type as a work table.

Some of the most ambitious mahogany pillar and claw tables have a lobed tip-up top worked with shallow dished circles and frequently ornamented with engraved brass and mother-of-pearl inlay (Col. pl. XXIV). So many survive that they must have been made in large numbers. Dealers and auctioneers call them supper tables, although, as R.W. Symonds observed, 'the sinkings could not have held close-fitting supper dishes because they overlap'.[55] He was probably correct in believing that they were designed as tea tables, but their unusual character has led others to suggest that they were used for serving wine or even as games tables. A brief trawl of bills, inventories and similar sources has produced two possible contemporary references to this distinctive pattern of table. An inventory of William Linnell's stock-in-trade compiled in 1763 listed a 'mahogany plate fashioned tea board' followed by 'a round plain Do'[56] which, although ambiguous, might be relevant, while in 1762 William Gomm sold Richard Weddell 'a fine Mahogany Compass Cutwork Tea Table on Castors £5 10s'.[57] The word cut-work in this context is likely to imply carving.

London tradesmen's cards sometimes illustrate standard circular claw tables, but regrettably not with multi-dished tops; however, a card issued by William Russell, mahogany turner and cabinet-maker of Fetter Lane (fl.1754–70) depicts a tip-up table alongside a promising-looking lobed tray.[58] Furthermore, several tradesmen listed 'Tea Boards, Tea Trays...' among their stock, clearly indicating that these were distinct articles, so it may be that these extraordinary dish-topped tables were known in their day as tea boards. Frederick Hintz certainly advertised 'Tea-Tables, Tea-Chests, Tea-Boards etc all curiously made and inlaid with fine Figures of Brass and Mother of Pearl' in 1738.[59] Wisps of mystery remain. There is some trade-card evidence that tea tables may have been rather more widely produced by turners than by general cabinet-makers. Certainly the circular tops and pillars were lathe-turned, while batches of tripod legs could have been bought ready-made. Depressingly little is known about the makers and precise dating of tripod tea tables; although (or perhaps because) so many were produced they are notoriously difficult to document, while labelled London examples are unknown.

Thirty-four mahogany pillar and claw tables decorated with engraved brass inlay have been recorded; many also display mother-of-pearl details. By far the largest number (23) have lobed tops worked with shallow circular depressions and a central cusped compartment. The number of con-joined dished indentations marching round the top varies from eight indentations (3) to ten (13) or twelve (6); five tables merely have lobed outlines and flat tops, while one spectacular example is designed with an elaborate arrangement of twenty sinkings (Pl. 145). The central panel normally possesses half the number of perimeter lobes, taking the form of quatrefoil, pentafoil or hexafoil; however, one table centres on a heart-shaped depression (Pl. 146) while two others have a circular hollow (Pl. 147–8). The compartments are outlined with brass

144. Perspective design by Thomas Malton for a supper table laid for a meal, 1782 (one would normally expect the top to be covered with a cloth)

145. Tea table, mahogany, having an unusually large number of sinkings, inlaid with a system of floral meanders, c.1750. *Mallett*

146. Tea table, mahogany with a heart-shaped central sinking and unique fronded scroll brass inlay, c.1755. *Phillips of Hitchin (Antiques) Ltd*

147. Tea table, mahogany, with circular dished centre and routine brass inlay including plates on the tripod, c.1755. *Malletts*

strings and the inner raised surface inlaid with various permutations of engraved brass shells, flower heads, foliate bosses, etc, alternating with pearl-shell motifs such as florets, acorns, birds and squirrels. Some tables bear a central brass plaque, one features the Royal Crown (Pl. 150), another engraved initials (Col. pl. XXIV). Overall, the character of the inlay displays a striking uniformity, although there are wide variations in technical quality.

It is common knowledge that the tops and stands of tripod tables are quite often married (Pl. 148); however, if the top and the base both feature brass inlay, the chances are that they have always been together. If this test of originality be applied, three forms of column support emerge: the balluster with ring turning (Pl. 152–3), the wrythen knop combined with a plain or fluted pillar (Pl. 154) and the pestle-shaped shaft (Col. pl. XXV). All are routine designs for the period, and although the limited range is interesting little can be read into this in terms of identifying workshop styles. The tripod bases also repay study. Two superb tables are raised on triquetra or Manx 'three-leg' supports in the form of stockinged human legs wearing buckled shoes (Pl. 155–6). They stand apart from the main group which has simple splayed legs and pad feet providing plain surfaces for engraved brass inlay. This decoration, confined to the knees and toes, consists mainly of foliate lapettes, engraved shells, stringing lines, florets, bell-flower pendants, etc. Once again a restricted repertoire of motifs is found, several of them allied to devices occurring on the tops. Tripods that diverge markedly from the standard design profiles are likely to have been married to the dished tops, although this is not invariably so.

Four other kinds of pillar and claw tables with brass-inlaid decoration of a rather different character have been recorded. An interesting octagonal flat-topped work-table has a wide border of interlacing strings, punctuated by Prince of Wales feathers executed in brass and mother-of-pearl, supported on a tripod with ornamental brass knee- and toe-caps (Pl. 157). Secondly, an otherwise routine 'pie-crust' tea table with leaf carving on the knees and ball-and-claw feet is embellished with a complicated curvilinear design executed in fine brass strings with pointed finials (Pl. 158). The delicate geometrical pattern is related to the flowing lines on a large drop-leaf dining-table (Pl. 76). Thirdly, a small round-topped tea table with a moulded rim raised on a carved tripod is inlaid with a meandering tendril between two circular strings enclosing a central plaque and flowerheads (Pl. 159). Finally, an extraordinary rococo example has a vigorously scrolled profile, the flat top outlined with a lively flame border, combined with flowers. This decoration is repeated as a central cartouche (Pl. 160). Although it lacks a 'pie-crust' edge, the top is obviously inspired by large silver salvers of the period, the spidery brass inlay attempting to simulate popular flat-chased ornament.

The following dish-topped tea tables with brass inlay have been recorded but are not among the examples illustrated in this survey:

Tea table, with a small drawer beneath the top.
   Sotheby's New York 22 April 1982, lot 350.
Tea table
   Christie's 27 June 1985, lot 210.
Tea table
   Sotheby's Parke-Bernet New York 2 Dec. 1978, lot 102; Christie's New York 20 June 1982, lot 143; Polly Peck sale, Phillips, 19 Feb. 1991, lot 72.
Tea table
   Country Life, 1 Dec. 1944, p. 946, repr.
Tea table
   Country Life, 9 March 1945, p. 419, repr.
Tea table, octagonal with pierced gallery.
   Christie's New York 29 Nov. 1983, lot 164.
Tea table
   From Plaw Hatch; Lady Lever Art Gallery, Liverpool (LL 4,605).
Tea table
   Roxburghe collection, illus. Edwards, III, p. 207, fig. 15; Sotheby's Parke-Bernet 2 Dec. 1978, lot 102.
Tea table, later stand.
   Christie's 27 Feb. 1992, lot 96.
Tea table
   Christie's New York 1 Nov. 1990, lot 113.
Tea table
   Phillips, 16 June 1992, lot 63; Norman Adams Ltd; private collection.

PILLAR AND CLAW TABLES

148. Tea table, mahogany with lively brass inlay, *c.*1760. The top is married to a fire-screen, tripod and pillar. *Charles Lumb & Sons*

149. Tea table, mahogany inlaid with brass and mother-of-pearl, possibly by Frederick Hintz, *c.*1740. *Ronald A. Lee*

150. Tea table, the top of Pl. 149, inlaid with a squirrel, basket of fruit and centring on an engraved Royal Crown.

PILLAR AND CLAW TABLES 119

151. Tea table, possibly by Frederick Hintz, c.1745, mahogany, inlaid with brass shells and mother-of-pearl bell flowers (one of the few tables of this type which has passed by family descent to the present owner). *Private collection*

152. Tea table, mahogany with modest brass and mother-of-pearl inlay, possibly by Frederick Hintz, c.1750. *Private collection*

153. Tea table, mahogany with simple brass and mother-of-pearl inlay, possibly by Frederick Hintz, c.1740–5. *The Trustees of the Victoria and Albert Museum*

154. Tea table, mahogany, the top outlined with simple brass strings, c.1755. *Malletts*

155. Triquetra tea table, mahogany with engraved brass and mother-of-pearl inlay, c.1750; closely similar in design to the only other recorded table of this pattern. *The Trustees of the Victoria and Albert Museum*

156. Detail of humanoid leg on Col. pl. XXVII, the shoe with a brass buckle. *Pelham Galleries*

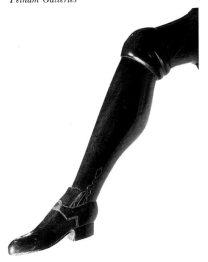

Tea-chests and dressing-boxes

Tea-chests might be thought a not especially promising subject; however, Chippendale published twelve designs in his *Director* and they were, certainly during the early Georgian period, often finished in the highest style of elegance. A surprisingly interesting group has emerged from our census of brass-inlaid furniture. From about 1730 onwards many silver tea services included a richly mounted tea-chest containing silver boxes for tea and sugar and sometimes even compartments for spoons, nippers, a cream-jug and knives.[60] A smart chest was obviously an essential part of the tea equippage, and a demand existed for specimens with ornaments of brass alongside the fashion for brass-inlaid tea tables, tea-boards and tea-kettle stands.

Many general furniture-makers advertised tea-chests, several also portraying them on their trade card. For instance, Landall & Gordon, cabinet-makers 'At ye Griffin & Chair' in Little Argyle Street, Westminster, issued a card which featured their shop sign and illustrated a tea-chest in the top left-hand corner, which suggests that they were promoting a special line (Pl. 12). Confirmation that this was indeed the case comes from a neat mahogany tea-chest outlined with simple brass strings and bearing the stamp 'T. LANDALL' (Pl. 13). Its present whereabouts is unknown but Roy Baxter, a previous owner, fortunately recorded details. The ambitious bombe tea-chest on Landall & Gordon's trade card is shown with little paw feet and inlaid decoration on the front, sides and flat top. It is in fact so strikingly similar to a group of (unsigned) brass-inlaid tea-chests that the interlocking evidence justifies their confident attribution to this firm. It is not known precisely when Thomas Landall was in partnership with Gordon (almost certainly the successful cabinet-maker, John Gordon, who later went into business with John Taitt) but their trade card seems to date from the early 1740s.[61] Close examination of the diminutive design (Pl. 161) reveals that the front centres on a shaped lock-plate with beaked bird-heads emerging from fronded scrolls and the corners have husk-like ornaments, sketchily repeated on the top and end panels. Because of the small scale these decorative details are simplified; however, they relate interestingly to the more elaborate brass-inlaid ornament on three tea-chests (Pl. 162–5) and two dressing boxes (Pl. 170–2).

A mahogany tea-chest of flat-topped bombe form with padouk cross-banding purchased by the Victoria and Albert Museum in 1965 has corner ornaments and lion-paw feet combined with brass edge mouldings comparable to those shown on Landall & Gordon's trade card (Pl. 162). Bird-head motifs are present on the handsome cast lifting-handle but the elaborate central engraved brass motif is entirely different, being a lively rococo composition featuring a pair of mermaids. An identical decorative scheme is found on a privately owned mahogany tea-chest which lacks cross-banding and has a replacement handle and in which the bombe curve is reversed (Pl. 163). A less ornate, slightly earlier solid mahogany bombe tea-chest in a private collection can also be attributed to Landall & Gordon because the brass lock-plate resembles the cartouche with fronded bird-heads depicted on their trade card (Pl. 164–5). The keyhole is covered by a brass flap which springs open to allow the key to be inserted when a small button hidden beneath baize, lining the underside, is pressed. When the lid is opened another pressure-operated spring catch is released which frees a small drawer concealed in the right-hand side of the plinth. This type of lock-catch and a love of mechanical contrivances is typical of much brass-inlaid furniture made at the time. The shallow drawer was almost certainly intended for keeping silver tea-spoons safe. An identical keyhole escutcheon with concealed cover released by a push button has been recorded on two handsomely fitted mahogany dressing-chests; the right-hand side of each case slides up to reveal a shallow full-length drawer hidden in a space

157. Work table, mahogany inlaid with brass and mother-of-pearl, *c*.1745–50. *Ronald A. Lee*

158. Tea table, mahogany with scalloped edging, the field inlaid with an elaborate design of brass strings, *c*.1755. *Vernay & Jussel*

159. Tea table, mahogany with brass inlay, *c*.1755. *Ronald A. Lee*

160. Tea table, mahogany with a wavy edge, and brass inlay simulating flat chasing on silver salvers, *c*.1760; an extraordinary example. *Vernay & Jussel*

161. Detail of tea-chest depicted on the trade card of Landall & Gordon, c.1745 (Pl. 12). *Trustees of the British Museum*

162. Tea-chest, mahogany with padouk crossbanding, possibly by Landall & Gordon, c.1745. *The Trustees of the Victoria and Albert Museum*

163. Tea-chest, mahogany inlaid with winged mermaids and a satyr mask, possibly by Landall & Gordon, c.1745. *Professor A.R. Hayward*

TEA-CHESTS AND DRESSING-BOXES

164. Tea-chest with drawer in base, mahogany, probably by Landall & Gordon, c.1745. *Private collection*

165. Detail of fronded bird-head lock-plate similar to the escutcheon on a tea-chest featured on Landall & Gordon's trade card (Pl. 161)

166. Tea-chest, possibly by John Channon, c.1750, padouk, the back and front inlaid with an eagle displayed; the rosewood lid is a later replacement. *M. Turpin Antiques*

beneath the internal compartments. Slightly different versions of the cartouche and fronded bird-head lock-plate occur on several bureau-cabinets (Pl. 149–53).

About 1750 Joseph Cooper, turner and cabinet small worker, issued a trade card advertising '... Powder Boxes, Tea Boards, Dressing Boxes & Tea Chests of the most Curious English & Foreign Woods...'[62] Finely figured and exotic timbers no doubt helped to make minor articles more attractive and saleable (and did not use up large amounts of rare veneers), and the addition of a little brass inlay would render them even more decorative. A luxurious padouk example cross-banded with ebony, now unfortunately lacking its original top (Pl. 166), is enriched with engraved brass acanthus foliage around the corners, while both front and back are embellished, below the strapwork escutcheon, with an eagle displayed (there is even a dummy keyhole at the back). An eagle also figures on the doors of the Murray writing-cabinet (Pl. 101); it was a popular motif, so too much should not be made of this, but it does link the tea-chest to mainstream brass-inlaid furniture.

An elegant, slightly earlier tea-chest faced with pretty panels of burr walnut defined by inlaid brass strings has brass mouldings and the asymmetrical engraved lock-plate incorporates a keyhole cover (Pl. 167). The plinth conceals a shallow drawer which closes against a large coil spring; when released, by pressing a brass button on the top edge of the case, the drawer is propelled open. The interior is partitioned into three wells, the smaller divisions at either end containing brass tea canisters with hinged lids and tin bottoms; the underside of the lid is lined with old marbled paper. A pair of burr elm tea-chests of the same period, cross-banded in walnut outlined with brass strings and corner beads, was sold at Sotheby's in 1992 (Col. pl. XXVIII); while a mahogany example of similar character (also with a plain escutcheon mount) but having in addition a side which slides upwards to reveal a hidden drawer was recently in the London trade (Pl. 168). Another much plainer version, with simple brass corner beads, and incorporating a secret drawer, is in the possession of Charles Lumb & Sons.

Standing slightly apart is a high-quality rectangular tea-chest inlaid with brass, mother-of-pearl and green-stained ivory (Pl. 169). It has the customary keyhole cover and drawer, the latter released by a spring catch on the top edge, opening in this instance to the left-hand side. Its present whereabouts is unrecorded but a black-and-white photograph captures its serene elegance.

Chippendale as usual has something of value to say, recommending in his prefatory

167. Tea-chest, burr walnut, with brass cannisters and a drawer for spoons in the base, c.1750. *Museum of Art, Rhode Island School of Design*

TEA-CHESTS AND DRESSING-BOXES

168. Tea-chest, mahogany with brass mouldings and inlay, c.1745–50. *John Keil Ltd*

169. Tea-chest, possibly by Frederick Hintz, c.1735–45, mahogany with brass, mother-of-pearl and bone inlay; a shallow plinth drawer opens on the left-hand side. *Ronald A. Lee*

notes to designs for tea-chests in the *Director* (1762) that 'the Ornaments should be of Brass or Silver'.[63] The reference may be to cast brass or silver mounts, but Chippendale was always alert to contemporary fashions and could well have been alluding to the taste for inlaid decoration. A tea-chest containing chinoiserie canisters and a circular sugar-bowl by the London silversmith Edward Wakelin (date-mark 1753) is inlaid with a design of strings, rosettes and foliage executed in engraved silver.

The evidence so far assembled, although interlocking, does not fit together quite as neatly as one might wish. However, the Landall & Gordon trade card, plus the tea-chest signed by Landall, indicates that this firm was certainly involved in the production of brass-inlaid cabinet small work. While four chests and two dressing-boxes can reasonably be attributed to their workshop, the ascription of further examples is speculative, while others appear to express very different house styles. The majority of London cabinet-makers supplied tea-chests, but when eventually the full story is unravelled it may well emerge that only a handful exploited brass inlay as a decorative technique.

Virtually identical mahogany dressing-boxes with ebony mouldings on the lids and stylised bird-head escutcheons are to be found in the Pinto collection at Birmingham Museum and Art Gallery (Pl. 170) and the Colonial Williamsburg Foundation (Pl. 172). Edward Pinto published his example as a drug cabinet but it seems more likely that both are dressing-boxes, because a specimen with a very similar interior illustrated on the late-eighteenth-century trade card of Charles Pryer is clearly identified as a dressing-box.[64] The lid of each is fitted with a looking-glass and the interiors partitioned into open and lidded compartments, including spaces at the front for an inkwell, sander and pen-tray. The right-hand side of the case pulls up to reveal a shallow, full-length secret drawer. They are in all probability similar to the slightly later 'mahogany Traveling strong Box with private partitions, drawer &c Compleat £2 18s 0d' which Thomas Chippendale invoiced to Lord Irwin in 1774 or 'a Mahog Travelling Box with brass lock & hinges £1 8s 0d'[65] which John Gordon supplied to the Duke of Gordon on 14 December 1748. The Birmingham box still contains several scent bottles with glass stoppers; it was probably originally raised on low bracket feet, because the keyhole cover is released by pressing a brass button beneath the base moulding. The design of the escutcheons (Pl. 171) suggest Landall & Gordon as makers.

Chairs

The three recorded patterns of chair with brass inlay are each interestingly different. Being a cabinet-maker and frame-maker, John Channon was perhaps seldom called upon to supply chairs, although one of his few surviving bills among the Scott of Harden papers shows that in 1769 he invoiced:[65]

12 Beach Chaires Carrott feet dyed with Matted seats	3	18	0
Six high Wooden Chairs	0	12	0

It is likely that he merely retailed and did not actually make this type of common furniture, which was normally produced by chair turners. By way of analogy, John Belchier (fl.1717–53), another leading figure, appears also to have concentrated on cabinet work and frames rather than the chair branch of the furniture trade.[67]

There is one chair that may be from the Channon workshop, which was acquired from a north-country source in the mid-1950s by H. Tweed Antiques, Bradford, and subsequently purchased by the Victoria and Albert Museum (Pl. 173). The frame bears the impressed number 05009 which is likely to be a dealer's stock mark –

170. Dressing-box, mahogany with ebony mouldings, attributed to Landall & Gordon, c.1745, on the evidence of the key plate. *Birmingham City Museums and Art Gallery*

171. Detail of lock escutcheon with spring-operated keyhole cover on the dressing-box in Pl. 170 (closely similar to the lock-plate on a tea-chest depicted on Landall & Gordon's trade card).

172. Dressing-box, mahogany with ebony mouldings, probably by Landall & Gordon, c.1745, presumably designed for travelling. *The Colonial Williamsburg Foundation*

Hamptons for instance used to punch such figures on their antiques. This exceptional padouk chair with its small proportions, vigorous curves and slightly quirky features such as the scrolls on the pedestal at the base of the splat, presence of carving on the rear legs and the exotic timber, suggested at one stage that it might have been made in one of the Canton workshops specialising in western-style furniture and imported as a blank for the decorative inlay to be added by English workmen. However, the beech seat-rails discredit this theory. The frame has many classic English design features, but the shaping of the seat gives it a rather Continental look, while the decoration of the splat has parallels in the well-known set of walnut chairs from Sutton Scarsdale with verre-églomisé armorial panels[68] and others with displays of heraldic inlay.[69] The engraved brass grotesque inspired by designs in Jean Berain's *Ouvres*, 1711, is extremely light, elegant and carefully fitted to the space. It centres on a crest 'issuing from a wreath a demi-horse forcene party per pale indented' which has not been

173. Armchair, possibly by John Channon, c.1740, padouk, the Berainesque inlay engraved with an unidentified British heraldic crest. *The Trustees of the Victoria and Albert Museum*

identified but in style of presentation is a typically British format, thus reinforcing the case for this being an English chair.

The reason for proposing a Channon attribution is the presence on the column bases of the signed bookcases at Powderham of brass plates directly copied from one of Berain's engravings. Although Berain's designs influenced the decoration of gun stocks, textiles, porcelain and Boulle work, English cabinet furniture tended to be rather insular at this period and it is perhaps unlikely that two firms both exploiting grotesque ornament and rare woods were active at the same date.

At St Michael's Mount in Cornwall there is a set of six mahogany side chairs having rectangular seats, straight legs with spandrel brackets and standard Director-style interlaced back-splats (Pl. 174). They do not correspond to any pattern book engravings but conform to a popular design type. The seat rails and front legs are inlaid with a simple lattice of brass hexagons and the brackets outlined with brass strings, while the 'ears' each have a spiral and leaf motif reminiscent of the inlay on a gate-leg table (Pl. 76 & 176). These chairs, unlike most brass-inlaid furniture, are domestic in character and not seeking to make a grand statement. They may well originally have been ordered by the St Aubyn family for their main seat (Clowance House, Praze, Cornwall), since St Michael's Mount was used mainly as a summer residence.[70] Another of their houses, Pencarrow, near Bodmin, has a clothes press from the same ensemble (Pl. 177). It is not clear whether the lattice inlay is intended to impart a gothic or chinoiserie flavour.

The last chairs are a pair with traceried splats and cluster-column front legs bought for Temple Newsam in 1963 (Pl. 175). The frames are inlaid with brass reeds, flutes, strings and mouldings. Doubts have been cast on their integrity because the rear seat-rail and pedestal are fashioned from a single board instead of being in two pieces, and on account of the construction of the front legs, the odd stretcher pattern and the nondescript sunk carving on the seat-rails. It is difficult to believe whole-heartedly in them but they are included in this survey as interesting specimens of taste.

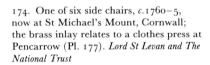

174. One of six side chairs, *c.*1760–5, now at St Michael's Mount, Cornwall; the brass inlay relates to a clothes press at Pencarrow (Pl. 177). *Lord St Levan and The National Trust*

175. Side chair, one of a pair, mahogany inlaid with brass stringing, flutes and reeding, *c.*1760. *Leeds City Art Galleries*

176. Detail of brass inlay on crest rail of chair illustrated in Pl. 174

Miscellaneous furniture

This chapter includes a dozen pieces that do not fit readily into the obvious categories. Unfortunately, none of them bears a trade label or name stamp, but several relate to the mainstream styles of brass-inlaid furniture. The only provenanced item is a mahogany clothes press at Pencarrow near Bodmin (Pl. 177) almost certainly originally commissioned, along with a set of chairs now at St Michael's Mount (Pl. 174), for Clowance House. It is a London-quality piece of traditional construction with 'stacked' bracket feet and sliding oak trays. The solid mahogany doors are inlaid with an overall design in brass strings copied from a pattern for glazing bars on a library bookcase in Chippendale's *Director*, 1762, pl. XC. The lattice border of brass hexagons corresponds to decoration on the frames of the set of chairs sharing the same provenance described in the previous section. Channon of course subscribed to the *Director* and had contacts in the West Country, but in the absence of documentation an attribution is hardly justified.

Nearly all furniture with brass inlay is of top London quality, so it is interesting to record a hanging corner cupboard (generally thought of as a provincial design type) with this form of decoration (Pl. 178). Admittedly, it is made of mahogany and displays fashionable detailing; however, the scrolling arabesques on the pilasters and doors are rather coarsely executed, which lends weight to the suggestion that it may have been produced in a regional centre. Another piece which might be provincial in origin is a mahogany architectural niche-cabinet in the form of a coved buffet with open shelves, three drawers in the base and flanking Corinthian columns. It was bought by Lord Leverhulme in 1913 and sold by his executors at the Anderson Galleries, New York in February 1924, lot 485. A rather dark plate in the auction catalogue is the only known illustration, but it shows that the column bases were inlaid with a stylised tulip design in brass strings.[71] The linear decoration on a gate-leg table (Pl. 76) offers the best stylistic analogy.

It will be recalled that in 1738 Frederick Hintz advertized a 'Choice Parcel' of furniture including 'Tea-Boards... inlaid with fine Figures of Brass and Mother of Pearl'. The intriguing term 'tea-boards' is ambiguous to modern furniture historians but could well refer to a tea tray. About twenty years ago, Asprey's had in stock an unusual lobed mahogany tray with a raised central reserve inlaid with mother-of-pearl husks combined with brass leaves and stringing (Pl. 179). I am assured that it was never the top of a pillar and claw table. The trade card of William Russell features a lobed tray[72] while a delftware tray dated 1743 in the Victoria and Albert Museum depicts a tea table set up with what appears to be a similar lobed tray.[73] On the available evidence it seems a fair assumption that Hintz made this example.

Another rare item connected with the service of tea is a triangular tea-kettle stand in the form of a mahogany board with low block feet and a raised profiled edge (Pl. 180). The rim and corners are decorated with brass stringing, while the field has three shaped ivory insets on which the feet of a tripod burner supporting a silver tea-kettle were intended to locate. The design of this possibly unique stand follows closely the form of commoner silver examples. There is no evidence that it was ever raised on a familiar pillar and tripod.

The celebrated Sam Messer collection[74] included a very superior dressing-table glass, the box base containing four small drawers and a fitted central cupboard (Pl. 181). The drawer fronts are decorated with fine silver metal strings and mother-of-pearl husks, fleur-de-lys, etc., while the door is inlaid with a pillared arch enclosing a triangle of very delicate intarsia executed in ivory, mother-of-pearl and ebony. The mosaic-work looks very Oriental, akin to the inlays on some imported games boards.[75]

177 (*opposite*). Clothes-press, mahogany, *c*.1760–5; the inlay on the doors is copied from a design for glazing bars on a bookcase in Chippendale's *Director*, 1762, while the border pattern is repeated on a set of chairs now at St Michael's Mount (Pl. 174); from Pencarrow, Cornwall. *Sir Arscott Molesworth-St Aubyn, Bt*

178. Hanging corner cupboard, mahogany with brass inlay, possibly provincial, c.1750–60. *Arthur Brett & Sons Ltd*

179. Tea board, attributed to Frederick Hintz, c.1740, mahogany inlaid with brass and mother-of-pearl. *Asprey*

180. Tea-kettle stand, mahogany, c.1740, inlaid with brass strings and ivory plaques (on which the feet of a silver tripod heater rested). *Leeds City Art Galleries*

181. Dressing table glass (detail), mahogany with pewter, brass, ivory and mother-of-pearl inlays, c.1755–60; the decoration is unusually refined and delicate. *The late Sam Messer*

182. Angle barometer, walnut case, the instrument by Charles Orme, Ashby-de-la-Zouche, dated 1741; this maker often used cases decorated with brass inlay. *Private collection*

The door opens to reveal a niche headed by a shallow drawer inlaid with a miniature lion rampant in ivory. The delicacy of the decoration and its Eastern flavour sets this dressing glass apart from other brass-inlaid furniture.

Several barometers with brass-inlaid cases are known. A fine instrument signed 'by CHARLES ORME of Ashby-de-la-Zouch 1741' is housed in a veneered walnut case outlined with brass strings and mouldings (Pl. 182).[76] Another barometer by this Leicestershire maker in a similar case is dated 1736.[77] There is no information as to where he bought or had his cases made. A mid-eighteenth-century mahogany stick barometer at the Victoria and Albert Museum has a pediment of rococo form set on tapered columns inlaid with brass, while the bulbous cistern cover is decorated in a mildly gothic taste with ogee and tracery motifs (Pl. 183). The instrument is inscribed: 'Made by G ADAMS at Tycho Brahe's Head in Fleet Street LONDON'. There were two makers of this name, father and son; however, the rococo impulses suggest it is likely to be by the elder man.

Finally, two clock-cases remain to be discussed. There is an entry in the account which John Channon sent in 1773 to the painter Richard Crosse for repairing,

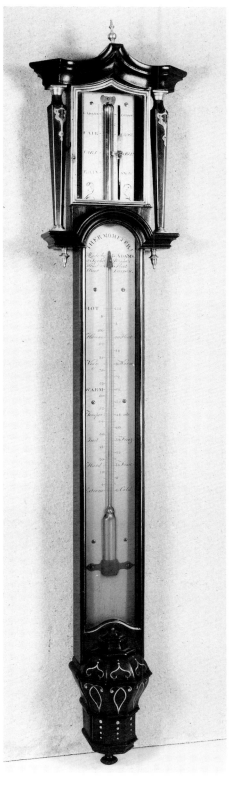

183. Barometer and thermometer, mahogany case with brass strings, the instruments by George Adams, London, c.1760. *The Trustees of the Victoria and Albert Museum*

134 FURNITURE SURVEY

184. Long-case clock, the movement by William Shepard of Millom, Cumbria, c.1765; the mahogany case is inlaid with brass strings and decorated with gilt mounts. *Partridge (Fine Arts) plc*

cleaning, lacquering and polishing a clock-case, but this was merely routine jobbing work. It has been suggested that Channon could have made the famous thirteen-foot-high Powderham clock housing an exceedingly elaborate musical movement by William Stumbels of Totnes, the celebrated Devon clockmaker.[78] There are payments totalling £105 to Stumbels in Sir William Courtenay's account book between 1743 and 1749, and of course there are two payments to John Channon for unspecified work. The Palladian-style walnut case on a bombé plinth is surmounted by golden emblematic figures. A Channon connection is however highly speculative. The possibility that he made the case for the celebrated 'Exeter Clock' (Col. pl. 1) is discussed on pp. 13–14. The fact that Nicholas Williams, joiner of Exeter, advertised that he sold clock-cases suggests that cabinet-makers in the city were trained in this branch of the trade.[79]

Two tall-case clocks, both at present in the London trade, are decorated with brass inlay. Partridge has a fine mahogany example thought to have belonged to Henry Hobhouse of Bristol, who owned the bureau cabinet illustrated in Pl. 70. The plinth and door are panelled with brass strings and quarter colonetts headed by bearded masks; the movement is by Shephard of Millom in Cumbria (Pl. 184). A second, much grander clock, acquired by R.A. Lee,[80] has a musical movement by John Jones, London. The rosewood case is lavishly mounted with ormolu and outlined with brass strings. Neither clock case relates closely to the mainstream tradition of brass-inlaid furniture. It is however worth drawing attention to their existence.

8. Workshop groups

Any attempt to identify different workshop groups and attribute them to one of the firms known to have specialised in brass-inlaid furniture must start with the Powderham bookcases, which are not only documented but signed and dated. Interestingly, the most prominent brass plates have been directly copied from a well-known engraving by Berain (Pl. 134) – a practice that was popular with continental designers and tradesmen. Accordingly, it is the finely detailed masks and the stylised shells amid scrolling foliage and border ornaments, rather than the mythological figures, that provide points of comparison with other furniture, while the elaborate key-pattern on the frieze and the dolphin feet furnish analogies with decorative features on the great back-to-back library table (Pl. 107 & 109). The resemblance is such that, although the dolphins on the bookcases are carved and gilt, not cast brass, it has even been suggested that this spectacular table was commissioned (some years later) as a centrepiece for the Powderham Castle library. It is in fact the two-part library table that creates a vital bridge between Channon's towering bookcases and the cluster of flamboyant furniture ornamented with brass which we have called the 'nymph and satyr' group (see p. 86). A further seven pieces can therefore be attributed with some degree of confidence to Channon's workshop.

Two ravishing collectors' cabinets on stands at Bristol (Col. pl. XIX) and the Victoria and Albert Museum (Pl. 113) also display certain features in common with the Powderham bookcases and the 'nymph and satyr' furniture. Both are exceptionally richly styled and have highly unusual engraved hinge- and lock-plates detailed with pairs of serpents (Pl. 115 & 122). The Victoria and Albert Museum model has, on the drawer fronts, a distinctive diaper pattern (derived from the inlays on Boulle furniture) which is echoed on the Murray writing-cabinet, while the vocabulary of ornament on the bottom door rail, the stand and apron is strongly reminiscent of the Powderham bookcases. The lock-plate on the niche door of the Bristol cabinet is delicately engraved with a *commedia del'arte* figure holding a club (Pl. 120) which is identical to a pair of figures on the Carlton Hobbs secretaire (Col. pl. VII), thus bringing this masterpiece into Channon's œuvre. There are also two tables with winged and helmeted warrior heads on lion's-paw cabriole legs (Pl. 84–6) matching the mounts on the knees of the Bristol cabinet, so they too can reasonably be ascribed to Channon on stylistic grounds. It also seems likely that, having slavishly used an engraving by Berain as the source for brass inlay at Powderham, Channon also copied Pineau's design for a table on the slope of the elegant bureau-cabinet illustrated in Col. pl. V.

This raises to fourteen the number of items attributed on stylistic evidence to Channon's workshop. An ambitious bombe tea-chest inlaid with an eagle (Pl. 166) akin to one displayed on the Murray writing-cabinet and rather coarsely engraved corner fronds which possess a similar quality to brass plates on the Powderham bookcases may also be linked to Channon, while the distinguished padouk chair with a Berainesque panel on the splat (Pl. 173) is more likely to be by him than by any of his rivals.

The trade card issued by Thomas Landall and John Gordon about 1740–5 portrays, in addition to their shop sign, a bombé tea-chest with brass inlay (Pl. 161), which suggests they were advertising a special line; indeed a tea-chest with brass stringing stamped 'T LANDALL' has been recorded (Pl. 13). Landall had been in business since 1724 and in the early 1740s formed an apparently brief partnership with John Gordon, who was trading on his own account by 1747. They made 'Tables, Chairs . . . & all sorts of Cabinet Work'. The tea-chest depicted on their card has a lock-plate in the form of twin fronded bird-heads flanking a cartouche with foliate corner motifs. This distinctive escutcheon occurs on a mahogany tea-chest (Pl. 165) and two travelling dressing-boxes (Pl. 170–2) which can, accordingly, be attributed to the partners working either together or separately. A further two bombé tea-chests (Pl. 162–3) resting on cast lion's-paw feet with brass mouldings and leafy corner ornaments, closely similar to the example on the trade card, can also be ascribed to the same workshop tradition.

John Gordon rapidly became a fashionable cabinet-maker, attracting lucrative commissions from the Dukes of Gordon and Atholl. Having been associated with a firm that made brass-inlaid furniture, he could well have continued to employ this decorative technique. It may be significant that one of his bills, dated 1748, refers to 'a Mahog Travelling Box with brass locks & hinges £1 8s 0d' which sounds similar to those in Pl. 170–2. He also supplied 'desks and bookcases'; brass inlay is not mentioned but one cannot help wondering whether he and/or his partner were responsible for four handsome mid-eighteenth-century bureau-cabinets embellished with distinctive stylised lock escutcheons (Pl. 67–70). Three also have on the slope corner ornaments of identical pattern. If the evidence of lock-plate design is accepted as an indication of common authorship it is possible to attribute nine items to the Landall/Gordon workshop tradition.

The next coherent sub-group centres on the bureau-cabinet branded underneath 'J GRAVELEY' (Pl. 50) which is likely to be a craftman's mark. True, it has not been found on other furniture, but then only one piece signed by Channon and one bearing Landall's stamp have so far been recorded. The drawer fronts and writing slope are decorated with exactly the same pattern of brass inlay as a secretaire illustrated in Pl. 54. The upper stages are different but the door frames of both are enriched with narrow frets and feature perching birds in the spandrels. They are unquestionably from the same workshop. A third bureau-cabinet, veneered in sabicu (Pl. 53), is more simply styled with brass strings on the drawers and less elaborate frets on the doors, but its proportions and general air of restraint display affinities with the other two secretaires in this group. Even more closely associated with the name-stamped cabinet are two highly sophisticated writing-tables (Pl. 80–3). The dark and light veneers on the slopes of the bureau and the tops of the tables appear to be the same, while the brass stringing, especially the looped border details with husks and inlaid dots, are closely matched.

The trickiest furniture to identify is the work of Frederick Hintz, who in 1738 advertised a sale of 'A Choice Parcel of Desks and Book-Cases of Mahogany, Tea-Tables, Tea-Chests, Tea-Boards, etc all curiously made and inlaid with fine Figures of Brass and Mother of Pearl'. The reason given for the sale was that 'the maker' intended 'soon to go abroad'. However, there is ample evidence that Hintz subsequently returned to England (p. 28), so his products do not all pre-date 1738.

The largest group of furniture 'inlaid with fine Figures of Brass and Mother of Pearl' are dish-topped tea tables, of which over twenty have been recorded. They are of uneven quality ranging from rather mean and shoddy (Pl. 152–3) to richly decorated examples (Col. pl. xxv & xxvii & Pl. 155–6) on elaborate pillar and claw supports.

The process of identifying which tea tables may have been made by Hintz is helped by a search for other types of furniture mentioned in his advertisement. The magnificent mahogany desk and bookcase illustrated in Pl. 55 has a strongly individual personality and is decorated with a combination of brass inlay and mother-of-pearl details; it must be short-listed for a Hintz attribution. The naturalistic brass 'figures' include a squirrel eating from a basket of fruit (Pl. 59), an unusual motif which occurs separately on the top of a tripod tea table (Pl. 150) elaborately enriched with brass and mother-of-pearl. An identical alternating pattern of engraved brass shells and pearl husks with dots between is found on two other tea tables (Col. pl. xxiv & Pl. 151) which can accordingly be assigned to Hintz, who was probably also responsible for two tables with florets rather than shells (Pl. 152–3), plus the solitary tea-board (Pl. 179) traced during our census.

It is hard to say how many more tea tables can be ascribed to Hintz, but at present he is the only tradesman definitely known to have produced them, so it is tempting to attribute the majority to his workshop. He also stocked tea-chests; only one inlaid with brass and mother-of-pearl has been located (Pl. 169), slender evidence for authorship, but in context Hintz is a strong candidate. It is worth mentioning that a Royal Crown is engraved on the central cartouche of the tea table with a squirrel and also features on the escutcheon of a lady's bureau (Pl. 78).

The impressive Kenwood secretaire might be included as a potential Hintz masterpiece on the strength of the tiny mother-of-pearl figures decorating the spandrels of the letter-holes (Pl. 62). However, the drawer handles, which match those on the cabinet on stand in the 'nymph and satyr' group (Pl. 112), the prospect door inlaid with a warrior similar to soldiers on the Bristol cabinet, and the nest of secret drawers suggest a cautious Channon attribution.

Although no more furniture in our survey can be linked to a maker, it remains to identify a few anonymous workshop groups. The splendid gateleg table embellished with stylised linear designs (Pl. 75–6) relates to inlay on the top rail of the St Aubyn family chairs and clothes press (Pl. 174 & 176). The mahogany silver-table from Haddo House (Pl. 74) and the walnut chamber table (Pl. 73) are decorated with very similar rosettes; they must surely be by the same hand. This leaves three important pieces of furniture which, through lack of convincing affinities, cannot be readily assimilated into any sub-group: the bureau-cabinet with a tortoiseshell veneered cornice (Pl. 47), the Ince Blundell artist's table (Pl. 89), and the anglo-oriental card table inlaid with brass and mother-of-pearl (Col. pl. x–xiii).

There is at present a dearth of evidence that the top London cabinet-makers were involved in producing brass-inlaid furniture. For instance, the copious documented commissions of Chippendale, the Linnells, Vile & Cobb or Ince & Mayhew reveal no hint that they ever employed this decorative technique although it must be said that the fashion had peaked by their heyday. There is, to be sure, a possibility that William Hallett occasionally favoured brass inlay as an option (Pl. 128 & 129), while John Gordon may also have used it, although in both cases proof is lacking. It certainly appears that this method of enrichment was regularly practised by only some half-dozen firms and exploited very occasionally by others. The brass marquetry is of uneven quality, ranging from rather coarse plates on the Powderham bookcases and several inferior tea tables to sophisticated work on the Murray writing-cabinet – well up to the standard of goldsmiths' heraldic engraving – which is likely to have been performed in a specialist shop. For example, an exquisitely detailed Bacchus mask appears on the Murray writing-cabinet (Pl. 101), one of the writing tables (Pl. 80) and a tea chest (Pl. 163) each of which are here attributed to a different cabinet-maker.

APPENDIX 1
The Wills of John and Martha Channon

The Will of John Channon (d.1779)
Public Record Office PROB 11.1058

In the name of God Amen
I John Channon of St Martin's Lane in the Parish of St Martin in the ffields in the County of Middlesex Gentleman being sick in Body but of perfect mind memory and understanding blessed be Almighty God to make this my last Will and Testament in manner following that is to say ffirst I desire all my just Debts and ffuneral Expences be in the first place duly paid and satisfied Item I give and bequeath unto my Brother Thomas Channon of the City of Exeter in the County of Devon the Sum of One hundred pounds of lawful money of Great Britain to be paid to him within twelve months after my decease Item I give to John Cambridge of St Martin's Lane aforesaid Cabinet Maker and <u>George Palmer of St Martin's Lane in</u>* the said Parish of St Martin in the ffields in the County of Middlesex aforesaid or the Survivor of them or the Exors or Administrators of such Survivor the sum of three hundred pounds of lawful money of Great Britain upon this special Trust and confidence to vest the same in Government Securities in their names as soon as conveniently maybe after my decease and to pay the Interest and Dividends thereof unto my said Brother Thomas Channon his Executors or Administrators during the Minorities of his three children Dorothy Thomas and John And upon further Trust to pay the said principal Sum of three hundred pounds unto the said three children in equal Shares of one hundred pounds each when they shall respectively attain the Age of Twenty one years And in case of the death of either of them during their minorities his or her Share to be divided and paid to the Survivor or Survivors of them Item I give unto my said Brother all my wearing Apparel Item I give unto my dear Wife Martha all and every my Leasehold Messuages or Tenements wheresoever situate subject to the payment of the yearly Rents payable therefrom To hold to her for and during the Term of her natural life only And from and after her decease to the use and behoof of my said Brother Thomas Channon his Executors Administrators or Assigns for all the residue of the several terms I have in my said Leasehold Estates Item all the rest residue and remainder of my Personal Estate household Goods Chattels Plate and other Effects of what nature soever I give to my said dear Wife Martha to and for her own proper use And it is my Will that the said John Cambridge and Edward Crase or either of them shall not be liable to any loss that may happen to my said Estate unless by their own wilful neglect... be accountable for the Acts or Receipts of the other of them but each for his own Acts and Receipts only and that they shall and may retain to themselves all reasonable Costs and Charges which they may be put to in and about the Execution of this my Will Item I give to my said Trustees the sum of five pounds each for their trouble herein And I do appoint my said Trustees Executors of this my last Will and Testament And Lastly I do hereby revoke all former and other Will or Wills by me at any time heretofore made and do declare this only to be and contain my last Will and Testament In Witness whereof I have hereunto set my hand and Seal the Twenty ninth day of July in the year of Our Lord One thousand Seven hundred and Seventy five John Channon Signed Sealed published and declared by the said Testator as and for his last Will and Testament in the presence of us who in his presence and at his request and in the presence of each other have subscribed our names as Witnesses hereto P A Gray Leicester ffields   Ar Hewetson his Clerk

This Will was proved at London the third day of November in the year of our Lord one thousand seven hundred and seventy nine before the Worshipful George Harris Doctor of Laws Surrogate of the Right Worshipful Peter Calvert Doctor of Laws Master Keeper or Commissary of the Prerogative Court of Canterbury lawfully constituted by the Oath of John Cambridge one of the Executors named in the said Will to whom Administration was granted of all and singular the Goods Chattels and Credits of the deceased he having been first Sworn duly to Administer power reserved of making the like grant to George Palmer the other Executor named in the said Will when he shall apply for the same
* origl. wrote on an Erazure

The Will of Martha Channon (d.1797)
Public Record Office PROB 11.1295

In the name of God Amen
I Martha Channon of the Parish of St Martin in the ffields in the County of Middlesex Widow do make this as my last Will and Testament revoking all former Wills of what kind soever and first I give my Soul to God my Creator my Body to the Earth from whence it came I desire all my just Debts to be paid as soon as convenient and my Body to be buried in Kensington Church Yard as near my late husband John Channon as possible the Expence to be as frugal as my Executrixes (herein after mentioned) shall think fit and I appoint my two dear and valuable ffriends Miss Anne Towne and Miss Margaret Towne Spinsters of Henrietta Street in the Parish of St Paul Covent Garden in the County of Middlesex my two Executrixes In Trust to this my last Will and Testament and first I give (as a small token of gratitude) to Miss Anne Towne abovementioned my Silver Soup Ladle I give to Miss Margaret Towne above mentioned for the same cause my four tooth and egg Candlesticks my best Snuffers and Snuffer pan my two Silver plated Candlesticks and flatt and chamber do with Snuffers and Extinguisher belonging to it I give to Dammaris [?] Henrietta Sim daughter of my dearly beloved Anna Henrietta Sim and of John Sim Attorney at law of Mark Lane in the City of London five Guineas I likewise give and bequeath to my good ffriends Mrs Mary Price Widow and Mr John Price her Son of May's Buildings

in the Parish of St Martin in the ffields in the County of Middlesex one Guinea each for a Ring as a small token of my Regard and if the above mentioned Mrs Mary Price dies before me the Guinea I leave her shall be given to her daughter Winifred Price I give and bequeath to my ffriend Miss Casandra Everitt now living with the abovementioned Miss Townes one Guinea for a Ring in remembrance of me I give to my Maid Servant Ann Mullett if living with me at my death five pounds I give to James Scadding of the Parish of St Mary Magdalen in Taunton in the County of Somerset carpenter and Joiner but now of London my Share of check's Mortgage whatever shall arise from it to be placed in the ffunds the Interest of which the said James Scadding and Elizabeth his Wife to enjoy for their lives and at the decease of both of them to be equally divided between the three Sons of James Scadding which is John James and William or the survivors of any of the three let James Scadding observe I do not wish him to go to law for it without a real prospect and if any thing is gained by it – pray God – bless and prosper it to those I have bequeathed it I give to Elizabeth Scadding wife of James Scadding my clay coloured Lutestring Gown and my Straw coloured Sattin Petticoat two striped common Muslin Aprons both the same Muslin but one scolloped the other plain if then living at my death I give to my niece Martha Howard my blue watered Tabby Gown and Coat my common black Silk NightGown two common Muslin Aprons striped and the same only one scolloped and the other plain my common black Silk cloak four of my Shifts in wear my two flannel petticoats and my two upper Petticoats I shall then have in common wear if living at my death I give and bequeath to Peggy Towne Scadding Daughter of the above James Scadding (and Martha deceased) my Gold Watch Chain Seals and all unto belonging to be delivered to her at the age of one and twenty I likewise give to the abovementioned Peggy Towne Scadding all my household ffurniture Plate Linnen China wearing apparel Jewels Trinketts and Ornaments Book Debts and Bonds and Notes of Hand and whatever I may have in the Hands in short all my monies and everything I shall die possessed on and all and every part of it to be put in the hands of my two Executrixes beforementioned that is Miss Ann Towne and Miss Margaret Towne for the use of Peggy Towne Scadding for them to dispose of any part they shall think will be for the best advantage for the use of the said Peggy Towne Scadding (my watch accepted) and whatever may be thought proper to sell the monies arising therefrom to be added to whatever money there maybe and placed (by my executrixes abovementioned) —— for the use of Peggy Towne Scadding the Interest of which or any part of the interest shall be laid out for the Education of the abovementioned Peggy Towne Scadding at the discretion of the two abovementioned Excutrixes and all that shall remain at the time Peggy Town Scadding arrives at the age of one and twenty the Interest of which she shall then receive during her life and at her death to her child or children born in wedlock but if she should marry prudent and her husband capable of making her the value to be properly settled for her entire use for her life and then to the child or children of them then the money may be drawn and if the said Peggy Towne Scadding should die married without children she shall have it in her power to leave the money to whom she pleases but if she dies before the age of one and twenty all that she shall benefit from what I leave her shall be divided between her three Brothers or the survivor in the manner following James Scadding one half the other half between John and William Scadding and in case the said Peggy Towne Scadding dies before the age of one and twenty my watch to be given to her Brother James Scadding but in that case he is not to receive it till the age of one and twenty witness my hand this 29 of Janry 1791

M Channon   Witness Mary Bordil   C Wemys

March 9 1795 Martha Channon adds this as a codicil I give and bequeath unto Anna Henrietta Sim wife of John Sim Attorney four pounds and to my two Executrixes Miss Ann Towne and Miss Margaret Towne five pounds each and to their Sister Martha Towne two Guineas for a Ring and to Mrs Robinson of Cranbourn Passage two Guineas for a Ring in memory of an old ffriend

Appeared Personally William Winchester of the Strand in the Parish of St Martin in the ffields in the County of Middlesex Stationer and William Nixon of St Martin's Lane in the said Parish and County aforesaid and jointly and severally made Oath as follows that they knew and were well acquainted with Martha Channon late of the Parish of St Martin in the ffields in the County of Middlesex widow deceased for some time before her death which happened in the Month of July last and that during such their knowledge of and acquaintance with the said deceased they have often seen her write and write and subscribe her Name and have thereby become well acquainted with the manner and character of her handwriting and subscription and having now carefully viewed and perused the paper writing hereunto amended purporting to be and contain the last Will and Testament as also a codicil thereto of the said deceased the said will beginning thus 'In the name of God Amen I Martha Channon in the Parish of St Martin in the ffields in the County of Middlesex widow do make this my last Will and Testament . . . this my watch to be given to her Brother James Scadding but in that case he is not to receive till the age of one and twenty witness my hand this 29 of Janry 1791 and thus subscribed M Channon' the said Codicil beginning thus 'March 9 1795 Martha Channon adds this as a Codicil and adding thus 'and to Mrs Robinson of Crambourn Passage two Guineas for a Ring in Memory of an old ffriend' they severally say and depose that they verily and in their consciences believe the whole Body Said and contents of the said codicil to be of the proper handwriting of the said Deceased and also observing the words 'ffive Pounds' written after the obliteration of the words 'two Guineas' in the eighteenth line of the second side of the said will they depose that they believe the Words so written to be the proper hand writing of the said Martha Channon Widow deceased Wm. Winchester On 23 Day of August 1797 the said Wm. Winchester was duly sworn to the truth of this Affidavit before me J Sewell Senr Prost. Geo: Silk M P. W Nixon On 25th Day of August 1797 the said William Nixon was duly sworn to the truth of this Affidavit before me J Fisher Senr Prost J Walker M P

This Will was proved at London with a codicil on the twenty sixth Day of August in the Year of our Lord one Thousand seven hundred and ninety seven before the worshipful John Sewell Doctor of Laws Surrogate of the Right Honourable Sir William Wynne Knight Doctor of Laws Master Keeper or Commissary of the Prerogative Court of Canterbury lawfully consistuted by the Oath of Margaret (by mistake in the will called Margret) Towne Spinster out of the Executrixes named in the said will to whom Administration was granted of all and singular the Goods Chattels and Credits of the deceased having been first sworn duly to administer power reserved of making the life Grant to Ann Towne Spinster the other Executrix named in the said Will when she shall apply for the same

[In the margin to the left of the last paragraph appears a note as follows:]

Proved at London with a Codicil the 13th day of August 1812 before the Worshipful Samuel Pearce Parson Doctor of Laws Surrogate by the Oath of Anne Towne Spinster the surviving Executor to whom admin was granted having been first sworn duly to Admin.

APPENDIX 2
Accounts, letters and inventories

References to John and Otho Channon and the Powderham bookcases in the Courtenay Manuscripts at the Devon County Record Office and in the muniment room at Powderham Castle

Account Books in the Devon County Record Office

1508M Devon/v5 *Receipts and Payments Book: General 1737–49*
   Entry f. 104 for April 29 1741
   'to Jno Channon part on Acct £50.0.0'
1508M Devon/v10 *Cash Book 1745–52*
   Entry f. 68 'pd Otho Channon a Cabinet-makers Bill (in 1745) £14.5'
   Entry f. 156 'pd Otho Channon in full of a Bill for Chairs, & a Mahogany Table £33.10.0'
1508M Devon/v20 *Ledgers*
   Entry f. 25 'Otho Channon of Exeter Chairmaker 1745 By a bill delivered £14.5.0 Oct. 12 1748 To cash pd him in full' 1751 Aug. 23 To Cash pd him in full for a Mahogany Table & Chairs £33.10.0
1508M London/v21 *Ledger of the Accounts of the Honble Sir William Courtenay Bart with Tradesmen & others in London*
   Entry f. 42 'Mr Jno Channon Cabinet maker By his Bill deliver'd beginning
   20 Feb. 1756, and ending ye 31st of July following £45.8.4'
1508M Devon/v36 *Account Books*
   Entry f. 264 '1743 March y 25 pd Otho Chanon(sic) in full of all demands £27.13.0'

Inventories in the Devon County Record Office and at Powderham Castle

An Inventory & Appraisement & full & Singular the Household Goods (Except ye Jewels, Paintings & other Goods & Things of & belonging to the Right Honourable Lord Viscount Courtenay deceased; at Powderham Castle, Exwell Farm and the Dolphin and Bonetta Yatchs(sic), as also the Household Goods & Furniture at Ford and the House in Exeter, taken in the months of June, July, August and September 1762. (Muniment Room, Powderham) v/1/38 (box no. 9)

lists f. 37 the contents of the library as follows:

'Two Manchineel Book Cases carv'd gilded & inlaid wth Brass
One mahogany Do. enrich'd & fluted Pilasters
Two Mahogany Do plain wth close Pediments & carv'd Capitals
A Cedar Medal Case Carv'd & Gilded
A Marble Chimney Piece & Slab wth wood ornaments, Tabernacle, Frame, wth a Bust Standing on a Bracket & a Landscape
A Large square mahogany Table wth fret enrichment, & clawd Feet
8 Mahogany Stools
Mahogany Pillar & Claw reading Table
Mahogany steps
Four green hair silk Damsk Curtains
An Alarum
Orrery, Globes, Telescopes, & other Mathematical Instruments'

(The total valuation of the contents of library came to £525; the total valuation of the contents of Powderham Castle came to £3,477 18s 6d)

An Inventory of all the Household goods, Linnen, Plate, China, etc. belonging to the Right Honble Lord Viscount Courtenay Deceas'd at Powderham Castle, Exwell Farm, In the Dolphin Yacht, Boats & Boat House, at the Belvieudier, Ford House at Newton & Courtenay House in Exeter taken in February 1789 (Muniment Room, Powderham Castle) v/1/38 (box no. 8)

Library
Two inlaid bookcases
Three Mahogany ditto with wire doors
One ditto with table of coins
One open bookcase
one writing table & eight stools
Mahogany steps & 2 Elevating desks
A Concave mirror on pillar & claw stand
An Orrery
A pair of large globes
A pair of smaller ditoo

A celestial globe
Three telescopes
A silver ink stand
Bath stove grate fender shovel, tongs, poker & brush
A peice of painting over the chimney peice
Two bronz'd figures over ditto
Four mahogany cases
Two wingd vessels
A peice of painting

'An Inventory of the furniture, Plate, Linen, China, Books, Paintings, Horses, Carriages, Plants, Shrubs, Farming Stock, and other Effects belonging to the Right Honble Lord Viscount Courtenay of Powderham Castle and Exwell Farm in the County of Devon taken Novr 1803 by Wm Hicks'

Devon County Record Office Courtenay Ms. 1508 M/London Family Household and Personal (1)

f. 14 No. 24 Library '2 Book cases with curtains inlaid gilded Caps & pediments with block cornices and other enrichments brass wire pannels, Silk curtains'

Correspondence and bills addressed to Mrs Anne Fenwick of Hornby Hall, Lancashire
Lancashire Record Office, Preston: RCHy 2/6/8

Dear Madm

I Shoud have answerd your Obleigeing Letter Sooner but Mr Channon has been in pursuit of Some Vast Curious and Valuable pictures which at last he has purchased its our Bless'd Savour and Six of his Apostles Supposed by the best Judges to be done by Raphel Urbin the Size of the pictures and frames together is 19 by 14 in neat Carv'd and Gilt frames the price is thirteen Guineas in all probability worth three times the Money but as Mr Channon was Requested by you he woud take no advantage and if you please to Order it they Shall be Sent Down for you to See and if you dont like them Mr Channon will keep them him Self he Coud not Get them to Send without Buying them and that you Shoud be Convinced of his Readiness to Serve you and their being a great bargain he will take them if Disliked by you so pray Send an answer as soon as Conveniant. I hope by this time you are a little more Settled but in particular I hope you Enjoy your Health as it and ever will be wish'd by me Mr Channon Joyns in Best Respects to your Self and Good Mr Butler which Concludes me Dear Mad'm Your truely affectionate Obleig'd Obedient Humble Ser't at all Commands.

London August 1766   *M. Channon*

Madam

I have Sent the Pictures of Our Saviour & Six of the Apossels Together with the parcles Carefully pack'd Please to Order the Man that Unpacks them to Strike Out the Sides of the Case a little way with his hammer then he may take them out Easey Altogether and If you Should not like my Purches please to Desire him to take Notice how the Slips are tack to the Sides to prevent there Rubing they Cost me Thirteen Guineas was You to Give An Hundred Guineas to the Best Painter in England it is not in his Power to Equel them Please to Faviour Me with a line how you Receive them.

My Wife Joynes in best Respects to you and Mr Butler & am Y'r most Obedin't Humble Serv't John Channon

St Martins lane
16th Aug't 1766

Dear Mad'm

I have been in Sommesetshire for this month past. Came to town last thursday and was greatly Surprised to find by your letter the pictures did not please as we thought the subject suited and they done by one of the Greatiest Masters and not to be follow'd. I have venture to say if you were to Give five Hunderd Guineas if desir'd Mr Channon this day to Unpack them they were not at all pack'ed as we had done and I am sorry to Say they are rub'd so much that the very ... dish Moulding is Quite Defac'd. I was Extreamly sorry to find them so as they are not fit to Show until they are Repair'd and was loth to Give you an Account that Might be any way Displeaseing you or to Occasion your anger to those who pack'ed them for when Mr Channon pack'd them the Slips was nail'd to Each of the frames and the pictures Seperate from Each Other so that they had no Caseing upon Each Other whereas now they did which was they Occasion of their Rubin – Mr Channon and Patty Joyn with me in Best Respects and are Glad to hear you have your health and hope to hear the Continuance of it which will be a happiness to Mad'm.

London Sept 23rd 1766   Your Obleig'd
                                  Obediant Humble Ser't at
                                  all Commands M. Channon

[Endorsed]

December 19th 1769
M Channons
acknowledgmt
for £7 being ye
shares of their
Lottery Tickets

			£	s	d
A:	L	16th	1:	–:	0
M:	R	16:	1:	–:	0
E:	J	16:	1:	–:	0
J:	L	16:	1:	–:	0
Jas:	Chas:	16	1:	–:	0
G:	B	9th	2		
			7:		0

Addressed to: Mrs Fenneck

                 Mrs: Ann Fenneck

                             To John Channon

By Cash Paid for two Pictures Gilt
Frames   5   5   0
To a Small pare of Garrendoles painted
    flack White and 'Brass Norsels & brasshold'
    fases & screws to Do   0   15   6

To 21 ft ½ packing case paper at 3½	0	6	3½
Paid Porteredge & Warehouse Roome to the Carsel Inn	0	1	8
	£6	8	5½

Madam

If you have a Desire for any Perticuler Picture or Pictures please do lett me know what will suite for it offen falls in my way to Meet with Some Very Good I shall take A pleasure to Obledge you Without any fee or Reward. My Wife Joynes in best Respects and I am Yr. most Obedient Humble Serv't

John Channon

St Martin's Lane

N.B. The Brass Norsels belonging to the Garrendoles is In the paper Parsel.

Hon,ard Mad'm

I was vastly Uneasy at your Silence and Much fear,d You was ill but thank God I have now the pleasure to hear you are Recover'd. I can Venture to say none wishes you the true Enjoyment of Life more than My self

the frames of the pictures were Much Damag'd and they Remain the same as when we Rec'd them I am Sorry Mad'm you did not like them as Mr Channon Made no Doubt when he Bought them that they woud meet with your approbation they were done by so great a Man as Raphell Urbin and a Subject as he thought woud please you I hope Dear Mad'm you will not be Displeas's at the Liberty I have taken of Encloseing Your Bill – Mr Channon and Patty joynes with me in best Respects to your self and Mr Butler wishing you the Continuance of your Health and every other Blessing and am Dear Good Mad'm your Obleig. Obediant Humble Sev't at all commands.

London February 17th 1767   *M. Channon*

June 18 1766

By Cash pd. for two pictures in Carv'd and Gilt frames	5	5	0
To a Small pr of Jourandoles painted flack-white with Brass Nossells Holdfasters and Screws to do.	0	15	6
To 21 ft and ½ of packing-case at 3½ per ft	0	6	3½
Pd porterage and ware-house room to the Castle in Wood Street	0	1	8
August 15th To a packing Case to the 7 pictures and porterage to the Inn	0	4	0
Sept 9th By Cash pd. for Carriage and Porterage of the pictures from the Inn to My House		15	6
	£6	17	11½

My Dear Good Mad'm

I have hardly Strength to hold My pen had it not been for bad health I Shoud have Answer'd Your very kind and Obleigeing letter Sooner but I have the Fever and Ague ever since Easter-tuisday which has brought me allmost to Death and what is Still very bad that in the very weak State I am in I Expect every Hour to be brought a bed we Rec'd the money Safe last week Mr Channon Joyns with me in best Respects to your Self and Good Mr Butler and beg you will Excuse My enlargeing at presant and I hope you will be kind anough to Remember me in Your prayers as I hope all My Good Christian friends will do and the Unworthy as I am yet I do asure you of mine for your health and Every Happiness so must Conclude My-Self with the Greatiest truth and Sincerity Dear Good Madam your truely Affectionate Obleig'd Obediant Humble Seer't at all Commands

M. Channon
1767
London June 27th

Patty presents her Duty to
you and is Much obleig'd for your
kind Remembrance of her

[Endorsed]

Set down ye 14th of July.
June 27th 1767
Mrs Channon's
letter acknowledged
rec't of money: £7 7s 0d
Pd by Mr Errington
being in full of
their Bil of £6 17 11½
3s:sent to Miss Patty
ye rest to Mr C for
Interest: viz: 6s

Dear Mad'm

I beg the thousand pardons for not answering your Letter Sooner and am Extreamly uneasy that I shoud be so Unfortunate to be the Means of your Disquiet but we have Safely Rec'd the Seven pound Answerable to your Draft but the truth was Mr Channon laid it in his Buroe and forgot to send it in time but you know Mad'm that coud prove of no Disadvantage and Since we did Receive it I have been so Extreamly Busy that I have hardly had a Moments time but had I Considerd the Consiquence I would not for the world have Made you Uneasy for on the Contirary there is nothing but I would do to give you pleasure and believe me Mad'm this is the Truth of my heart I am Vastly Glad to hear you hold so well and thank God we are all verry well and my little Boy is Charmingly and fonder of his Father than of any Body he is not able walk yet but I hope the Spring and warm weather will Forward him he has Cut 12 teeth but in that he has suffer'd verry severely

Last week it was Excessive Cold here and a great deal of snow fell and since and at present its pretty tollerable Mr Channon Patty and (even my little Boy) all Joyne with me in Best Respects and Return you the Compliments of the Season and am Dear Mad'm Your truely Sincere affectionate and Obleig'g Obediant Humble Ser't at all Commands.

M. Channon
London   December 19th 1768

We beg the favour
you will please to present our
kindiest compliments
to good Mr Butler
I shall be glad to know if
the aventurers have been successfull

APPENDIX 3

Thomaas Treslove payment

Royal Bank of Scotland, Drummonds 1768 ledger
1–2, fol. 257. Account of Mr Thomas Treslove
18 June John Channon £9.14.0.

[There is a monument to Thomas Treslove at
St Peter's, Northampton, dated 1785].

Bill to Walter Scott

Scottish Record Office GD 157/659
Walter Scott of Harden Papers (Lord Polwarth)

1769 Nov 18th	Scott Esq Bought of John Channon			
	A Wallnuttree Chest of Drawers on Castors	3	10	0
	A Mahog'y Sideboard table	3	0	0
	12 Beach Chaires Carrott feet dyed with Matted seates	3	18	0
	Six high Wooden Chairs	0	12	0
	A spider leg table (erased)			
		£11	0	0

Received at the same time the Contence in full pr John Channon.
   [The absence of packing charges suggest this furniture was
ordered for a London house.]

Bill to Richard Crosse

Victoria and Albert Museum Library
86 GG 23 (Crosse accounts)

1773 Mr Crosse To John Channon					Dr
June 20th	To Repaireing a Mahog'y Clock Case head a New frett to Do Cleaning & Lackering the Capitles & bases & Varses & pollishing Do a Cover Screwes &c	0	6	6	
	To repaireing a Serpintine teatable a New frett to Do Scrapeing & pollishing Do alover	0	5	6	
July 12	To a 5ft Bedsteed Stout Mahog'y Pillers fine Wood Carv'd on strong Castors the best Double horse cloath Sicking bottom & Laceing line. Compas rod & base latts & a Scerpintain Cutt Cornish Compleate	6	16	6	
	To 55 yds of the best Crimsen Moreene at 2s – 9 pr yard	7	11	3	
	To 102 yds of the best cover'd lace	1	9	3	
	To 8 yds of brown hesings to Back line the head & teaster	0	10	6	
	To 2 Torsels	0	3	0	
	Buckram to back line the Vallins	0	17	0	
	Brass Rings Silk tape thread Studds tax &c	0	10	6	
	Carried Forward	18	10	0	
	Brought Forwards	18	10	0	
	To Makeing the Furniture and Covering the Cornishses	2	12	6	
	To 3 Men & fixing up the bedsteed & furniture at Yr House tax &c	0	5	0	
	Cash paid for a Bedwrinch left at Yr House	0	2	0	
	To a paper case to the teaster of Cateredge paper	0	2	0	
		£21	11	6	

Octo'r 18th 1773
   Rec'd the Contents in full & all Demands
                                                        pr John Channon
£21 11 6

APPENDIX 3
John Channon's fire-insurance policy

Guildhall Library, Sun Insurance Office registers
MS. 11976, vol. 130, pp. 2–3.
Policy No. 172993   9 January 1760
Premium £1.70
Renewal dated Xmas 1760

John Channon on the West side of St Martin's Lane Cabinetmaker on his household Goods Utensils & Stock in trade in his now Dwelling house only/Brick/ situated as aforesaid not exceeding five Hundred Pounds	500
Glass in trade therein only not exceeding one hundred pounds	100
On his Household Goods Utensils & Stock in trade in a Brick house only behind the aforesaid in his own Possession not exceeding one hundred & fifty Pounds	150
Wearing Apparel therein only not exceeding fifty Pounds	50
Glass therein only not exceeding fifty Pounds	50
On his Utensils & Stock in trade in a timber workshop only in the yard behind the aforesaid not exceeding one hundred & fifty Pounds	150
C Gascoigne – C Bewicke – J Fisher	£1,000

APPENDIX 4

The inlaid room at Mawley Hall

Sarah Medlam

An ensemble of woodwork which clearly relates to the group of brass-inlaid furniture and in particular to the Powderham bookcases, though the channels of connection are not clear, is the panelling in the inlaid drawing room at Mawley Hall, Shropshire. The house, which has been attributed to Francis Smith of Warwick (1672–1738), was completed in 1730 for Sir Edward Blount, Bart. and survives substantially unchanged. The interiors display ambitious and idiosyncratic decorations, including plasterwork attributed to the Italian stuccoist Francesco Vassalli and a unique serpentine banister to the finely carved woodwork of the staircase, the risers of which are inlaid with decorative stringings in lighter woods and roundels. As early as 1910 H. Avray Tipping in an article on Mawley was pointing out the similarities between the carved trophies of fishing and gardening on the staircase here and the same motifs carried out in plaster at Powderham two decades later.[1]

The inlaid drawing-room is quite small, forming a *cabinet*, with exceptional woodwork, including doors and door-cases, pilasters and panelling, of walnut, inlaid with dark and light woods and with brass inlay on the half-columns flanking the main door (Pl. 185), which is the closest known parallel to the work on the columns of the Powderham bookcases.

The room is a square, the floor set with a central octagon of parquetry.[2] There are three doors, each with ten fielded panels outlined with cross-bandings. Above two are broken scrolled pediments and fielded, framed panels as overdoors, set with trellised marquetry enclosing formal flower heads. The third door, set in the wall opposite the windows, is the centrepiece of the room in terms of decoration, the chimney-piece clearly in this interior playing a lesser role. The door is flanked by attached Doric columns, supporting a deep frieze with, above, a broken curved pediment, very reminiscent of the pediments of the Powderham bookcases. The scale of this doorway in such a small room, and the richness of its decoration, are sumptuous. The pillars are veneered with walnut and other woods, the bases showing fluting 'drawn' with brass stringing. Brass inlay features again at the top of the pillars, as flower-heads strung between pairs of flutes, and as rosettes, diamonds and curved stringing inlaid into collars at the top of the columns, and the abaci (Pl. 186). The same repertoire of motifs is repeated in the mouldings of the segmental pediment. The frieze, including the blocks heading each column, is decorated with strapwork in marquetry of woods, the design above each column centring on a roundel inlaid with a figure in ivory. This marquetry in wood is not immediately reminiscent of any furniture in the group, but relates to the Bennett bureau (Pl. 46).

The walls of the room show dado panels in walnut outlined with bolection moulding. Above this the walls are set with panels, the fields now filled with silk. It may be that the original scheme was for tapestry, which would have given greater weight to the walls than is now apparent.

The overmantel has undergone some adaptation and now features an inset panel carrying a carved and gilt mirror, the frame embellished with additional small panels of marquetry, the whole of it probably German, dating from the later eighteenth century.[3] This panel is set between pilasters, with interlinked marquetry panels outlined in stringing in dark and light woods on a light ground, each filled with a single motif such as an animal or an urn. Between the pilasters and above the mirror is an oval panel showing in marquetry the arms of Sir Edward Blount and those of his wife, Apollonia Throckmorton, whom he married in 1722. The wall opposite the chimney-piece is balanced by a similar bay, the armorial panel between the pilaster capitals being echoed by a marquetry panel with the monogram of Sir Edward and his wife.

Unfortunately no documentation on the creation of this exceptional room survives.[4] That Sir Edward had a particular eye for the decoration of his house is evident from the choice of such flamboyant plasterworkers and woodworkers. The family were Catholics, and though this might suggest opportunites for contact with the Continent, precise parallels for the inlaid drawing room are difficult to find. At first glance one is reminded of interiors such as those at Ottobeuren,[5] but no closer comparisons can be made, though we know that the Mawley stuccoist, Vassalli, worked at Mannheim in 1720[6] and that Francesco Serena, a stuccoist who had worked at Ottobeuren, was working at Ditchley in the late 1720s.[7] In Britain, undoubtedly the nearest comparative pieces are the bookcases at Powderham. If we believe from this that Channon had a hand in the creation of the marquetried room at Mawley, he must have had access to craftsmen who also worked in the dark/light strapwork tradition reminiscent of the late seventeenth century, and in a style which used separate marquetry motifs, as if taken from a design book, in a manner which can hardly be paralleled in British work of the first half of the eighteenth century.

APPENDIX 4   145

185. The main door from the inlaid drawing-room at Mawley Hall, Shropshire, c.1730. *R. Galliers-Pratt*

186. Detail of brass inlay on the column capitals and marquetry in the frieze. *R. Galliers-Pratt*

Notes

1. Introduction

1. 9 March 1945.
2. *Country Life*, 7 May 1948.
3. *Country Life*, 13 January 1950.
4. *Country Life*, 16 February 1956.
5. *Country Life*, 13 September 1956.
6. *Country Life*, 18 October 1956.

2. The Channon family of London and Exeter

1. Burney Collection of Newspapers, 363b, British Library, *The Craftsman*, 24 July 1742.
2. Burney 381b, *The Daily Advertiser*, 23 November 1742. Mr Eade was still lodging with Channon in January 1743 and published a subsequent advertisement in the same paper on 14 January 1743 (Burney 379b).
3. There are copies of this publication in the National Art Library (48.H.6) and the British Library (10.Tab.45).
4. Mormon Index for London under Frances Channon, taken from the baptism register for St Martin's-in-the-Fields.
5. *The Apprentices of Great Britain 1710–1762*, extracted from the inland revenue books of the Public Record Office, London, for the Society of Genealogists, 1921–8, vol. 13, p. 155.
6. *Exeter Freemen 1266–1967*, ed. M.M. Rowe and A.M. Jackson, Devon and Cornwall Record Society, Extra Series 1, Exeter, 1973, p. 264.
7. Westminster Local History Library, Poor Rates 1737, F 495, f. 65, under St Martin's Lane in Bedfordbury Ward.
8. *The Apprentices of Great Britain*, vol. 46, p. 155; *Exeter Freeman*, p. 234.
9. ibid.
10. *Boyd's Marriage Index*, Society of Genealogists; registers of St Sidwell, Exeter: marriages.
11. The twins survived less than a month and were buried on 1 December 1699. Correspondence between N.S.E. Pugsley, Exeter City Librarian, and John Hayward, Deputy Keeper of Woodwork, July–September 1965, archives of the Furniture and Woodwork Collection, Victoria and Albert Museum. The entries have been checked in the microfilm of the registers of St Sidwell, Exeter, baptisms, deposited in the Devon County Record Office.
12. See also *Devon & Cornwall Marriage Licences 686–1704*, p. 528, licence granted 8 October 1697; registers of St Sidwell, Exeter, marriages 1569–1733 MFC 46/10; *Devon and Cornwall Marriage Licences 1704–23*, p. 16, licence granted 5 October 1705.
13. St Sidwells Exeter, baptism register 1569–1733, MFC 46/10.
14. Correspondence between N.S.E. Pugsley and John Hayward.
15. B.F. Cresswell, *Exeter Churches*, Exeter, 1908.
16. Devon County Record Office, Exeter Poor Rate Book, 159b(1), 1708–32; Otho Channon's name occurs as a contributor on f. 29 (1708), f. 114 (1709), f. 153 (1710), f. 207 (1711), f. 244 (1712), f. 345 (1713), f. 381 (1715), f. 475 (1732).
17. Correspondence between N.S.E. Pugsley and John Hayward.
18. P. Ziegler, *The Sixth Great Power, Barings, 1762–1929*, London, 1988, p. 14.
19. Quoted in R. Newton, *Eighteenth Century Exeter*, Exeter, 1984, p. 22.
20. Ziegler, pp. 14–15.
21. Correspondence between N.S.E. Pugsley and John Hayward; Mormon index for Exeter. St Sidwell, Exeter, baptism and burial Registers, 1733–79, MFC 46/10, 11. Otho Channon's will was proved in 1756, and that of Otho Channon senior was proved in 1740. Both passed through the Court of the Principal Registry of the Bishop of Exeter and were preserved in the Probate Registry at Exeter (which was destroyed in 1942; unfortunately, neither of these wills was transcribed).
22. *The Apprentices of Great Britain*, vol. 21, p. 4062; *The Freemen of Exeter*, pp. 260, 271, 274.
23. Devon Record Office, Powderham Ms. account books 1739–49, 1508M Devon/v5 f. 104.
24. ibid.: loose letter enclosed between ff. 93–4.
25. Devon County Record Office, Powderham Ms. 1508M Devon/v10 account books 1745–52, f. 68;/v36; account books, f. 264.
26. ibid., 1508M/vz account books 1727–36;/v5 account books 1737–49, f. 67.
27. ibid., account books 1745–52, f. 156.
28. 1508M/v21, ff. 1, 42.
29. Westminster Local History Library, rate books for the parish of St Martin's-in-the-Fields.
30. *A Copy of the Poll for a Citizen for the City and Liberty of Westminster begun to be taken at Covent Garden 22 November to 8 December 1759*.
31. Westminster Local History Library, rate books for the parish of St Martin's-in-the-Fields.
32. Kensington Local History Library, St Mary Abbots burial registers, entry for 17 July 1797. (I am grateful to Francie Downing for this reference.)
33. *The Apprentices of Great Britain*, vol. 16, p. 3094; vol. 32, p. 6359.
34. ibid., vol. 23, p. 4413.
35. ibid., vol. 30, p. 923. A Thomas Channon of the parish of Wilton, Taunton, married Mary Strong on 23 November 1756, *Register of Wilton, Taunton, Somerset*, transcr. J.H. Spencer, Taunton, 1890, p. 136. In 1747 one Thomas Channon married Phillis Collins at St Mary Magdalen, Taunton, *Somersetshire Parish Registers*, Marriages X, ed. W.P.W. Phillimore, St Mary Magdalen, Taunton, 1907, p. 33. Curiously, the same marriage is recorded in the registers of St Sidwell, Exeter, for 12 June 1764, which is given also as the date of the christening of Thomas's daughter Mary.
36. Public Record Office PROB 11.1058.
37. Guildhall Library, Sun Insurance Company Ms. vol. 130, p. 283.
38. Mormon Index, London, under Channon; see appendix 2.
39. Martha Channon's will is in the Public Record Office. PROB 11.1295.
40. Gilbert 1978(2), p. 12.
41. Preston Record Office, RCHy 2/6/8.
42. See advertisement in the *The Craftsman* quoted on p. 5.
43. Drummonds Bank, London, 1768, ledger I–Z, f. 979.
44. Scottish Record Office, Scott of Harden Papers (Lord Polwarth) G.D.157/659.
45. National Art Library, Ms. Accounts of Richard Crosse, 86.GG.23.
46. P.R.O. PROB 11.1058. Only the entry for the christening of Mary Channon, daughter of Thomas on 12 June 1764 has been traced to date.
47. Beard and Gilbert, p. 142.
48. *The Craces: Royal Decorators 1768–1899*, ed. M. Aldrich, Brighton, 1990, p. 5.
49. Kensington Local History Library, St Mary Abbots burial register, entry for 29 October 1779. The entry is under John Shannon who was described as of 'St Martens [sic] lane'. The burial book records that he died at the age of 73 and was buried 'close to the stone in the wall in the old ground facing Mr Harrison's house, Church Lane'. There is no surviving record of a gravestone or its inscription and no record that the Channons owned property in Kensington. (I am

NOTES TO PAGES 11–25   147

indebted to Francie Downing for this reference.)
50 PROB 11.1295.
51 Two members of the Scadding family are recorded in the published Marriage Registers of St Mary Magdalen, Taunton; John Scadding in 1735 and Richard Scadding in 1779. *Somersetshire Parish Registers*, ed. W.P.W. Phillimore, Marriages X, pp. 15, 70.
52 Kensington Local History Library, St Mary Abbots marriage register, entry for 14 August 1776. James Scadding married Martha Bouchier. (I am indebted to Francie Downing for this reference.)
53 ibid. She was described as sixty-four at the time of her death. (I am indebted to Francie Downing for this reference.)

3. Channon's rivals and the London market for brass-inlaid furniture

1 See p. 9.
2 Quoted by C.N. Ponsford, *Time in Exeter*, Exeter, 1978, p. 109.
3 R. Newton, *Eighteenth Century Exeter*, Exeter, 1984, p. 24.
4 Ponsford, pp. 73ff.
5 E. Croft-Murray, 'The Ingenious Mr. Clay', *Country Life*, vol. 104, 1948, pp. 1378–80.
6 See p. 5. This advertisement appeared on 23 November 1742.
7 See p. 5. This advertisement appeared on 24 July 1742.
8 *A Copy for the Poll for a Citizen for the City and Liberty of Westminster begun to be taken at Covent Garden 22 November to 8 December 1749*. According to this source, other cabinet-makers in the City and Liberty of Westminster included John Fish, Benjamin Goodison, William Harris, George Nix, Samuel Shallford and John White in Long Acre; John Yeats in St Martin's Lane; Thomas Parker and John Worthy in Hemings Row; John Dobson in St Martin's Court; Samuel Stain in Pall Mall; William Fenton in Suffolk Street; James Wilson in Castle Court; James Comery in Castle Street; Christopher Wallis in Dirty Lane; George Bates in Whitcombe Street; Joseph Shelton in Villers Street; Edmund Hardy in Russell Court; George Smith in Castle Street; William Kirk in the Strand; John Cerne in Middlesex Court; Peter Le Mayre in Mercer's Street; John Robinson in Bear Street; James Newton in Red Lion Court; Francis Stuart in Coventry Court; Alex Dingwall in Leicester Fields; Thomas Edwards in Chandos Street; Peregrine Tate in Banbury Court; Alexander Henderson in Castle Street; James Moncur in Coventry Court; John Harding in the Hay Market; and Ephraim Jackson in Charles Court. In addition carvers included William Linnen[sic] ⟨Linnell⟩ in Long Acre; Aaron Jones in Castle Street; James Wallis in James Street; Charles Angier and John Dubourg in Long Acre; Thomas Latham in Cross Lane, Long Acre; Joseph Cotton in Leg Alley; John Elkrington, Chapel Alley, Long Acre; James Wittle(sic) ⟨Whittle⟩, Castle Street, carver; Christopher Mason, Charles Court, a carver and gilder; and John Harris, Vinegar Yard, a picture-frame maker. Another neighbour was the upholsterer Paul Saunders in Hartshorne Lane.
9 White, p. 205.
10 T. Friedman, *James Gibbs*, London, 1984, p. 261.
11 White, p. 197.
12 ibid., 37–8, 399.
13 R.W. Symonds, 'Gerrit Jensen, Cabinet-Maker to the Royal Household', *Connoisseur*, April 1935, pp. 268–74.
14 G. Jackson-Stops, in *Treasures from the Royal Collection*, The Queen's Gallery, London, 1988–9, pp. 98–9, fig. 94.
15 *Boughton House: The English Versailles*, ed. T. Murdoch, London, 1992, pl. 79, pp. 133–4, 223.
16 Symonds, 'Gerrit Jensen', p. 269.
17 Legal affidavits to the executors of Ralph, 1st Duke of Montagu, Boughton House.
18 Edwards and Jourdain, pp. 91–2; J.D.U. Ward, 'The Work of Coxed and Woster in Mulberry Wood and Burr Elm', *Apollo*, November 1941, pp. 104–6.
19 Heal fig. 12, p. 230.
20 V&A W.66-1924; Symonds 1958 (1).
21 This is now in the Saloon at Erddig but originally stood on the pier of John Meller's State Bedroom. John Loveday refers to it in his diary of a tour in 1732, *Guide Book to Erddig*, The National Trust, 1977, p. 17.
22 I am grateful to Francie Downing for researching the evidence for brass-inlaid furniture in contemporary sale catalogues in the British Library, the National Art Library, and at Christie's. Edgeley Hewer's catalogue (Lugt 387) is in the British Library. He died on 6 November 1728 at the age of 36. He was a Fellow of the Royal Society (Musgrave's obit.; Political State of Great Britain, XXXVI, 496; Historical Register Chronicle, 58).
23 Sir William Stanhope's sale catalogue is in the National Art Library, 23.V.V.; see also R. Edwards, 'An Eighteenth Century Sale Catalogue', *Country Life*, vol. LXIII, 19 May 1928, pp. 737–9.
24 The advertisement appeared in *The Daily Journal* 18 April 1735; British Library, Burney 309b. William Hubert may be connected with the Huguenot family of that name who were based in the Strand at this time (see T. Murdoch ed. *The Quiet Conquest: The Huguenots 1685–1985*, Museum of London, 1985, pp. 110–11).
25 British Library, Burney 305b.
26 P.R.O. PROB 11.701; the will is dated 14 December 1739.
27 Announcement in the *London Daily Post and General Advertiser*, 2 March 1741; British Library, Burney 355b.
28 Announcement in the *General Advertiser*, 22 April 1751.
29 Announcement in the *London Evening Post*, 3–5 February 1737; British Library, Burney 372b.
30 W.37-1953. The 'mahogany Desk and Bookcase' was lot 13 on the fifth day of Sir William Stanhope's sale.
31 E.2320-89; Beard and Gilbert pp. 503, 708. Kelsey and Potter supplied Hoare with a mahogany bed-table, a screen on pillars and claws, and a fine mahogany bed enriched with carving (V&A archives, Furniture and Woodwork Collection).
32 This formerly belonged to Roy Baxter. The sale catalogue of Hon. Col. John Mercer, late of Denmark Street, Soho, and Nicholas Hawksmoor, is in the British Library.
33 Announcement in the *Daily Post*, 22 May 1738, Burney 332b.
34 L. Boynton, 'William and Richard Gomm', *Burlington Magazine*, vol. CXXII, June 1980, p. 396; Johnston, *John Channon*.
35 Beard and Gilbert, p. 434; Johnston p. 39. A bass viol with seven strings bearing the label of 'Frederick Hintz, Ryder's Court, 17 Leicester Fields, London, 1760' is in the V&A 169-1882, see G. Thibault, J. Jenkins, J. Bran-Ricci, *Eighteenth Century Musical Instruments: France and Britain*, Victoria and Albert Museum, London, 1973, p. 44, no. 24.
36 E. Edwards, *Anecdotes of Painting*, London, 1808, cited by Claxton-Stevens p. 18. There is further information on G.M. Moser in Snodin.
37 Beard and Gilbert, p. 905.
38 Hayward 1965, p. 13; Beard and Gilbert, p. 364.
39 Hayward 1965, p. 23.
40 Gilbert 1978(2), pl. 212.
41 Heal Collection, British Museum, 28.121; Snodin, pp. 179–80.
42 Christie's archives retain annotated copies of both these catalogues.
43 I am grateful to John Harris for bringing this catalogue to my attention; an annotated copy is in the Christie's archives.
44 National Art Library 23.L.
45 Both notices appeared on 23 May 1775; British Library, Burney Collection 631b, 634b. I am grateful to Susanna Avery for these references.
46 Advertisement in the *Public Advertiser*, 3 August 1776, found by Susanna Avery; Burney 642b.

4. The continental context: Germany

1 Symonds 1956 (1).
2 Two carved frieze panels of the late sixteenth century from a house near Exeter (now in the collections of the Victoria and Albert Museum), follow engravings by Jan Vredeman de Vries. They were discussed by Anthony Wells-Cole in 'An Oak Bed at Montacute: A Study in Mannerist Decoration', *Furniture History*, XVII, 1981, p. 15.
3 E.A.G. Clarke, *The Ports of the Exe Estuary 1660–1860*, Exeter, 1960, p. 95.
4 Philip Ziegler, *The Sixth Great Power*, London, 1988, p. 15.
5 Clarke, p. 51.
6 He left his home in Mühlheim in 1731; Huth p. 6.
7 Greber, p. 30: 'Er legte sich aufs Gravieren, auf die Mosaik in Holz und auf die Mechanik mit so gutem Erfolg, dass er bald von den

Geschicktesten Cabinetmachern gesucht und reichlich belohnt wurde.'
8. Greber, p. 30.
9. Greber, p. 31: 'Er hatte ein Mosaik in Holz erfunden, arbeitete für eigene Rechnung und seine Kunstarbeiten wurden von den Cabinetmachern sehr gesucht und reichlich bezahlt.' In view of Hintz's established trade in brass inlaid furniture by 1738, Ludwig's claim for his grandfather may be ambitious.
10. Boynton, p. 396. (The authors would like to record their thanks to Lindsay Boynton for help in the preparation of this chapter. His own article on the connections between the Moravian community and the trade of cabinet-making in London is forthcoming.)
11. Greber, p. 38.
12. Huth, pl. 1.
13. Greber, p. 38.
14. For a detail of the engraved plaque see Greber, pl. 4.
15. Huth, p. 30.
16. For tables with this mechanical device see Huth, pl. 139–48. The last shows the same mechanism on a drawing for a neo-classical table published in the *Journal des Luxus und der Moden* as late as May 1795.
17. Huth, p. 29.
18. Huth, pl. 36.
19. Huth, p. 9.
20. Huth, p. 6.
21. Huth, p. 10. Huth makes the point that this would have allowed Abraham Roentgen to maintain contact with workshops such as those of Chippendale and of Ince & Mayhew, and to be aware, if he had not been earlier, of their published designs.
22. Huth, p. 10.
23. At this time he evidently had a German apprentice. In the account books of the Lutheran Church of the Savoy (1754–70) a payment of 5 gns. was made to 'Hintz und den jungen Schmidt bei ihm verbunden' on 31 May 1738 (Victoria Library, Westminster, 90/46).
24. Lindsay Boynton was the first to establish Hintz's membership of the Moravian community and to point out the significance of this for the exchange of ideas and development of techniques (Boynton, p. 396). Much of the detail of Hintz's life was established by Janet Halton, Librarian at the Moravian Church House, Muswell Hill. The authors would like to record their gratitude to Janet Halton for her help and guidance on matters of detail and of general Moravian history. Without her help this account of Hintz's life could not have been written.
25. Information from Mrs Halton. For a note on the setting up of the first group see Colin Podmore, 'The Fetter Lane Society', *Proceedings of the Wesley Historical Society*, XLVI, part V, p. 126.
26. ibid.
27. Podmore, p. 142. At that time John Wesley was interested in the movement.
28. There are gaps in the Moravian Church archives at various times in the 1740s.
29. *Brown Book*, p. 233. Moravian Church archives. The Brown Book is a compilation of various sources of material relating to the Fetter Lane Society.
30. *Pilgrim House Diary*, 22 November 1746. Moravian Church archives. The Diary covers the period July 27 1743–8, but there are some gaps.
31. ibid.
32. *Pilgrim House Diary*, 29 November 1746.
33. *Gemeinhaus Diary*, 1747, 16th week. Moravian Church archives. This records that they were married 'according to ye Liturgy of the Church of England' (for which a dispensation was needed) and that it was conducted 'in ye presence of all ye English Brethren and Sisters', this last comment suggesting some extensive travelling among the members of the English community.
34. The minutes of the 'Helpers' Conference' (a meeting held every ten days or so to deal with church matters) of 20/31 July 1747 records Hintz as 'expected tonight or tomorrow'. Moravian Church archives.
35. Minutes of the Helpers' Conference, Monday March 14 1747/8.
36. ibid.
37. *Brown Book*, p. 118. She was baptised on the day of her birth, 28 June.
38. *Brown Book*, p. 413.
39. ibid.
40. Fragmentary diary of the life of Ann Hintz. Moravian Church archives.
41. ibid. This 'diary' is a retrospective account of her life and dates are not mentioned.
42. The reference to him as 'cabinet maker' in 1751 may record the community's memory of his training rather than his current employment. Both Hintz and his wife attended the weekly Helper's meetings fairly regularly in 1749–50, but their attendance tailed off in 1751. He seems to have become preoccupied with business worries and the minutes for 12 September 1750/1 record that 'Br Hintz cannot get through his business'.
43. Minutes of the Helpers' Conference, 24 February 1752: '6. Bro. Hintz has opened his shop in Newport Street, Some of his Bills were brot. into the Conference.'
44. *The Universal Director or the Nobleman's and Gentleman's True Guide* by Mr Mortimer, London, 1763, part II, p. 51. Lindsay Boynton has pointed out that the reference in Anthony Bailes, *Victoria & Albert Museum, Catalogue of Musical Instruments, vol. II, Non-Keyboard Instruments*, London, 1978, p. 5 to Hintz as also 'selling furniture' in 1763, is not substantiated by the entry in the directory, which records him at 'the corner of Ryder's Court, Leicester Fields'.
45. *Brown Book*, p. 233. She was buried in the Moravian burial ground at Chelsea.
46. Elders' Conference Minutes, 25 April 1772 records the agreement to his being buried with his wife. That permission was needed suggests a split, and the Minutes of the Helpers', conference, 17 May 1772 record: 'it were to be wished we had a list of all those children who have been baptised by us and that if possible we might bring them into the lap of the Congn. as Nisbet, Hintz, Townsent and others'. Moravian Church archives.
47. The first record seems to be in Willibald Leo Freiherr von Lutgendorff, *Die Geigen-und Lautenmacher vom Mittelalter bis zur Gegenwart*, Frankfurt, 1913. On page 371 a label is printed, but by transcription, rather than photographically. The label appears to read clearly: 'F. Hinds/Maker/Ryder's Court, Leicester Fields/17 London 76'.
48. Huth, p. 8.
49. Greber, p. 34, quoting from the papers of the Herrnhag Helferkonferenz, 1741–5.
50. ibid.
51. Huth, pp. 36–7.
52. Nicholas Goodison, *Ormolu: The Life and Work of Matthew Boulton*, 1974, p. 5.
53. Daniel Defoe, *A Plan of the English Commerce*, London, 1728, pp. 218–19.
54. A. Hepplewhite, *The Cabinet-Maker's and Upholsterer's Guide*, London, 1788; prefatory remarks.
55. Kreisel and Himmelheber, p. 35.
56. ibid.
57. Kreisel and Himmelheber, p. 34.
58. Kreisel and Himmelheber, p. 48.
59. Kreisel and Himmelheber, p. 258.
60. *Meisterstücke Mainzer Möbel des 18. Jahrhunderts*, catalogue of an exhibition held at the Museum für Kunsthandwerk, Frankfurt-am-Main, 1988, p. 24.
61. Kreisel and Himmelheber, p. 26.
62. ibid.
63. Kreisel and Himmelheber, p. 27.
64. P.W. Meister, in *World Furniture*, London, 1975, p. 150.
65. E.T. Joy, 'Norwegian Furniture 1660–1820: its relationship with English styles', *Connoisseur*, CLXIX, 1968, p. 18.
66. *Mostra del Barocco Piemontese* (exhibition catalogue), Turin, 1963, p. 13.
67. It is interesting that Abraham Roentgen's wealthy brother-in-law, Bausch, had a business in Hamburg. Huth, pp. 10 and 12.
68. Joy, 'Some aspects of the London furniture industry in the eighteenth century', MA thesis, University of London, 1955.
69. Held in the information section of the Furniture and Woodwork Collection at the Victoria and Albert Museum.
70. Edward T. Joy, 'English Furniture Exports' I, II, in *Country Life*, 20 June 1952, pp. 1925–6, and 27 June 1952, pp. 2010–12; 'The Overseas Furniture Trade in the Eighteenth Century' in *Furniture History* (I), 1965, pp. 1–10.
71. E.T. Joy, 'Norwegian Furniture 1660–1820: its relationship with English styles', *Connoisseur*, CLXIX, 1968, pp. 18–21.
72. See the discussion of George Michael Moser in chapter 3, p. 21. The subject is also discussed by Richard Edgcumbe in Snodin, pp. 127–8.
73. Benno Forman, 'Continental Furniture Craftsmen in London: 1511–1625', *Furniture History* (VII), 1971, pp. 94–119.
74. Peter Thornton and William Rieder, 'Pierre Langlois, Ebéniste', *Connoisseur*, CLXXVIII, 1971, pp. 283–8; CLXXIX, 1972, pp. 105–12, 176–87, 257–65; CLXXX, 1972, pp. 30–5.
75. J.F. Hayward, 'Christopher Fuhrlohg, an Anglo-Swedish cabinet-maker', *Burlington*,

cxi, 1969, pp. 648–55; J.F. Hayward, 'A newly discovered commode signed by Christopher Fuhrlohg', *Burlington*, cxiv, 1973, pp. 704–11; J.F. Hayward, 'A further note on Christopher Fuhrlohg', *Burlington*, cxix, 1977, pp. 486–93.
76 Beard and Gilbert.
77 Beard and Gilbert, p. 852. The 1750 account to Earl Fitzwalter includes a 'Mahogany Campaign Desk', certainly a piece which would have included more than usual (if rather plain) brasswork. The German spelling of the name and the dates are from the records of the German church in the Savoy, quoted in Johnston, p. 36.
78 The account books (1754–70) of the Lutheran Church of the Savoy held at the Victoria Library, Westminster, refer to a payment in February 1741/2 to 'Schumacher', who may have been Martin Schumacher, the German cabinet maker from Ansbach.
79 Kreisel and Himmelheber, pp. 24–5 and pl. 2.
80 Beard and Gilbert, pp. 408–9.
81 Kreisel and Himmelheber, p. 95.
82 Kreisel and Himmelheber, p. 357.
83 Kreisel and Himmelheber, pl. 90, 91.
84 Kreisel and Himmelheber, pl. 52.
85 Kreisel and Himmelheber, pl. 847.
86 Kreisel, 1970 edn, pl. 842.
87 Kreisel and Himmelheber, pl. 848.
88 For a full discussion of the furniture from the Altona region see Annette-Isabel Kratz, *Altonaer Möbel des Rokoko und Klassizismus*, Hamburg, 1988.
89 Kratz, plates, passim.
90 *Kaiserlicher Kunstbesitz aus dem Holländischen Exil Haus Doorn*, Berlin, Staatliche Schlösser und Gärten, 1991, no. 89.
91 Kreisel and Himmelheber, pl. 792.
92 Kreisel and Himmelheber, pl. 784 illustrates the cupboard.
93 Illustrated and discussed in *Kunstmuseum Düsseldorf. Ausgewählte Werke*, Düsseldorf, 1977, no. IV-28.

5. The continental context: France

1 See Snodin; and J. Cornforth, 'French Style, English Mood', *Country Life*, 1 October 1992.
2 Cornforth. Other examples, including Norfolk House and Isaac Ware's work, are well documented in Snodin, and R. White, 'Isaac Ware and Chesterfield House', in C. Hind (ed.), *The Rococo in England: a symposium*, 1986, pp. 175–92.
3 *Guide Book to Erddig*, The National Trust, 1977, p. 13.
4 'The Imports of Great Britain from France', Louis Philippe Boitard; reproduced c24 in Snodin, p. 49.
5 Edward T. Joy, 'Chippendale in trouble at the Customs', *Country Life*, August 1924, 1951.
6 Snodin, p. 16.
7 The print is known in two states, the name of the engraver lacking in both, the difference being the addition of the numbering of the plates and the addresses of the publishers: (1) Berain, *c*.1700, and (2) Jacques Thuret, son-in-law of Berain, shortly after 1711. See R. Berliner, *Ornamentale Vorlageblätter des 16. bei 18. Jahrhunderts*, Leipzig, 1926, II, pl. 327; R.-A. Weigert, *Jean I Berain, Dessinateur de la Chambre et du Cabinet du Roi (1640–1711)*, Paris, 1936, II, no. 71, pl. XXVII, fig. 48. (I would like to thank Michael Snodin for his discovery of this link and Peter Fuhring for providing information on this source.)
8 Künstgewerbemuseum, Schloss Köpenick, Berlin. (Thanks to Dr Burckhardt Göres.)
9 *Grand Oppenord*, series KK, LL.
10 Illustrated in Verlet, *Les Bronzes Dorés Français*, Paris, 1987, p. 83, pl. 85.
11 For example, a pair of female faces at each corner of a chimneypiece of white marble in the Grand Salon on the ground floor at the Chateau of Bercy, now in the Hotel Schickler, Paris, illustrated in F. Contet, *Les Vieux Hotels de Paris*, Paris, 1909 onwards, and the chimneypiece from the gallery at the Chateau of Meudon now in the Cronstedt Collection, Stockholm, illustrated in Bruno Pons 'Le décor de l'appartement du Grand Dauphin au Château Neuf de Meudon (1909)', *Gazette des Beaux Arts*, VIe periode, tome cxvii, Fev. 1991, pp. 59–76. (Many thanks to Christian Baulez for suggesting these sources for designs for chimney-pieces.)
12 For example, the caryatids on the chimneypiece in the Salle du Conseil (by Gobert or Leblanc, 1748) are in the form of female figures, representing truth and justice, which turn towards each other. Each has a cartouche behind the face which recalls the Channon *espagnolettes*. The chimney-piece in the Chambre du Dauphin, 1747, has very finely cast and chased bronzes of Flora and Zephyr, attributed by Nolhac to Caffieri, but possibly supplied by Gobert or Leblanc (illustrated in Verlet, *Les Bronzes Dorés Français*, Paris, 1987, p. 79, pl. 77).
13 Archives Nationales O^1 1774, pièce 105. Another example, though less similar, of male figures exists in the small satyrs in bronze on the chimney-piece from the Salle de Compagnie at the Petit Hotel de Villars, Paris.
14 I would like to thank Michael Snodin for drawing my attention to the relationship between French *espagnolettes* and the design of the London furniture mounts. Also see 'La mode des espagnolettes Oppenord à Juvarra', in *Antologia di Belle Arti, Mélanges Verlet*, 1985, nos. 27–8, 3rd vol.
15 The design is conserved in the Cabinet des Estampes, Bibliothèque Nationale, Paris, illustrated in F. Souchal, *Les Slodtz*, Paris, 1968, pl. 72a.
16 Bookcase, one of a pair, attributed to Charles Cressent, Gulbenkian Museum, Lisbon, illustrated in Pierre Kjellberg, *Le Mobilier Français du XVIIIe Siècle: Dictionnaire des Ebénistes et des Menuisiers*, Paris, 1989, p. 201 and Pradère, pl. 93, p. 133.
17 I would like to thank Didier Aaron for drawing the armoire to my attention and Christian Baulez for permitting me to look closely at the Versailles armoire.
18 I would like to thank Peter Fuhring for drawing this source to our attention. This set of prints, claimed to be designs by Berain, engraved by the otherwise unknown Mersonau in Paris, were sold by J. Nicholls, the Minories, Aldgate. Mersonau and other French plates re-issued by Nicholls were put out again about 1728 or earlier by John Pine in *The Compleat Book of Ornaments* (Snodin, cat. c3, p. 42). Fuhring notes that the compositions are considered by Weigert to be of an unknown author, whose name has been substituted by that of Berain. Fuhring suggests that 'commercial reasons must have been instrumental in using French names to sell otherwise anonymous compositions, taken from several different French, Italian and probably English sources'.
19 Though originally these were positioned at each of the four corners, one is now missing.
20 Illustrated in Pradère, p. 118. (I would like to thank M. Maurice Segoura for providing information and the photograph of this commode, now in a private collection.)
21 Commode à tombeau with five drawers, 1730–40, stamped François Mondon. The bronze mounts follow the curve of the carcass at each corner – the female heads follow a convex shape approximately in alignment with the middle of the three rows of drawers, and are surmounted by two leaf motifs above the cresting. This additional section follows the convex profile in alignment with the top drawer. (I would like to thank M. Didier Aaron and M. Bill Pallot for allowing me to examine this commode, and for their interest in this project.)
22 Commode en tombeau, bois de violette, Christie's Monte-Carlo, 19 June 1988, no. 118, and illustrated in Kjellberg (note 16 above), p. 632.
23 Illustrated in Pradère, pp. 111–13. These are attributed to Gérard on the basis of another *bureau plat* stamped N.G. in the Toledo Museum of Art, Ohio. (I would like to thank Lee Mooney, Toledo, Dr Sigrid Sangl, Munich, and M. Rossi, Paris, for providing information about this group.)
24 Thanks to Albert Neher of the Furniture Conservation Section, Victoria and Albert Museum, for this observation.
25 Chasers working for the cabinet-maker Charles Cressent included Guillaume Lonbard and Pierre Vandnesanne, both *fondeurs-ciseleurs* who chased *espagnolettes* for him (Pradère, p. 130).
26 Peter Fuhring, 'Designs for and after Boulle furniture', *Burlington Magazine*, June 1992.
27 See Carolyn Sargentson, 'Markets for Boulle furniture in early eighteenth century Paris', *Burlington Magazine*, June 1992.
28 Pradère gives biographies and archival references for these cabinet makers.
29 See Mlle M.-J. Ballot, *Charles Cressent, Recueil de Documents Inédits*, Archives de L'Art Francais, Paris, 1969.
30 The Earl of Waldegrave.
31 no. 155. Two large armoires with tortoiseshell marquetry with two large doors at the front and small doors on either side, all

decorated with gilt bronze figures, valued at 4,000 *livres* Archives Nationales, Minutier Central, CXXI, 306, 17 August 1736, cited in Pradère, p. 112. Gérard's chasers included Olivier de Rouvray and Louis Regnard, *ciseleurs*, rue des Arcis.
32 Cited in Pradère, p. 130.
33 Svend Eriksen, *Neoclassicism*, 1974, pp. 271–6.
34 Archives Nationales, Y1899.
35 H. Ottomeyer and P. Proschel, *Vergoldete Bronzen Die Bronzarbeiten des Spätbarock und Klassizmus*, Munich, 1986, II, pp. 647–8.
36 Goodison, p. 21. (I would like to thank Helena Hayward for drawing my attention to this.)
37 ibid.
38 Goodison, pp. 22–3.
39 Goodison, pp. 23 and 175 (note 50).

6. Furniture manufacture and workshop organisation

1 M. Berg, *The Age of Manufactures: Industry, Innovation and Work in Britain 1700–1820*, Glasgow, 1985.
2 R. Campbell, *The London Tradesman*, London, 1747, pp. 169–76.
3 Campbell, p. 170.
4 Campbell, p. 172.
5 B. Cotton, *The English Regional Chair*, Woodbridge, 1992, p. 23 and passim.
6 P. Kirkham, 'Samuel Norman: a study of an eighteenth century craftsman', *The Burlington Magazine*, August 1969, pp. 506–13.
7 H. Hayward and P. Kirkham, *William and John Linnell: Eighteenth Century London Furniture Makers*, London, 1980, pp. 168–80.
8 Kirkham, p. 506.
9 Hayward and Kirkham, pp. 171–2.
10 Kirkham, pp. 507–8.
11 The exact status of this advertisement print is not clearly understood.
12 6 December 1744, *Daily Advertiser*; British Library, Burney 397b.
13 Quoted in chapter 3, pp. 18–19.
14 This obsession with mahogany was reinforced by Percy Macquoid's division of the eighteenth century into several 'Ages' of woods, the 'Age of Mahogany' being the name he gave to the period covered by this study.
15 There are approximately 80 different types of mahogany which grow in the West Indies.
16 D. Learmont, 'The Trinity Hall Chairs, Aberdeen', *Furniture History*, XIV, 1978, p. 6, no. 14, pl. 14.
17 F. Lewis Hinckley, *The Directory of the Historic Cabinet Woods*, New York, 1960, p. 125.
18 22 February 1702, *The London Gazette*.
19 Amboyna – *Pterocarpus indicus*; Campeachy wood or logwood – *Haematoxylon campechianum*; Ebony – many varieties imported; Grenoble, either Indian or European (European Grenoble is French walnut – *Juglans regia*, but Indian Grenoble is not identified); Guiney Wood or Guiney Redwood – *Dracontomelum spp.*; Manchinele or Manchineel – *Hippomane mancinella*; Nicarago – possibly a group of woods from the Nicaraguan cedar, lignum vitae and mahogany; Porto Bello – ?; Padauk or Padouk – *Pterocarpus spp.*
20 Taken from the *Daily Advertiser*, *Daily Journal*, *Daily Post and Advertiser*, *General Advertiser*, *General Evening Post*, *London Courant*, *London Evening Post*, and the *Public Advertiser* from 1730 to 1760.
21 'Grenoble' could refer to a region now part of modern Switzerland, which specialised in the production of clock-cases, or, more likely, it is a reference to the type of timber (French walnut, from the same area).
22 *General Advertiser*, 9 February 1748; British Library, Burney 428b.
23 *Daily Advertiser* 10 February 1744; Burney 381b.
24 The identification of the timbers was undertaken by Jo Darrah of the Scientific Section. The pieces of wood taken were approximately 5 mm × 5 mm × 3 mm, some smaller and some a little larger, with the grain running with the longest dimension. Sections were prepared as follows:

(1) The density and the colour of a fresh surface were recorded;

(2) The sample was boiled in water for ten minutes to soften the tissues;

(3) It was (where possible) divided into two parts, one used for the cross section, the other for the radial and tangential sections;

(4) The sample was mounted in the required alignment in water on a freezing platform (cryostat) and embedded in ice. The sections were cut with a microtome. The process was repeated to prepare the other two sections;

(5) The sections were examined in transmitted light at ×50, ×125 and ×320 magnification, using when necessary crossed or half-crossed polars.

All the visible characteristics of the three sections were noted down. The woods were identified initially using the Forest Products Research Laboratory wood identification cards. When possible the identification was confirmed by comparing the unknown with a reference slide or with photographs of sections. The South Carolina University Computer system was not particularly useful but helped to confirm the identity of one sample. In all eighteen samples were prepared and identified.
25 Absolute identification is difficult from the necessarily small samples.
26 Unless the match of the wood of the pilasters is absolute with that of the carcase, it may simply be that the nineteenth-century restorer chose the standard eighteenth-century wood.
27 This piece has not undergone scientific identification of timbers, so all identifications are open to dispute.
28 Padouk is a nineteenth-century name which came into common usage about 1838. In eighteenth-century inventories and advertisements there are references to Red wood, which may indicate the same wood.
29 *Chlorophora tinctoria (H.)*, from the West Indies.
30 Possibly Padouk, of which there are many species.
31 *Madeira* is the Portuguese word for 'wood'.
32 This is a reference to *bois violet* or kingwood, a species of *Dalbergia spp.* from tropical America.
33 Taken from 'An Inventory & Appraisement & full & Singular the Household Goods (Except ye Jewels, Paintings & other Goods & Things) of & belonging to the Right Honourable Lord Viscount Courtenay deceased; at Powderham Castle, Exwell Farm and the Dolphin and Bonetta Yatchs [sic]; as also the Household Goods Furniture at Ford and the House in Exeter, taken in the months of June, July, August and September 1762'. V/1/38 box no. 9 (Muniment Room at Powderham Castle).
34 See Kenneth Lemmon, 'The Hunt for New Plants', in *The Garden, A Celebration of One Thousand Years of British Gardening*, London, 1979, p. 94.
35 Krzysztof Pomian, *Collectors and Curiosities: Paris and Venice 1500–1800*, transl. Elizabeth Wiles-Portier, Cambridge, 1987, p. 105.
36 *Guide to the Lady Lever Art Gallery, Port Sunlight*, London, 1989, p. 64.
37 W37-1953.
38 One, a nineteenth-century copy of the Boulle Trianon commodes, was with Carlton Hobbs in autumn 1992.
39 For a discussion of this piece see pp. 79–82.
40 Philip Zea, *New England Furniture*, ed. Brock Jobe and Myrna Kaye, Boston, Mass., 1984.
41 V&A, W18-1952.
42 W37-1953.
43 A bureau-desk at the Victoria and Albert Museum, W29-1959, of about 1710, uses walnut for the carcase of the small drawers behind the fall-front.
44 This was the term used by Chippendale in the 1754 edition of his *Director* to describe a very similar form of furniture.
45 Commode, veneered with lacquer, about 1750, Victoria and Albert Museum, Jones Collection, 1094–1882.
46 See the Walsh brass of 1752 at Curry Rivel, Somerset, illustrated in M. Norris, *Monumental Brasses – The Craft*, London, 1978, pl. 263.
47 *Le Bronze*, Paris, 1910, pl. XXX, LV.
48 It is significant in this context that Thomas Chippendale was describing the mounts on some of his furniture designs as intended for execution in brass or silver (*The Director*, 3rd edn, pl. CXXII, 'Designs of Cabinets').
49 See Snodin, G13, p. 112; E13, p. 70; the candlesticks by Moser are in the Victoria and Albert Museum, M.329 & A-1977.
50 N. Goodison, *Ormolu – the work of Matthew Boulton*, London, 1974, p. 20.
51 E. Griffin, *William Palmer, Master Engraver 1737–1812*, privately printed, 1990.

7. Furniture survey

1 Heal, figs. 11–13.
2 Goodison 1969, pp. 195–6.
3 27 June 1957, lot 80.
4 Symonds 1958 (1).

NOTES TO PAGES 59–144

5 This letter was sold to the Victoria and Albert Museum with the bureau.
6 Partridge (Fine Art) Ltd, *Summer Exhibition Catalogue*, 1988 (7); Christie's, 18 November 1982, lot 125.
7 18 July 1975 (lot 51).
8 See correspondence with Anne Fenwick (appendix 2).
9 Edwards, vol. 1, p. 145, fig. 49.
10 First identified by Helena Hayward (Hayward 1982).
11 Details of Gordon's commissions are in Beard and Gilbert, pp. 355–7.
12 Partridge (Fine Art) Ltd, *Summer Exhibition Catalogue*, 1988 (13).
13 Christie's, 15 November 1990, lot 42, and 19 November 1981, lot 94.
14 S. Sitwell, *Conversation Pieces*, London, 1936, pl. 26.
15 The Crown motif also occurs on a pillar and claw table (fig. 173) and Samuel Bennett's secretaire (fig. 48).
16 Observation by Carlton Hobbs's restorer.
17 *Country Life*, 27 January 1950.
18 C.L. Crossman, *The China Trade*, Princeton, 1972, pl. 116, illustrates the interior of a shop in Canton making furniture in the western style.
19 Tove Clemmensen, 'Some Furniture Made in China in the English Style, Exported from Canton to Denmark, 1735, 1737, 1738', *Furniture History* XXI (1985), pp. 174–80.
20 'The Indian Period of European Furniture: III', *Burlington Magazine*, November 1934, p. 213.
21 Carlton Hobbs, *Catalogue Number Three*, 1992 (21).
22 Victoria and Albert Museum E2320.89.
23 Clemmensen, fig. 6.
24 Gilbert 1978 (2), pl. 400, illustrates a breakfast-table of this kind which Chippendale supplied to the Earl of Dumfries in 1759.
25 Symonds 1950, p. 106.
26 Information kindly supplied by Michael Snodin.
27 Symonds 1956 (2).
28 The above (unverified) information is taken from Christie's catalogue, 6 July 1989, lot 163. See Fonthill sale lot 62.
29 Symonds 1956 (1), p. 287.
30 See designs from 1762 edition for a toilet table, pl. CXVIII; also a pair of cabinets, pl. CXXII.
31 P. Macquoid, *The Age of Mahogany*, 1906, p. 146, fig. 128.
32 Photographs in Temple Newsam files under 41/1988.
33 No. K.3425.
34 Hayward 1965, p. 17.
35 Hayward 1966, p. 69.
36 Clive Ponsford, *Devon Clocks and Clockmakers*, 1985, p. 71.
37 Information from Lucy Wood.
38 P. Ward-Jackson, *English Furniture Designs of the 18th Century*, London, 1958, fig. 185.
39 Boynton, p. 401, pl. 32.
40 J.F. Hayward, 'A China Case Attributed to Thomas Chippendale', *Connoisseur*, June 1962, p. 111, fig. 3.
41 Sold at Christie's, 14 November 1991 (lot 209).
42 Partridge, Lewis and Simmons, *Specimens of Old English Furniture*, New York (n.d., c.1905), no. 35, pl. XVIII.
43 Ralph Edwards, when visiting Powderham in the 1940s to examine some family portraits, was the first professional furniture historian to notice the signed tablets (letter to Major Arthur Bull in Temple Newsam files – 23/85).
44 Hayward 1966.
45 Devon County Record Office: Powderham MS account books 1739–49, 1508M Devon/V5, f. 104.
46 Hayward 1966, p. 66, fig. 3.
47 The inventories kept in the muniment room at the castle: box no. 9.
48 Girouard, p. 21.
49 F. Lewis Hinckley, *Directory of Historic Cabinet Woods*, New York, 1960, p. 60.
50 Identified by Michael Snodin.
51 T. Malton, *A Compleat Treatise on Perspective*, part 2, 1783, fig. 28.
52 Leeds Record Office: RD/AP1/143/118.
53 Susan Stuart, 'Prices for Workmen in Lancaster', *Regional Furniture* II (1988), p. 19.
54 Gilbert 1978 (2), p. 159 and pl. 470.
55 Symonds 1945, p. 418.
56 H. Hayward and P. Kirkham, *William and John Linnell*, London, 1980, p. 174.
57 Beard and Gilbert, p. 350.
58 Heal, p. 154.
59 *Daily Post*, 22 May 1738.
60 One of the most comprehensively fitted tea-chests made by Paul de Lamerie in 1735 is in the Temple Newsam collection. J. Lomax, *British Silver at Temple Newsam and Lotherton Hall*, Leeds, 1992 (125).
61 Details of John Gordon's life and work are summarised in Beard and Gilbert, pp. 355–7. He invoiced tea-chests to several clients in the 1740s and 1750s.
62 Heal, p. 41.
63 *The Gentleman and Cabinet-Maker's Director*, 1762, note to pl. CLIX, which features six designs for tea-chests; the 1754 edition included two more plates for tea-chests, CXXVIII and CXXIX.
64 E.T. Joy, 'Furniture Shops in Georgian London', *Connoisseur Year Book 1960*, p. 20, fig. 3.
65 Gilbert 1978 (2), p. 268; Scottish Record Office: GD44/49/20/2.
66 Scottish Record Office: GD157/659.
67 Beard and Gilbert, pp. 59–60, provide a summary of his life and work.
68 Edwards, I, p. 256, fig. 93.
69 Edwards, I, p. 256, figs. 90–2.
70 Information from Jeremy Pearson.
71 I am grateful to Lucy Wood for information about this piece.
72 Heal, p. 154.
73 Elizabeth Garrett, *At Home: The American Family*, New York, 1989, p. 42, illus.
74 Sold at Christie's 5 December 1991.
75 Gilbert 1978 (2), pl. 407.
76 Goodison 1969, pp. 192–6 and col. pl. III.
77 Information from Sir Nicholas Goodison.
78 Girouard, p. 21, fig. 9.
79 *The Protestant Mercury: or the Exeter Post Boy*, 18 May 1716.
80 Sotheby's New York 1 February 1992, lot 50.

Appendix 4

1 *Country Life*, 2 July 1910, p. 23.
2 The floor, apart from the clear addition of the mirrors, to be discussed below, is the one element in the room which is disturbing. The fact that it does not follow the square shaping of the room might suggest that the woodwork was originally designed with an octagonal cabinet in mind.
3 The chimney-piece itself is rather awkward, with the tapering marble caryatid plinths on either side looking somewhat squat.
4 A fire destroyed all the house records in 1808, as quoted from family sources by Geoffrey Beard in *Decorative Plasterwork in Great Britain*, London, 1975, n. 177. The only early description of the panelling comes from *Passages from the Diary of Mrs Philip Lybbe Powis of Hardwick House, Oxon., A.D. 1756 to 1808*, ed. Emily J. Climenson, London, 1899, p. 139.
5 Kreisel and Himmelheber, pl. 305–7. Mrs Lybbe Powis (supra) in her general comments on Mawley speaks of 'a thousand nick-nacks from abroad, as one generally sees in Catholic families', suggesting that the Blounts did travel. The sending of Catholic sons to France and the Low Countries for education was standard practice, but little is known of education in the German states.
6 Alistair Laing, 'Foreign Decorators and Plasterers in England' in *The Rococo in England, a Symposium*, ed. Charles Hind, London, 1986, p. 29.
7 Laing, p. 37.

Select bibliography

Beard and Gilbert
: Geoffrey Beard and Christopher Gilbert (eds.), *Dictionary of English Furniture Makers 1660–1840*, Leeds, 1986.

Boynton
: Lindsay Boynton, 'William and Richard Gomm', *Burlington Magazine*, June 1980, pp. 395–400.

Christie's 1989
: Christie's, Catalogue, *Important English Furniture*, 6 July 1989, lot 163.

Claxton-Stevens
: Christopher Claxton-Stevens, 'Channon Revisited', *British Antique Dealer's Association Hand Book, 1990*, 1989, pp. 18–22.

Claxton-Stevens and Whittington
: Christopher Claxton-Stevens and Stewart Whittington, *Eighteenth Century English Furniture: The Norman Adams Collection*, Woodbridge, 1983.

Coleridge
: Anthony Coleridge, *Chippendale Furniture*, London, 1968.

Edwards
: Ralph Edwards, *The Dictionary of English Furniture*, 3 vols., London, 1954.

Edwards and Jourdain
: Ralph Edwards and Margaret Jourdain, *Georgian Cabinet-Makers*, (rev. edn.) London, 1955.

Fitz-Gerald
: Desmond Fitz-Gerald, *Georgian Furniture* (Victoria and Albert Museum Large Picture Book), London, 1969.

Fitz-Gerald and Thornton
: Desmond Fitz-Gerald and Peter Thornton, 'Abraham Roentgen "en-glische Kabinett-macker" and some further reflections on the work of John Channon', *Victoria and Albert Museum Bulletin*, October 1966, vol. II, no. 4, pp. 137–47.

Gilbert 1978 (1)
: Christopher Gilbert, *Furniture at Temple Newsam House and Lotherton Hall*, Leeds, 1978.

Gilbert 1978 (2)
: Christopher Gilbert, *The Life and Work of Thomas Chippendale*, London, 1978.

Girouard
: Mark Girouard, 'Powderham Castle, Devon – I', *Country Life*, 4 July 1963, pp. 18–21.

Goodison 1969
: Nicholas Goodison, *English Barometers 1680–1880*, London, 1969.

Goodison 1974
: Nicholas Goodison, *Ormolu: The Work of Matthew Boulton*, London, 1974.

Greber
: Josef Maria Greber, *Abraham und David Roentgen, Möbel fur Europa*, 2 vols., Starnberg, 1980.

Hayward 1965
: John Hayward, 'English Brass-inlaid Furniture', *Victoria and Albert Museum Bulletin*, January 1965, vol. I, no. 1, pp. 10–23.

Hayward 1966
: John Hayward, 'The Channon Family of Exeter and London', *Victoria and Albert Museum Bulletin*, April 1966, vol. II, no. 2, pp. 64–70.

Hayward 1982
: Helena Hayward, 'Delight in Nature', *Country Life*, 3 June 1982, p. 1622.

Heal
: Ambrose Heal, *The London Furniture Makers 1660–1840*, London, 1953.

Huth
: Hans Huth, *Roentgen Furniture, Abraham and David Roentgen, European Cabinet-Makers*, London, 1974.

Johnston
: Donald Johnston, *John Channon and the German Community in London*, unpublished Christie's Fine Art Course thesis, 1990.

Kreisel and Himmelheber
: Heinrich Kreisel and Georg Himmelheber, *Die Kunst des Deutschen Möbels: Spatbarock und Rokoko*, Munich, 1983.

Lomax
: James Lomax, 'Symbols and Secrecy', *Country Life*, 10 March 1988, pp. 136–7.

Ponsford
: Clive Ponsford, *Devon Clocks and Clockmakers*, Newton Abbot, 1985.

Pradère
: Alexandre Pradère, *French Furniture Makers: The Art of the Ebéniste from Louis XIV to the Revolution*, London, 1989.

Snodin
: Michael Snodin (ed.), *Rococo Art and Design in Hogarth's England* (Victoria and Albert Museum exh. cat.), London, 1984.

Symonds 1945
: R.W. Symonds, 'Tip-up Tables', letter in *Country Life*, 9 March 1945, pp. 418–19.

Symonds 1946
: R.W. Symonds, 'Tea and Supper Tables', *The Antique Collector*, May–June 1946, pp. 84–90.

Symonds 1948
: R.W. Symonds, 'Furniture of the Nobility (1700–50)', *Country Life*, 7 May 1948, pp 930–1.

Symonds 1950
: R.W. Symonds, 'A George II Writing Cabinet', *Country Life*, 13 January 1950, pp. 104–6.

Symonds 1956 (1)
: R.W. Symonds, 'A Magnificent Dressing-Table', *Country Life*, 16 February 1956, pp. 286–8.

Symonds 1956 (2)
: R.W. Symonds, 'Back-to-Back Writing-Tables', *Country Life*, 13 September 1956, pp. 533–4.

Symonds 1956 (3)
: R.W. Symonds, 'Re-Discovering Old Furniture', *Country Life*, 18 October 1956, pp. 891–3.

Symonds 1958 (1)
: R.W. Symonds, 'Two English Writing Cabinets', *Connoisseur*, April 1958, pp. 83–7.

Symonds 1958 (2)
: R.W. Symonds, 'An English Commode of Rare Design and Quality', *Leeds Arts Calendar*, no. 39, 1958, pp. 3–8.

White
: E. White, *Pictorial Dictionary of British 18th Century Furniture Design: The Printed Sources*, Woodbridge, 1990.

Yorke
: James Yorke, 'John Channon Cabinet-Maker', *Antique*, Winter 1989, pp. 55–8.

Notes to the plates and figures

Colour plates

I MUSICAL CLOCK
made by Jacob Lovelace (d.1766) and exhibited in London in 1739. Lithograph, 1833.
The clock was apparently 10′ high and 5′ wide and weighed half-a-ton or more. When exhibited again in the nineteenth century in London it was described as follows:
'The celebrated Exeter clock is not only a timepiece, striking the hours of the day and chiming the quarters, but it is a perpetual almanack, telling the days of the week and month; leap year when it happens; showing the phases of the moon and its age; moreover, it will be silent if required; and when agreeable, will play a variety of tunes on an organ; Saturn presiding as conductor, and beating time, and Fame and Terpsichore moving to the air. It has also a most musical peal of six bells, with ringers; a moving panorama allegorical of day and night; and a guard of two Roman soldiers, who salute, with their swords, Apollo and Diana as they appear. The soldiers' heads are actually turned when the bells ring – as well they may be.'
Jacob Lovelace was a fellow parishioner of Otho Channon (1698–1756) of St Stephen's, Exeter, where Otho was churchwarden in 1735–6.
LIT: Liverpool Museums Bulletin, vol. 12, 1963–4; Ponsford, 1978; idem., 1985; Alan Smith, 'The Exeter Lovelace Clock', *Antiquarian Horology*, June 1966, pp. 78–85.
PROV: Devon and Exeter Institution Library, Exeter.

II PEDESTAL
Detail of a brass- and tortoisehell-inlaid ebony boulle marquetry pedestal (one of pair), attributed to André-Charles Boulle c.1700. The configuration of inlay on a round column is similar to that found on the Powderham bookcases and in the inlaid room at Mawley Hall (columns flanking the doorway into the hall).
PROV: Hubert de Saint-Senoch; Christie's, New York, 4 November 1992.

III COMMODE
Veneer of rosewood, gilt-bronze mounts, stamped F.L. The corner mounts on this and other French Régence commodes and *bureaux plats* provide the model for those used on the V&A medal cabinet.
PROV: Maurice Segoura; private collection.

IV & VII BUREAU-CABINET
Padouk with brass mouldings and inlay, c.1740.
Oak and pine carcase, mahogany drawer linings. The reverse side of the door and floor of the central pigeon-hole are inlaid with a cypher JEP. The harlequin figures engraved on the prospect are repeated on the Bristol cabinet (Pl. 120).
H. 91; W. 42; D. 26″.
LIT: Symonds 1958 (1) pl. 2–11; *Country Life*, 2 Oct. 1975, p. 850, pl. 1; Carlton Hobbs, *Catalogue Number Two*, 1991 (20).
PROV: Lady Pott, Clifton Hampden, Abingdon, Berks.; Christie's 27 June 1957, lot 157; H. Blairman & Sons; Lord Samuel of Wych Cross; Sotheby's 17 Nov. 1989, lot 50; Carlton Hobbs Ltd.

V BUREAU-CABINET
Mahogany with brass mouldings and inlay, c.1740–5.
Oak and pine carcase, mahogany drawer linings. Handles not original, the bracket feet restored.
H. 88; W. 43; D. 24″.
The inlay on the slope is taken from a design for a table (pirated from Nicholas Pineau) in Batty & Thomas Langley's *City and Country Builder's and Workman's Treasury of Designs*, 1740, pl. CXLIII (see Pl. 65).
LIT: Hayward 1982, pl. 1.
PROV: Sotheby's New York 17 Nov. 1979; Wellington Antiques; Asprey; private English collection.

VI BUREAU-CABINET
Mahogany with brass inlay, chequered strings and stellar ornament, c.1745. The divisions between the small drawers in the prospect pull out to reveal secret compartments.
H. 102; W. 51; D. 25″.
LIT: Partridge (Fine Art) Ltd, *Summer Catalogue*, 1988 (13); Claxton-Stevens, p. 20, repr.
PROV: By descent from Henry Hobhouse, Queen's Square, Bristol; Partridge (Fine Arts) Ltd; private collection.

VIII–IX HARLEQUIN GAMES TABLE
Mahogany with brass inlay, c.1745.
Of triple flap design, the first top banded with harewood and inlaid with scallop shells, serves as a backgammon and chess-board; the second flap is baize-lined with counter-wells for playing cards; the rising till is fitted with letter-holes and five short drawers.
H. 30; W. 30; D. (closed) 14$\frac{1}{2}$″.
Fifteen pieces of multi-purpose mechanical furniture are depicted on the advertisement sheet of Potter, London, fig. 13.
PROV: Colonel William Stirling of Keir; Christie's 15 Nov. 1990, lot 59.

X–XIII CARD-TABLE
Padouk, inlaid with brass and mother-of-pearl, c.1735–40.
The top opens to reveal a baize-lined playing surface dished for candlesticks and counters; there is a small frieze drawer in one end; concertina action underframe.
H. 28; W. 32$\frac{1}{2}$; D. (closed) 16″.
An almost identical pair of tables, but lacking brass string panels on the frieze, were sold at Sotheby's, 18 Nov. 1983, lot 46.
PROV: Sotheby's New York 29 Oct. 1983, lot 76; Christie's New York 25 Oct. 1986, lot 147; French & Co.; Christie's 9 July 1992, lot 47; Neil Sellin.

XIV–XVI SIDEBOARD TABLE
Padouk with brass mouldings and inlay, c.1745–50.
Oak carcase, later marble top.
H. 34; W. 126; D. 47.
Originally one large table, dismantled and reassembled as two tables in about 1861; rebuilt as a single side table 1991.
LIT: Carlton Hobbs, *Catalogue Number Three*, 1992 (21).
PROV: The Lords Delamere, Vale Royal, Cheshire; Christie's 25 Sept. 1980, lots 106 and 107; Ronald A. Lee; Carlton Hobbs Ltd; private collection.

XVII–XVIII WRITING-CABINET*
Mahogany with padouk cross-banding, profuse gilt-brass mounts and inlay, c.1750.
Oak and pine carcase, Cuban mahogany drawer linings; constructed in three parts with robust iron hooks and eyes at the back; the central niche cupboard houses 17 secret drawers and compartments.
H. 96; W. 44; D. 29″.
LIT: Symonds 1950, pl. 1–7; Symonds 1956 (1), pl. 2; Edwards, vol. 1, p. 144, pl. 45; Coleridge, pl. 64; Claxton-Stevens and Whittington, col. pl. 17a,b,c; Claxton-Stevens, pl. 4–5; Yorke, pp. 56–7, repr; Lomax, pl. 1–5; C. Gilbert, 'The Channon Cabinet', *NACF Review 1986*, pp. 126–7, repr.
EXH: Royal Academy, London, *English Taste in the 18th Century*, 1955/6 (180).
PROV: By descent to Sir William Keith Murray

---

* The presence of an asterisk * indicates that the timber(s) have been microscopically identified.

of Ochtertyre, Perthshire, Scotland; Christie's 30 June 1949, lot 130; Norman Adams Ltd; Major Arthur Bull; bought by Leeds City Art Galleries (23/85).

XIX–XX CABINET ON STAND
Mahogany, yew, ebony with brass mounts, mouldings and inlay, c.1735–40.
H. 86; W. 36½; D. 17½".
Oak carcase and inner structures. The main lock-plates are engraved with Roman heroes (copied from prints by H. Goltzius, 1586), the inner lock with a harlequin figure which occurs also on the secretaire in Col. pl. VII. The helmeted warrior masks ornamenting the knees are found also on two tables. Pl. 84 & 86.
LIT: Hayward 1966, p. 68, pl. 4; Coleridge, pl. 66.
PROV: Moss Harris & Sons; William Redford (Antiques); Gerald Kerin Ltd; bought by Bristol Museums and Art Gallery, 1966 (7481).

XXI BACK-TO-BACK LIBRARY TABLE
Mahogany with kingwood cross-banding, gilt-brass mouldings, mounts and inlay; oak and pine carcase, c.1750–5.
H. 36; W. 61; D. 27½".
The two halves have become separated; the half now in America had lost several mounts, including the dolphins and side lifting handles; these have now been recast from the V&A table.
(a) LIT: Symonds 1956 (1), pl. 3–10; Symonds 1956 (3), pl. 7; Hayward 1965, p. 14, pl. 5 and 13; Coleridge, pl. 61–2; Fitz-Gerald (39).
EXH: Musée des Arts Decoratifs, Paris, 1959, Le Siècle de l'Elegance (75); V&A, Rococo Art and Design, 1984 (L2).
(b) LIT: Yorke, pl. 1.
PROV: Possibly Alderman Beckford, Fonthill Splendens.
(a) Temple Williams Ltd; H. Blairman & Sons; bought by the V&A (w. 4-1956).
(b) Sir George Holford, Dorchester House; Malletts (advert Connoisseur, Oct. 1933, p. x); Charles Angell, Bath; Sotheby's 3 July 1936, lot 128; Major Boulton (advert Apollo, Dec. 1940); Sotheby's 12 Feb. 1965, lot 88; Christie's 6 July 1989, lot 163; private American collection.

XXII COMMODE*
Mahogany; oak, pine with brass inlay and mounts c.1750.
The gothic-pattern frets in-filled with black wax; unlaminated white-oak drawer fronts, the bottoms of framed flush-beaded panel construction.
H. 35; W. 55; D. 27".
LIT: Symonds 1956 (3), pl. 1–4; Symonds 1958, pl. 1–4; Gilbert 1978 (1), no. 222.
PROV: By descent from Lt Col. Evelyn W. Thistlethwayte, Southwick Park, Hants (whose ancestor subscribed to Chippendale's Director, 1754) to his nephew H.F.P. Borthwick-Norton, whose widow, Eva, sold it at Harrod's Sale Room, 29 May 1956; Temple Williams Ltd; bought by Leeds City Art Galleries (28/57).

XXIII POWDERHAM BOOKCASE
See Pl. 4 & 132–43

XXIV TEA TABLE
Mahogany with brass and mother-of-pearl inlay, c.1745.
H. 28½; Diam. 27".
PROV: Aldridges, Bath, 1 July 1986; Sotheby's 14 Nov. 1986, lot 51; Meyer Keyser Ltd.

XXV TEA TABLE
Mahogany inlaid with brass. c.1750.
H. 27½; Diam. 26½".
LIT: Claxton-Stevens & Whittington, pp. 288–9, repr; Claxton-Stevens, p. 19, repr.
PROV: Sir Alfred Chester Beatty; Walter Chrysler Jnr; Parke-Bernet New York 29 April 1960, lot 89; Malletts; Sotheby's 16 July 1982, lot 89; Norman Adams Ltd; private collection.

XXVI TEA TABLE
Mahogany with brass inlay, c.1755.
H. 23; Diam. 27".
A small brass shield is engraved JEG.
PROV: Edward James, West Dean Park; Christie's 2–6 June 1986, lot 204; Sotheby's 5 May 1989, lot 51; Rogill Fine Art.

XXVII TRIQUETRA TEA TABLE
Mahogany with brass and mother-of-pearl and brass inlay, c.1750.
H. 28; Diam. 28".
PROV: Edward James, West Dean Park; Christie's 2–6 June 1986, lot 205; Pelham Galleries; Sotheby's 17 Nov. 1989, lot 42; Weber-Brown.

XXVIII PAIR OF TEA-CHESTS
Burr elm with walnut cross-banding, brass inlay and mouldings, c.1740–50.
W. 10¾".
Another virtually identical example was sold at Sotheby's 17 July 1992, lot 180.
PROV: Sotheby's 14 Feb. 1992, lot 4.

2. The Channon family of London and Exeter

A FAMILY OF OTHO CHANNON OF EXETER, SERGE-MAKER
It is possible that Otho Channon, Innholder (see fig. B), and Otho Channon, Serge-maker, were the same person and that he changed his occupation between 1719 and 1724. If so Otho Channon, joiner (1697–1756, see fig. C) and John Channon, cabinet-maker (1711–79, see fig. D) were probably his sons by different marriages and therefore half-brothers. The recurrence of twins (see figs. B & D) would reinforce this suggestion.

B FAMILY OF OTHO CHANNON OF EXETER, INNHOLDER

C FAMILY OF OTHO CHANNON (1697–1756) OF EXETER AND LONDON (?), JOINER

D FAMILY OF JOHN CHANNON (1711–79) OF EXETER AND LONDON, CABINET-MAKER
It is possible that John Channon's wife Martha was a relative of his mother, particularly as one of his daughters was named Dorothy Martha after both. This helps to confirm that John Channon, cabinet-maker, was the John Channon born in 1711, even though the St Mary Abbots burial register suggests that he was 73 at the time of his death (he would have been 68 if he was indeed born in 1711). Experience of eighteenth-century records suggests that his age was incorrectly given at the time of his death.

1 TITLE-PAGE
Robert Furber's Twelve Months of Flowers and Fruit, folio, London, c.1732.
Robert Furber (1674–1756) was a gardener at Kensington Gore 'over against High Parke Gate near Kingsinton'. Furber issued the first printed gardener's catalogues in book form and his Twelve Months of Flowers, the first illustrated trade catalogue, was published in 1730. This edition combines that publication with the Twelve Months of Fruit, which appeared in 1732. The illustrations were based on the work of the Flemish painter Pieter Casteels (1684–1749). The subscribers included Otho Channon, almost certainly John Channon's master and half-brother, and George Lacy, who was responsible for hand-colouring the plates. In 1742 John Channon sold reprints of this publication for two guineas a set from his premises in St Martin's Lane.
LIT: John Harvey, 'Nurseries, Nurserymen and Seedsmen', in The Garden, A Celebration of One Thousand Years of British Gardening, London, 1979, p. 108.
PROV: National Art Library, V&A.

2 PAGE FROM THE RATE BOOK
Parish of St Martin's-in-the-Fields, showing the first entry for John Channon in St Martin's Lane, Bedfordbury Ward, in 1737. Other names of interest recorded in the rate books on the previous and subsequent pages to the entry for John Channon include the French dealer William Hubert (d.1740) and from 1740 the French sculptor Louis François Roubiliac (1702–62).
PROV: Westminster Local History Library (F. 495).

3 PLAN OF THE CITY OF EXETER
By John Rocque, 1744, showing the location of St Sidwell's parish, 755 × 1,888 mm.
John Rocque, surveyor and printseller, was based at Old Round Court, on the north side of the Strand. Best known for his Survey of London (see Pl. 7), Rocque also produced maps of other provincial cities including Bristol and Norwich. Rocque played an important part in the dissemination of the rococo style by publishing the latest books of engraved ornament from Paris. In 1759 he still supplied 'A Book of Ornaments'

by Brunetti, first published in London in 1736, for which he himself had engraved several plates. The plan of Exeter includes in the borders views of Exe Bridge, the guildhall, the cathedral, the castle, the city hospital, the workhouse and the custom house.
PROV: British Library.

4 BOOKCASE
One of a pair, supplied by John Channon in 1740 for the library, Powderham Castle.
Padouk with carved giltwood mounts and inlaid brass decoration.
H. 151; W. 98.5; D. $40\frac{7}{8}$.
For a full description see pp. 106–13.
LIT: mentioned in the manuscript inventories of the contents of Powderham
Castle, 1762 and 1789 (see appendix 2). A payment to John Channon on 29 April 1741 'part on Acct £50' may be for this commission (account books of Sir William Courtenay, Devon Record Office 1508 M Devon /v5); Hayward, 1966; Yorke.
PROV: Made for Sir William Courtenay, later 1st Viscount Courtenay (1709–62), possibly in anticipation of his marriage in April 1741 to Lady Frances Finch, daughter of Rt. Hon. Earl of Aylesford; acquired by the V&A in 1987 as acceptance in lieu in situ.

5 OVERMANTEL IN THE OLD LIBRARY
(now the Gold Drawing Room), Powderham Castle, attributed to Otho Channon, c.1740.
Mahogany(?) with carved giltwood ornaments.
The overmantel and wooden fireplace surround appear to be of mahogany. The landscape is contained in an eared frame incorporating a Greek key pattern in raised gilt-wood, which is less sophisticated than the motif inlaid in brass on the Channon bookcases. The carving of the festoons of fruit on the fireplace surround is close in character to the festoons on the pediments of the Powderham bookcases. Likewise, the twin cherubs' heads which support the broken pediment flanking the tabernacle are echoed in the engraved brass plaques occupying a similar position above the capitals on the bookcases.
LIT: In the 1762 inventory of the contents of Powderham Castle this is described as 'A Marble Chimney Piece & Slab with wood ornaments, Tabernacle, Frame, wth a Bust standing on a Bracket & a Landscape' (see appendix 2); Girouard.
PROV: Made as part of the creation of this room as a library in c.1740, the overmantel has been attributed to the Channon workshop, although much of the execution is of a lower quality than the bookcases. Payments to Otho Channon on 25 March 1743 and 12 Oct. 1748 for £27 13s and £14 5s respectively may relate to this commission, although it seems more probable that the overmantel would have been installed before the bookcases. There is no surviving evidence of the identity of the bust which originally stood on the bracket, nor has the painter of the landscape been identified. The Earl of Devon, Powderham Castle.

6 BRASS PLAQUE
from one of the bookcases supplied by John Channon for Powderham Castle. Tony North has suggested that the high-quality Gothic lettering on the two brass plaques was engraved by a craftsman who specialised in executing monumental inscriptions (see p. 56).
LIT: and PROV: as for Pl. 4.

3. Channon's rivals and the London market for brass-inlaid furniture

7 ST MARTIN'S LANE AND THE SURROUNDING AREA
from John Rocque's *Survey of London*, 1746, showing the location of John Channon's premises and those of earlier and rival cabinetmakers.
1. John Channon from 1737 to 1779, then his widow until 1784; 2. William Hubert until 1740, then his widow until 1751; 3. Gerrit Jensen until 1715; 4. Thomas Chippendale until 1753; 5. William Vile and John Cobb from 1750; 6. William Hallett from 1752. St Martin's Lane emerged as the new centre of the cabinet-making trade during the first half of the eighteenth century, servicing London's growing West End. It was also the centre of exchange of the latest continental styles with its proximity to the print shops of Great Newport Street and the Strand, and the presence of St Martin's Lane Academy and Slaughter's coffee house, both of which attracted artists and craftsmen, particularly foreign artists and craftsmen who were working in London.
LIT: Hugh Phillips, *Mid-Georgian London*, London, 1964, pp. 107–17; G. Wills, *English Furniture, 1760–1900*, Enfield, 1971, frontispiece.
PROV: Museum of London.

8 WRITING-COMMODE
from Montagu House, Bloomsbury. attributed to Gerrit Jensen, c.1692. veneered with ebony, kingwood, pewter, brass and copper.
W. $37\frac{1}{2}$; D. $27\frac{1}{2}$".
The writing-commode, which is part of a pier set of a pair of commodes and mirrors, contains nine drawers and is inlaid in the Boulle technique with ornamental decoration inspired by the designs of Daniel Marot, in particular from the *Nouveaux Livre d'Ornements propres pour faire en broderie et petit point* and the *Nouveaux Livre d'Orfeverie*, which were published in 1702.
Marot was based in London during the 1690s and it is probable that his designs were circulated here before they were published. Montagu House was the London home of Ralph, 1st Duke of Montagu (1737–1809), former ambassador at Versailles, and thus the furnishings were in the latest French taste.
LIT: Tessa Murdoch, ed., *Boughton House, The English Versailles*, London, 1992, pl. 79, pp. 133, 223.
PROV: The Duke of Buccleuch and Queensberry, Boughton House.

9 NICHE DOOR ON BUREAU-BOOKCASE BY SAMUEL BENNETT
The marquetry is executed in boxwood set into burr walnut, c.1725.
The marquetry incorporates, in the spandrels of the central arch, two Royal Crowns each containing a Maltese cross. This panel decorates the door of a central inner cupboard which is flanked by pigeon-holes and smaller drawers.
LIT: Beard and Gilbert; Symonds 1958(1).
PROV: Acquired by the V&A in 1924 (W. 66-1924).

10 BOULLE WRITING-TABLE
Veneer of tortoiseshell and brass on a pine carcase, c.1695.
H. $30\frac{1}{2}$ × W. 45 × D. 26".
This is one of the earliest French Boulle writing-tables to be recorded in an English collection. In 1726 it stood in the best bedchamber at Erddig, North Wales, and it can still be seen in the saloon there today.
LIT: The Diary of John Loveday, 1732; *Guide Book to Erddig, Clwyd*, The National Trust, 1977, p. 17; M. Drury, 'Early Eighteenth-Century Furniture at Erddig', *Apollo*, vol. 107, 1978, p. 46.
PROV: John Meller, Erddig; The National Trust from 1973.

11 ADVERTISEMENT PRINT SIGNED POTTER
Engraving.
$10\frac{3}{4}$ × $7\frac{3}{4}$".
This advertisement may record furniture produced by a Thomas Potter, who was in partnership with John Kelsey in the late 1730s. The range of carcase furniture illustrated includes several pieces with sophisticated sprung mechanisms which are normally associated with continental production (see Pl. 18,20) but recently similar English pieces have come to light (Pl. 87–8) and Christie's 25 Feb. 1993, lot 117.
PROV: Acquired by the V&A in 1989 (E.2320-89).

12 TRADE CARD OF LANDALL & GORDON
5 × $3\frac{1}{2}$".

This card of c.1745, which depicts their shop sign, also features a tea chest suggesting that this may have been a special line. A tea-chest impressed T. LANDALL has been recorded (Pl. 166), while three others of bombé form with brass inlay and paw feet similar to that portrayed on their card are known (Pl. 162–4).
LIT: Heal, p. 93.
PROV: British Museum, Sir Ambrose Heal Collection.

13 TEA-CHEST
Mahogany with brass strings, c.1745. Impressed along the top edge 'T. LANDALL'.
The trade card of Landall & Gordon, cabinet-makers in Little Argyle Street, London, depicts a more ambitious brass-inlaid tea-chest (Pl. 12).
PROV: Thought to have passed through a London sale room in the 1980s, now known only from a photograph supplied by Roy Baxter.

14 DRAWING OF A BOULLE ARMOIRE
Attributed to John Vardy, c.1746.
$8\frac{1}{4} \times 6\frac{1}{8}''$.
Inscribed with scale in feet.
This drawing is attributed to Vardy by comparison with the signed drawing, c.1746, in the collection of the Royal Institute of British Architects of a *bureau-plat* and a *cartonnier* (see Snodin, C15, p. 46; P. Ward Jackson, *English Furniture Designs of the Eighteenth Century*, London, 1984, no. 45) which was then in the collection of Richard Arundale at Allerton Park. The *bureau plat*, which is by Bernard van Risenburgh II, is now at Temple Newsam House. It seems likely that this armoire was in a British collection in the 1740s and it is possible that it was in the same collection as the *bureau plat* and the *cartonnier*.
PROV: V&A acquired in 1857, mus. inv. no. 66 (earlier provenance not recorded).

15 BOULLE WRITING-TABLE
Veneer of tortoiseshell and brass on a pine carcase.
Supplied by Thomas Chippendale in 1759 for Dumfries House.
H. $32\frac{1}{2}$; W. 46; D. 20.
This French writing-table was supplied to the 5th Earl of Dumfries for Dumfries House in 1759 at a cost of fifteen guineas.
LIT: *French Connection: Scotland & the Arts of France*, Edinburgh, 1985, p. 59; Gilbert 1978 (2), pl. 212.
PROV: Dumfries House, Scotland.

4. The continental context: Germany

16 TRIPOD TABLE
Abraham Roentgen, Herrnhag, c.1745. This table relates closely to the English pieces, though the baluster stem seems thinner than those used on the English examples.
LIT: Greber, pl. 9; Huth, pl. 8.

17 DETAIL OF THE TOP OF 16
The top shows the technique of brass inlay which Roentgen learned from Hintz during his time in London.
LIT: Greber, pl. 8; Huth, pl. 9.

18 HARLEQUIN-ACTION WRITING- AND GAMES TABLE
Abraham Roentgen, Herrnhag, c.1750. Fruitwood with brass inlay. Other tables with this mechanism, made by Roentgen in the early years of his career, are known and are illustrated in Greber.
LIT: Fitz-Gerald & Thornton; Franz Adrian Dreier, 'Klapptisch von Abraham Roentgen' in *Kunst und Antiquitäten*, III/80, pp. 51–3.

19 DETAIL OF THE POTTER ADVERTISEMENT PRINT
See notes to Pl. 11 for details. While English furniture historians tend to think of such mechanisms as deriving from Germany, German scholars working on Roentgen clearly see this aspect of his work as an English importation.

20 READING STAND
Abraham Roentgen, Neuwied, c.1750–60. Fruitwood with brass mounts. This type of table, with adjustable top, was produced by Roentgen over a number of years, some in a very plain fashion but others decorated with marquetry of metal and mother-of-pearl, of a richness which took them quite away from their English prototypes. Greber illustrates a number of these more decorative pieces.
LIT: Greber, pl. 54.

21 BUREAU-CABINET
Attributed to Michael Kümmel, Dresden, c.1750. Veneered in kingwood, with marquetry of mother-of-pearl, brass and ivory. This piece shows how the bureau form, which originated in England, could become in Germany the vehicle for the most elaborate and sophisticated marquetry. The complicated shapes of the carcase work of this piece provide a challenge to the workmen cutting and laying the marquetry, but the play of light achieved by so much curvature in the carcase allows the reflections on the brass and the mother-of-pearl to be seen to greatest advantage. The complexity of this technique demands skills close to those needed for the making of boulle marquetry.

22 TOP OF A GAMES TABLE
Martin Böhme, Berlin, c.1720. Walnut, with marquetry of other woods and engraved brass and pewter. Queen Sophia Dorothea was the daughter of George I, who was married in 1706 to Frederick William I of Prussia. The decoration of the table includes the monogram FWSD, surrounded by the Garter ribbon with the motto 'Honi soit qui mal y pense', the marquetry of this section using engraved brass and pewter.
LIT: Kreisel, pl. 17.

23 LARGE CLOTHES-PRESS
Brunswick, c.1731–5. Walnut, with inlay of ivory and engraved pewter, including the monogram of Duke Ludwig and his wife. This cupboard is said to have come from Schloss Salzdahlum. It is a very grand version of the clothes-presses which stood in public areas such as stair landings and passages in less grand houses. The use of engraved pewter was a reasonably common and perhaps earlier variant of the inlay of engraved brass in Germany.
LIT: Kreisel, pl. 96.

24 BOOKCASE
Johann Georg Nestfell, Wiesentheid, 1725. Marquetry of walnut, with gilt-wood capitals and bases to the columns and trellis work in brass, with the monogram of Count Rudolf Franz Erwein. This piece, though differing in detail from the decoration of the Powderham bookcases, is remarkably close in form, and shows the same desire for ostentatious statement. The complicated 'cageing' of the columns is an even more elaborate version of the stringing on the Powderham pieces and on the door-case columns at Mawley Hall.
LIT: Kreisel, pl. 220.

25 MEDAL CABINET
Hanover or London, c.1740–50. Walnut and gilt-wood, with the arms of George II. This piece clearly suggests a difficulty in attribution. In the 1970 edition of Kreisel, this was illustrated as a piece possibly made in London. By 1983 it was omitted from the edition revised by Himmelheber. It is clearly a piece which needs careful study.
LIT: Kreisel, *Die Kunst des Deutschen Möbel*, Munich, 1970, band II, pl. 842.

26 CABINET
Christian Friedrich Lehmann, Copenhagen, 1755, for Frederick V of Denmark. Veneered in exotic woods on cedar, with carved giltwood. The form and decoration of this derives from the traditions of Dresden. Christian Friedrich Lehmann was German-born, moving to Copenhagen as court cabinet-maker to Frederick V of Denmark. The English library tables with brass inlay represent a rare English essay in the flamboyant curves which are so brilliantly handled on the lower section of this piece.
LIT: Kreisel, pl. 842.

27 DETAIL OF BRASS INLAY ON A CORNER CUPBOARD
Berlin, c.1750. Veneered in cedar with

NOTES TO THE PLATES AND FIGURES

brass stringing outlining marquetried scrolls. The corner cupboard of which this is a detail is one of a number of pieces at Schloss Charlottenburg, Berlin, which use brass inlay, often in the form of simple stringing. Frederick William I of Prussia, who died in 1750, was married to Sophia Dorothea, daughter of George I.
LIT: Kreisel, pl. 784, illustrates the whole piece.

5. The continental context: France

28 PARQUET
Tortoiseshell and brass marquetry, from Royal Swedish coach made in Paris in 1696 by Oppenordt after designs by Berain. The shell motifs are very characteristic of French design until the Régence.
PROV: Royal Palace, Stockholm, Livrustkammaren.

29 POWDERHAM BOOKCASE
Detail of upper section of column (see note to Col. pl. II).

30 BRISTOL CABINET
Detail of cockerel-heads escutcheon which is similar to the escutcheons used by the Boulle workshops, for example the commode illustrated in Pl. 31.

31 COMMODE
Detail of cockerel-heads escutcheon from a pair of commodes in sarcophagus form made in the Boulle workshops, veneered with marquetry of ebony and brass, gilt-bronze mounts.
PROV: Delivered by André-Charles Boulle for the Chambre du Roi at Trianon 1708–9 (Musée de Versailles).

32 MEDAL CABINET
Kingwood, gilt-bronze mounts. The central female figure has some similarities with the pair of espagnolettes used on the V&A library desk.
PROV: Delivered by Antoine-Robert Gaudreaux and the brothers Slodtz for the Cabinet Intérieur of Louis XV at Versailles (Musée de Versailles).

33 BUREAU PLAT
Ebony, gilt-bronze mounts, attributed to Noel Gérard. The corner mounts are of the same model as used on the commode illustrated in Col. pl. III (see note).
PROV: Bayerisches Nationalmuseum, Munich.

34 ARMOIRE
One of pair, première-partie marquetry of ebony, tortoiseshell and brass, gilt-bronze mounts. The bronze mounts at the foot and top of this piece seem to bear some relation to the Bristol cabinet (a similar use of vases), to the Potter advertisement sheet (reclining figures on a pediment), and to the V&A library desk (dolphin mounts).
PROV: Gévigny Collection; Beloselsky-Belozersky Collection; Christie's, Monaco, 18 June 1992, lot 212; the other in contrepartie at the Musée de Versailles.

6. Furniture manufacture and workshop organisation

35 BOOK-MATCHED VENEER
Padouk veneers on plinth of the Powderham bookcase, 1740.
PROV: Lord Courtenay, Powderham Castle; V&A.

36 TORTOISESHELL MOULDING
Detail of tortoiseshell on the cornice of bureau-cabinet illustrated in Pl. 47.
PROV: V&A.

37 MASTIC INFILL
Detail of brass fretwork and mastic infill on base of the Southwick Park commode (Col. pl. XXII).
PROV: Leeds City Art Galleries.

38 JOINT CONSTRUCTION
Diagrams showing dovetails and rebate joints. The dovetails are based on an interior drawer from the bureau-cabinet illustrated in Pl. 47; the rebate joint is based on the drawer construction of the Southwick Park commode illustrated in Col. pl. XXII.
Drawn by Andrew Green, 1993.

39 DETAIL OF SMALL DRAWER
Interior drawer from the cabinet in Pl. 47 showing thinness of timber and setting of base.
PROV: V&A.

40 DETAIL OF DRAWER CONSTRUCTION
Detail of the base of a drawer from the Southwick Park commode (Col. pl. XXII).
PROV: Leeds City Art Galleries.

41 CAST-BRASS CAPITAL
Detail of Corinthian capital from the cabinet on stand illustrated in Pl. 113. This shows two-piece casting held together by pegs.
PROV: V&A.

42 DETAIL OF BRASS INLAYS
The engraved brass inlays on lower section of the cabinet on stand illustrated in Pl. 113.
PROV: V&A.

43 BRASS-INLAID GUNSTOCK
Detail of cast-brass inlays from the stock of a gun by Griffin, English, about 1740.
PROV: V&A.

7. Furniture survey*

44 & 46 BUREAU-CABINET
Walnut with various inlays, c.1725. The inside of the door is inlaid with the inscription: SAMUEL BENNETT / LONDON FECIT. The interior decorated with arabesque marquetry including two Royal Crowns (Pl. 9).
H. 108; W. 38; D. 21".
LIT: O. Brackett, Catalogue of English Furniture and Woodwork, London, 1927, vol. III (1094); Heal, pl. 15; Edwards, vol. I, p. 137, pl. 31 and 32.
PROV: V&A (W.66-1924).

45 BUREAU-CABINET
see Col. pl. IV & VII.

47–9 BUREAU-CABINET*
Mahogany with an oak carcase, padouk cross-banding, brass inlay and tortoiseshell veneer lining the cornice, c.1740.
H. 99; W. 37; D. 23".
A section of the central pilaster slides back to reveal the key-hole; a slide in the writing-bed conceals a central well. The plaster Venus and wooden flaming-vase finials are not original.
LIT: Hayward 1965, p. 12, pl. 2; Fitz-Gerald & Thornton, pl. 12; Fitz-Gerald (no. 36); M. Tomlin, English Furniture, London, 1972, pl. 86.
PROV: John Noble Taylor; Jacob Carrington; Alan Good, Glympton Park, Oxon; Sotheby's 2–3 July 1953, lot 281; Vyse Millard; Partridge (Fine Art) Ltd; bought by the V&A (W.37-1953).

50–2 BUREAU-CABINET
Padouk with partridge wood cross-banding and brass inlay c.1740–5. The base branded: J. GRAVELEY. Interior of upper stage shelved above two rows of small drawers and pigeon-holes. Allied to Pl. 54 and two writing-tables Pl. 81 & 83.
LIT: Hayward 1965, p. 15, pl. 6.
PROV: Sotheby's 12 July 1963, lot 84; J.A. Lewis; now known only from photographs.

53 BUREAU-CABINET
Sabicu inlaid with brass, c.1745.
H. 85; W. 39; D. 21".
PROV: Shafto (Antiques) Harrogate; Charles Lumb & Sons; R.A. Cookson; Charles Lumb & Sons; Apter Fredericks Ltd; private American collection.

54 BUREAU-CABINET
Mahogany with brass inlay, c.1735. Displays certain features in common with a walnut secretaire bearing the trade label of John Belchier (Christie's, 18 Nov. 1982, lot 125), but is even more closely allied to the Graveley secretaire (Pl. 50).
Known only from a photograph in the V&A archive (N.3015).

55–60 BUREAU-CABINET
Mahogany with brass and mother-of-pearl inlay, c.1745–50. The squirrel and basket of fruit motif occurs on a tea table (Pl. 150); the 'tassels' are inlaid and engraved mother-of-pearl.
H. 102; W. 41; D. 24".
PROV: By descent from Rev. R.L. Parker to his grand-daughter. Mrs V.M. Brooks of Henley; Sotheby's 18 July 1975, lot 51; private American collection.

158 NOTES TO THE PLATES AND FIGURES

61–4 BUREAU-CABINET
Mahogany with brass mouldings and engraved brass and mother-of-pearl inlay, c.1745–50.
Oak and pine carcase, mahogany drawer linings. The spandrels of the letter-holes inlaid with mother-of-pearl motifs; a niche cupboard in the upper stage houses a nest of secret drawers. The handle plates correspond to those on Pl. 112.
H. 104; W. 50; D. 25″.
LIT: Symonds 1948, pl. 1–2; Hayward 1965, p. 20, pl. 10.
PROV: Joseph Steinberg; Malletts; bought by the Iveagh Bequest, 1959 (IBK 1054).

65 DESIGN FOR A TABLE
The inlay on the slope of the bureau-cabinet (Col. pl. V) is taken from a design for a table (pirated from Nicholas Pineau) in Batty & Thomas Langley's *City and Country Builder's and Workman's Treasury of Designs*, 1740, pl. cxliii.

66–7 BUREAU-CABINET
Mahogany with brass inlay, c.1745.
The prospect contains fluted pilaster secret compartments.
H. 110; W. 57″.
The mirror plates, bracket feet and apron with stellar inlay all restored.
LIT: Claxton-Stevens, p. 20, repr.
PROV: The Palling family, Brownshill Court, Painswick, Glos.; Phillips 14 June 1988, lot 59; Jonathan Harris (Antiques).

68 BUREAU-CABINET
Mahogany with brass inlay, carved and gilt festoons on the pilasters, c.1745.
The door must originally have framed a mirror.
PROV: H. Morton Lee; Malletts (known only from a cutting in Ronald A. Lee's albums).

69 BUREAU-CABINET
Mahogany with brass inlay, c.1745.
H. 59; W. 34″.
Gilt-enriched looking-glass surround missing.
PROV: Sotheby's New York 17 Sept. 1988, lot 818; Sotheby's 7 May 1993, lot 131.

70 BUREAU-CABINET
see Col. pl. VII.

71 SLAB TABLE
Walnut with brass mounts, c.1725.
Pine carcase, inlaid marble top.
H. 30; W. 29; D. 19″.
PROV: Ronald A. Lee; private collection.

72–3 CHAMBER TABLE
Walnut with brass inlay on the top, c.1735–40.
Oak carcase and drawer lining, the side lifting handles possibly not original. Designed as a centre table.
H. 28; W. 36; D. $23\frac{1}{2}$″.
LIT: G. Wills, *English Furniture 1550–1760*, Enfield, 1971, p. 240, repr.
PROV: John Keil Ltd; M. A. Pilkington.

74 TEA TABLE
Mahogany with brass inlay, c.1740.
H. $27\frac{1}{2}$; W. $32\frac{1}{2}$; D. $21\frac{1}{2}$″.
LIT: A.A. Tait (ed.) *Treasures in Trust*, 1981, p. 89, pl. 69.
PROV: Haddo House, Aberdeen (National Trust for Scotland) (79.5002).

75–6 GATELEG TABLE
Mahogany with brass inlay, c.1750.
The inlay is a little like that on the crest rail of chairs at St Michael's Mount (Pl. 176).
PROV: Ronald A. Lee; Nigel Grimwood; Robert Bradley (Antiques); Jeremy Ltd; private collection.

77 WRITING-DESK
Mahogany parcel gilt with brass inlay and mouldings, c.1750.
H. 30; W. 49; D. 25″.
Similar to a writing-table at Holkham Hall, Norfolk, illustrated in Edwards, III, p. 246, pl. 14.
PROV: Mallett & Son.

78–9 BUREAU
Rosewood with brass inlay and a marquetry star motif, c.1740–5.
The lock escutcheon engraved with a Royal Crown, which also occurs on a tea table (Pl. 150) and the Samuel Bennett secretaire (Pl. 9).
PROV: Mr Young; G. Noel Butler (Antiques); H. Morton Lee (Antiques); Robert Smith.

80–1 WRITING TABLE*
Padouk, cross-banded in partridge wood and inlaid with brass, c.1740–5.
Oak carcase, padouk legs, fitted with a writing-slide above the frieze drawer; closely similar to a table now in San Francisco, Pl. 83. Allied to the Graveley secretaire.
H. $30\frac{1}{2}$; W. $30\frac{1}{2}$; D. 20″.
LIT: Hayward, 1965, p. 13, pl. 3 and 7; *Casa d'Oro*, 53, 10 Nov. 1967.
PROV: Ronald A. Lee; Harrods Ltd; bought by the V&A (W.44-1947).

82–3 WRITING-TABLE
Padouk, cross-banded in partridge wood and inlaid with brass, c.1740–5.
The central cartouche is engraved with the crest of the Marsh family of Langden and Denton in Kent. There is a closely similar table at the V&A (Pl. 81). Allied to the Graveley secretaire.
H. $29\frac{1}{2}$; W. 34; D. 23″.
LIT: C. Gilbert, 'The Hochschild Collection', *Sotheby's Art at Auction 1978–9*, p. 222, pl. 4.
PROV: The Marsh family; Malletts (advert. *Country Life*, 15 March 1973, p. 34); Gerald Hochschild; Sotheby's 1 Dec. 1978, lot 31; Phillips & Harris; The Fine Arts Museums of San Francisco (78.90).

84–5 CENTRE TABLE
Padouk, c.1740–5.
H. 29; W. 46; D. 25.
The warrior mounts on the knees and fronded lion's-paw feet are identical to the cast-brass mounts on the Bristol cabinet and stand (Pl. 118) and a side table (Pl. 86).
PROV: Jonathan Harris and Ronald A. Lee.

86 SIDE TABLE
Padouk with brass mounts c.1740–5.
The warrior masks and lion's-paw mounts are identical to those on the Bristol cabinet and stand (Pl. 118) and also occur as carved enrichment on a centre table (Pl. 85).
PROV: Leonard Knight Ltd; Ronald A. Lee (known only from a photograph in R.A. Lee's albums).

87–8 BREAKFAST TABLE
Mahogany; pine, c.1745–50.
Fitted with a loose tray which by means of brass catches can be either lowered into the deep framing or raised to table-top height. The flaps designed as hinged slides.
H. 36; W. 32; D. 28″.
Corresponds to a model on the Potter advertisement sheet (Pl. 11).
PROV: Denys Wrey Ltd; Christie's 16 July 1992, lot 133; bought by Leeds City Art Galleries (30/1992).

89 ARCHITECT'S TABLE
Rosewood, with brass mounts and stringing, c.1740–5.
The mounts on the cabriole legs are ornamented with a grotesque mask, those on the aprons with a putto head; three of the candle nozzles replicated.
H. 30; W. 34; D. $20\frac{1}{2}$″.
EXH: V&A, *CINOA International Art Treasures*, 1962 (116); Temple Newsam, Leeds, *Country House Lighting*, 1992 (105).
PROV: The Ince Blundell family; Ince Blundell Hall sale (Salisbury & Hammer) 15–17 March 1960, lot 990; Godden of Worthing Ltd; Ronald A Lee; National Museums on Merseyside (1965.276).

90 TWO CHIPPENDALE DESIGNS
Chippendale included two plates of wildly curvilinear furniture in the 3rd edition of his *Director*, 1762, pl. CXVIII and CXXII (right). It is possible that he served the London trade as a freelance professional furniture designer and so could conceivably have designed the 'nymph and satyr' group.

91–102 WRITING-CABINET
SEE COL. PL. XVII–XVIII.

103–5 WRITING-CABINET
Mahogany; oak, pine, with brass mounts and inlay, c.1740–5.
H. 89; W. 49; D. 31″.
LIT: Symonds 1948, pl. 3–6; Symonds 1950, pl. 2; M. Jourdain & F. Rose, *English Furniture: the Georgian Period*, London, 1953, pl. 19 and 94; Symonds 1956 (1), pl. 1.
PROV: Mrs Matthews; Christie's 11. Nov 1919, lot 111; Moss Harris & Sons; Lord Leverhulme; Anderson Galleries, New York, Leverhulme sale, pt 1, 9

NOTES TO THE PLATES AND FIGURES

Feb. 1926, lot 21; Fundacao Madeiros, Lisbon.

106–9 BACK-TO-BACK LIBRARY TABLE
see Col. pl. XXI.

110 COMMODE
Mahogany; oak, pine with gilt brass mounts, c.1750.
H. 34; W. 54; D. 26″.
LIT: Coleridge, p. 39, pl. 63.
PROV: (?) Partridge (Fine Arts) Ltd; bequeathed to the Fitzwilliam Museum, Cambridge, by Louis Clarke (M.27-1961).

111 COMMODE
Rosewood, with winged gilt-brass handles of familiar pattern, c.1745–50.
H. 42; W. 42″.
LIT: P. Macquoid, *Age of Mahogany*, 1906, p. 146, pl. 128.
PROV: H. Oatway Esq (known only from the above illustration).

112 CABINET ON STAND
Mahogany with gilt brass mounts, c.1750.
The clear-glazed door probably fronted originally by a looking glass. The handle-plates correspond to those on the Kenwood secretaire (Pl. 61). A very similar lower stage of a cabinet on stand is recorded in the V&A photographic archive (K.3425).

113–17 CABINET ON STAND*
Cuban mahogany, oak carcase veneered in padouk with brass mounts, mouldings and inlay, c.1740.
Engraved lock-plates and hinges, the top drawer fitted for writing, the cornice headed by cast-brass busts of Roman emperors.
H. 92; W. 53; D. 26″.
The interior, fitted originally with tiers of shallow shelves, has been gutted; the looking-glass plates replaced, the fluted pilasters are modern copies. An illustration in Sotheby's sale catalogue (1962) shows it prior to restoration.
LIT: Hayward 1965, p. 10, pl. 1, 9, 11, 12; Fitz-Gerald (37); Coleridge, pl. 60; G. Wills, *English Furniture, 1550–1760*, Enfield, 1971, Col. pl. 30.
PROV: Mrs Amy Guest; Sotheby's 2 Feb. 1962, lot 157; J.A. Lewis & Son; bought by the V&A (W.7-1964).

118–27 CABINET ON STAND
see Col. pl. XIX–XX.

128 CABINET ON CHEST-OF-DRAWERS
Sabicu or mahogany, parcel gilt with brass inlay, c.1747.
The interior fitted with a row of six small drawers with letter-holes above and adjustable shelves over.
H. 96; W. 56; D. 20.
Possibly associated with bank-account payments to William Hallett between 1747 and 1752.
LIT: P. Macquoid, *English Furniture in the Lady Lever Art Gallery Collection*, 1928, vol. III (289), pl. 72; *Apollo*, Jan. 1980, p. 29, pl. 12.
EXH: Royal Academy, London, *English Taste in the 18th Century*, 1955/6 (94); Musée des Arts Décoratifs, Paris, *Siècle de l'Elegance*, 1959 (21).
PROV: Sir James Dashwood, Kirtlington Park, Oxon, and by descent to Sir Charles Dashwood; D.L. Isaacs (Antiques); Lord Leverhulme; National Museums and Galleries on Merseyside (LL.4416).

129 The commode was bequeathed to The National Trust by John Hayward; it has a later marble top.

130 CHINA CABINET
Mahogany, parcel gilt, the door-frame inlaid with engraved brass c.1760.
H. 70½; W. 49½; D. 21″.
There is an anonymous drawing for this cabinet at the V&A (D.1356-1897) illustrated by P. Ward-Jackson, *English Furniture Designs of the Eighteenth Century*, London, 1958, pl. 185.
PROV: By descent to C.F.J. Beausire of Liverpool, accepted by H.M. Government in lieu of estate duty and allocated to Liverpool City Council in 1973 (now National Museums and Galleries on Merseyside) (8976).

131 COLLECTOR'S CABINET
Mahogany, kingwood and tulipwood with red tortoiseshell, engraved brass inlay and ormolu mounts, c.1770–5.
The rosewood stand dates from c.1800. The central medallion of Liva Drusilla, wife of Augustus, is inspired by a Roman coin.
H. 21; W. 40; D. 11.
Possibly by George Haupt working to a design by Sir William Chambers.
PROV: Pelham Galleries.

132–43 BOOKCASE*, one of a pair by John Channon, 1740.
Padouk ornamented with brass mouldings and inlay, gilt carving; oak and pine carcase. Each bears a brass tablet inscribed: 17 J. CHANNON 40. The main plates are copied directly from an untitled suite of grotesques, published by Berain in Paris, c.1700. V&A (E.4149. 1906).
H. 150; W. 90; D. 36″.
Associated with a part-payment of £50 'on account' to John Channon on 29 April 1741. Recorded as being made from the West Indian timber manchineel in the Powderham inventory of 1762. Moved in about 1800 from the upstairs library to an anteroom on the ground floor.
LIT: Girouard, p. 21, pl. 10; Hayward 1966, pp. 64–70, pl. 1 and 2; Coleridge, pl. 65; Yorke, p. 58 repr.
PROV: By descent from Sir William Courtenay to the present Lord Courtenay; accepted by H.M. Government in lieu of inheritance tax and acquired by the V&A in 1987 on condition that the bookcases remain in situ at Powderham Castle (W1-1A 1987).

144 DESIGN FOR A SUPPER TABLE
From Thomas Malton, *A Compleat Treatise on Perspective*, part 2, 1783, fig. 28.

145 TEA TABLE
Mahogany with brass inlay, c.1750.
H. 27; Diam. 29″.
PROV: Malletts; Gerald Hochschild; Sotheby's 1 Dec. 1978, lot 30; Phillips & Harris.

146 TEA TABLE
Mahogany with brass inlay, c.1755.
Unusual heart-shaped central dish.
PROV: Phillips of Hitchin (Antiques) Ltd.

147 TEA TABLE
Mahogany with brass inlay, c.1755.
H. 27; Diam. 23″.
PROV: Sotheby's 31 Jan. 1975, lot 82; Malletts.

148 TEA TABLE
Mahogany with brass inlay, c.1760.
The top is married to the tripod stand of a fire screen.
PROV: Charles Lumb & Sons.

149–50 TEA TABLE
Mahogany inlaid with brass and mother-of-pearl, c.1740.
The central cartouche is engraved with a Royal Crown, which occurs also on pl. 79; inlaid details include a squirrel and basket of fruit motifs which feature on the secretaire (Pl. 60).
PROV: C. Fredericks; Ronald A. Lee; Chandris.

151 TEA TABLE
Mahogany inlaid with brass and mother-of-pearl, c.1745.
H. 27½; Diam. 26″.
PROV: Historic private collection in Worcestershire.

152 TEA TABLE
Mahogany inlaid with brass and mother-of-pearl, c.1750.
H. 27½; Diam. 24″.
PROV: private collection.

153 TEA TABLE
Mahogany with brass and mother-of-pearl inlay, c.1740–5.
H. 27½; Diam. 26½″.
LIT: Hayward, 1965, p. 69, pl. 6.
PROV: Claude Rotch; bequeathed to the V&A (W.22-1962).

154 TEA TABLE
Mahogany with brass inlay, c.1755.
Gilt flutes on the pillar.
PROV: Malletts.

155 TRIQUETRA TEA TABLE
Mahogany with brass and mother-of-pearl inlay, c.1750.
H. 29; Diam. 28″.
PROV: The Earl of Wemyss, Elcho Castle, Perth, Scotland; Walter Chrysler Jnr; Parke-Bernet New York 6–7 May 1960, lot 504; Jeremy Ltd; Symons Galleries; Malletts; given to the V&A by Brig. W.E. Clarke (W.3-1965).

156 TRIQUETRA TEA TABLE
see Col. pl. XXVII.

157 WORK TABLE

NOTES TO THE PLATES AND FIGURES

Mahogany inlaid with brass and mother-of-pearl, c.1745–50.
H. 27; Diam. 25".
PROV: Ronald A. Lee; S. Sainsbury; Christie's 13 April 1989, lot 133.

158 TEA TABLE
Mahogany with brass inlay, c.1755.
PROV: Ronald A. Lee; Vernay & Jussel; private American collection.

159 TEA TABLE
Mahogany, inlaid with brass, c.1755.
Diam. 21½".
PROV: Sotheby's 5 Oct. 1973, lot 66.

160 TEA TABLE
Mahogany with brass inlay, c.1760.
The linear decoration simulates the flat chasing found on silver salvers.
PROV: Randolph Brett; Joel Wolff; J.A. Lewis; Vernay & Jussel.

161 TRADE CARD OF LANDALL & GORDON, c.1745
5 × 3½".
The card, which depicts their shop sign, also features a tea-chest, suggesting that this was a special line. A tea-chest impressed 'T. LANDALL' has been recorded (Pl. 13) while three others of bombé form with brass inlay, two having paw feet similar to that portrayed on their card are known (Pl. 162–5).
LIT: Heal, p. 93.
PROV: British Museum, Sir Ambrose Heal collection.

162 TEA-CHEST
Mahogany with brass mouldings and inlay, c.1745.
Cross-banded in padouk, oak bottom board, the interior divided into three compartments, the lid lined with red silk, original handle.
H. 7; W. 11.
The rather crowded brass inlay is closely matched on another example (Pl. 163). Both tea-chests have many features in common with one depicted on Landall & Gordon's trade card (Pl. 161) justifying a cautious attribution to this firm.
LIT: Hayward 1966, p. 69, pl. 5; G. Walkling, *Tea Caddies*, 1985, pl. 33.
PROV: H. Blairman & Sons; bought by the V&A (W.11-1965).

163 TEA-CHEST
Mahogany with brass mouldings and inlay, c.1745.
Cross-banded in mahogany, new lifting handle and lock, oak bottom; the interior originally partitioned into three compartments; the keyhole cartouche engraved with a mask.
H. 6½; W. 10½; D. 5".
The existence of an almost identical example (Pl. 162) suggests that both were made for stock. The bombé form, foliate corner ornaments and brass lion's-paw feet display affinities with a tea-chest depicted on Landall & Gordon's trade card (Pl. 161). The resemblance justifies a cautious attribution to this firm.
LIT: Fitz-Gerald & Thornton, p. 146, pl. 13.
PROV: Helena Hayward; Professor A.R. Hayward.

164–5 TEA-CHEST
Solid mahogany, c.1745.
The keyhole cover springs open when a button underneath is pressed; a catch operated by pressure from the lid releases a shallow drawer for silver spoons in the right-hand side of the plinth. The interior is divided into three compartments for black tea, green tea and sugar.
H. 6; W. 10; D. 6".
Identical lock-plates occur on two dressing boxes (Pl. 170–2) and several bureau-cabinets (Pl. 66–70). The fronded birds' heads flanking the keyhole correspond to the escutcheon on a tea-chest depicted in Landall & Gordon's trade card (Pl. 161), justifying a cautious attribution to this firm.
EXH: Witney Antiques, *An Invitation to Tea*, 1991 (53).
PROV: Witney Antiques; private collection.

166 TEA-CHEST
Padouk with brass inlay and base moulding, c.1750.
Veneered on an oak carcase with ebony banding; the later rosewood top bears a tablet engraved AJ; interior divided into three sections. The back and front bear identical decoration (including a dummy keyhole). An eagle displayed also occurs on the Murray writing-cabinet (Pl. 101).
H. 6¾; W. 11¾; D. 7¼".
PROV: M. Turpin Antiques.

167 TEA-CHEST
Walnut with brass inlay, c.1750.
Veneered on a mahogany foundation. The interior is divided into three sections, two containing brass canisters with hinged tops and tin bottoms. The plinth houses a shallow drawer, propelled open by pressing a brass button set on the top right-hand edge of the case, matched on the left by a non-functioning counterpart.
H. 7; W. 9½; D. 6".
PROV: W. Phelps Warren; Museum of Art, Rhode Island School of Design (85.075.13).

168 TEA-CHEST
Mahogany with brass inlay, c.1745–50.
The right-hand side slides upwards to reveal a shallow plinth drawer for silver spoons.
H. 7; W. 11; D. 7".
PROV: John Keil Ltd.

169 TEA-CHEST
Mahogany with brass and mother-of-pearl inlay and brass mouldings, c.1735–45.
A shallow plinth drawer on the left-hand side is released by a spring on the top edge; the keyhole cover (engraved with a basket of fruit) is released from the base. The top, front and back are inlaid with engraved brass, also leaf motifs in mother-of-pearl and green stained bone.
H. 6½; W. 11½.
PROV: Known only from a sale catalogue cutting in Ronald A. Lee's albums.

170–1 DRESSING-BOX
Mahogany with ebony mouldings and brass inlay, c.1745.
Identical in all respects with Pl. 172 except the bracket feet and mirror lining the lid are missing. Both were presumably made for stock. The square corner compartments lift out and have sliding lids, one contains three ceramic petrie dishes; other wells house glass bottles. A hidden compartment under the pen tray is revealed by moving the paper dividers. Concealed plinth drawer.
H. 5½; W. 18; D. 14".
LIT: *Apollo*, July 1955, p. 22, pl. 3; *Apollo*, April 1968, p. 289, pl. 4 and 5.
PROV: Bird Antiques; Edward Pinto; Birmingham City Museums and Art Gallery (T.862).

172 DRESSING-BOX
Mahogany with ebony mouldings and brass inlay, c.1745.
The keyhole cover is released by pressing a button underneath the centre-base moulding; the right-hand side pulls up to reveal a full-length shallow drawer in the plinth. The interior is fitted for dressing and writing; a looking-glass lines the lid.
H. 8½; W. 18; D. 14".
Identical, with the exception of the feet, to a box in Pl. 170. The same engraved brass lock-plate occurs also on a tea-chest (Pl. 170) and several bureau-cabinets (Pl. 66–70). The fronded bird heads flanking the central cartouche resemble a keyhole escutcheon on a tea-chest depicted on Landall & Gordon's trade card (Pl. 161) justifying a tentative attribution to this firm.
PROV: Ronald A. Lee; The Colonial Williamsburg Foundation (1967-583).

173 ARMCHAIR*
Padouk with brass inlay, c.1740.
Veneered beech seat rails, the splat inlaid with an unidentified British crest 'issuing from a wreath a demi-horse forcene party per pale indented'. The frame impressed 05009. The birds at the bottom of the inlaid panel are similar to a pair on the Graveley bureau (Pl. 52).
H. 36; W. 21; D. 19".
LIT: Hayward 1965, p. 13, pl. 4, p. 18, pl. 8; Fitz-Gerald, no. 38.
PROV: Tweed (Antiques) Bradford; Waddingham (Antiques) Harrogate (advert. *Connoisseur*, June 1956); R.A. Lee; presented to the V&A Museum by Brig. W.E. Clarke through the NACF (W.32-1959).

NOTES TO THE PLATES AND FIGURES

174 & 176 **CHAIR**, from a set of six
Mahogany with brass inlay, c.1760–5.
En suite with the clothes press at Pencarrow (Pl. 177).
H. 38; W. 21; D. 17".
PROV: Probably acquired for Clowance House, the principal Cornish seat of the St Aubyn family, and removed later to St Michael's Mount, the residence of Lord St Levan.

175 **CHAIR**, one of a pair
Mahogany with brass inlay, c.1760.
H. 38; W. 21; D. 17½".
LIT: Gilbert 1978 (1), no. 79.
EXH: Temple Newsam, *Thomas Chippendale*, 1951 (98).
PROV: By descent from Robert Reid, Moor Park, Harrogate, to his daughter, the Hon. Mrs J de Courcy; bought by Leeds City Art Galleries (12/63).

177 **CLOTHES-PRESS**
Mahogany with brass inlay, c.1760–5. Oak and pine secondary woods, the upper stage fitted with sliding trays. The inlay on the door panels is copied from a design for glazing bars on a bookcase in Chippendale's *Director*, 1762, pl. XC. The border pattern is repeated on a set of chairs also made for the St Aubyn family now at St Michael's Mount (Pl. 174).
H. 56; W. 47½; D. 23".
PROV: Probably ordered originally for Clowance House, the principal Cornish residence of the St Aubyns; by descent to Lt Col. Sir Arscott Molesworth-St Aubyn, Bt., Pencarrow, Bodmin.

178 **HANGING CORNER CUPBOARD**
Mahogany inlaid with brass, c.1750–60.
Oak back and bottom, three shelves within.
H. 41; W. 33".
PROV: Arthur Brett & Sons Ltd.

179 **TEA BOARD**
Mahogany inlaid with brass and mother-of-pearl, c.1740.
PROV: Asprey Ltd; Malletts (known only from a photograph supplied by Asprey).

180 **TEA-KETTLE STAND**
Mahogany inlaid with ivory and brass, c.1740.
H. ¾; W. 9½; D. 9½".
A rare object inspired by the design of silver tea-kettle stands.
PROV: Brand Inglis Ltd; Ronald A. Lee; bought by Leeds City Art Galleries (28/91).

181 **DRESSING-TABLE GLASS**
Mahogany decorated with pewter and brass stringing lines accented by mother-of-pearl and ivory details, c.1755–60.
The central cupboard is inlaid with an intarsia-work mirhab niche, the standards carved with blind gothic frets.
H. 29; W. 18; D. 9".
This form of toilet glass was known as a 'union suite'.
PROV: Ronald A. Lee; Sam Messer; Christie's 5 Dec. 1991, lot 51.

182 **ANGLE BAROMETER**
The instrument by Charles Orme, Ashby-de-la-Zouche, dated 1741.
Walnut case with brass mouldings and inlay.
H. 41¾".
Sir Nicholas Goodison has records of eleven angle barometers by Charles Orme with brass inlay, dated as follows: 1736 (2); 1740 (2); 1741 (4); 1742 (2); 1743 (1).
LIT: Goodison, p. 134, Col. pl. III and pp. 192–6.
PROV: Private collection.

183 **BAROMETER AND THERMOMETER***
The instruments by George Adams, London, c.1760.
Mahogany case with brass inlay.
H. 37½".
LIT: Goodison, p. 128, pl. 76.
PROV: The Dowager Viscountess Harcourt; Christie's 26 Oct. 1961, lot 9; given to the V&A by Brig. W.E. Clarke through the NACF (w.21-1961).

184 **LONG-CASE CLOCK**
The case, which has verre églomisé panels, is likely to have been made by a general cabinet-maker working in the north-west. H. 110.
PROV: Partridge (Fine Arts) Ltd.

Appendix 4

185 **MAWLEY HALL, SHROPSHIRE**
The door forms the main focus of decoration in the room after the armorial panels above the fireplace; this is the only area of decoration where brass is employed.

186 The scale of the motifs in brass is closely similar to those used on the Powderham bookcase. Both would seem to derive from Berain engravings of c.1700 showing columns with strapwork or mock fluting, although no detailed source has been traced.

Index

Adam, R. 4
Adams, G. 133
Allewelt, Capt. 84
Altona 34
Ancaster, Earl of 31
Anderson, D.N. 44
Ansbach 29
armoires 21–2, 32–43, 156, 157
Arundale, R. 21, 22, 156
Atholl, Duke of 70, 136
Augustus III 'the Strong' 29, 30

Babel, P. 15
back-to-back library table 1–2, 45, 91–6, 154
Bailey, Sir H. 23
Baker, M. 99
Baring, J. 8
barometer-cases 59, 133, 161
Bateman, R. 23
Bathurst, Lord 23
Baxter, R. 121
Beausire family 106
Beckford, W. 91, 94
Beecham, Lord 23
Belchier, J. 64, 126, 157
Bell, H. 59
Bell, P. 59
Bennett, S. 2, 17, 54, 59–60, 144, 155, 157
Bent, W. 44
Berain, J. 15, 38, 39, 40, 57, 89, 108, 110, 111, 113, 127, 129, 135, 159
Berlin 30, 32
Blairman, H. & Sons 2, 59
Blount, Sir E. 144
Böhme, M. 29, 30, 156
bookcases 1, 21, 33–4, 35; see also Powderham bookcases
Boson, J. 106
Borthwick-Norton, E. 96
Boulle, A.-C. 13, 17, 21, 22, 37, 39–40, 42, 52, 57, 61, 64, 99, 102, 103, 106, 129, 135, 153, 155
Boulton, M. 44, 56
Bristol Art Galleries cabinet 3, 18, 26, 38, 39–40, 60, 67, 82–3, 102–5, 135, 137
Britton, J. 91
Brooks, V.M. 64
Brunetti, G. 15
Brunswick 32–3, 34, 36, 156
Bull, A. 87
bureau-cabinets 25–6, 30, 34, 38, 59–74, 153–8 passim
Burnett, J. 8

cabinets 23, 33, 34, 35, 36, 49, 153–9, passim; see also Bristol, Murray, Victoria and Albert Museum cabinets
cabinets on stands 2–3, 15, 19, 34, 98–106, 154, 159
Caffieri, P. 40
Cambridge, J. 11, 138
Campbell, R. 45, 46
Carlton Hobbs Ltd bureau 17, 34, 50, 51, 79, 135; table 82
chairs 21, 30, 37, 46, 49, 126–30, 160, 161
Chaninge, H. 7
Chaninge, O. 7
Channon, Anne 7
Channon, Anne (b.1729) 8
Channon, Anne Jane (b.1766) 10
Channon, Caligula (b.1728) 8, 103
Channon, Dorothy 5, 7, 138
Channon, Dorothy Maria (b.1731) 8
Channon, Dorothy Martha (b.1766) 10
Channon, Elizabeth 5
Channon, Frances (b.1725) 5, 8
Channon, James (b.1708) 5, 7
Channon, John (b.1699) 7, 146
Channon, John (1711–79) 3–38 passim, 46–68 passim, 79, 82–3, 86, 92–113 passim, 123–44 passim, 146, 154, 155
Channon, John (b.1758) 10
Channon, John (b.1767) 10
Channon, Martha (1733–97) 10–12, 138–43 passim, 146
Channon, Otho (d.1740?) 5–7, 13, 146, 154
Channon, Otho (1698–1756) 5–10, 13, 15, 64, 103, 109, 140, 146, 153, 154, 155
Channon, Otho (b.1726/7) 8
Channon, Otho (1733–6) 8
Channon, Otho (b.1759) 10
Channon, Thomas 5, 7, 10, 11, 138, 146
Channon, Tiberius (b.1735) 8, 103
Channon, Titus Vespasian (1734–5) 8, 103
Channon, William (b.1699) 7
Chippendale, T. 2, 3, 10, 14, 21, 22, 34, 37, 86, 96, 114, 121, 124, 131–6, 137, 149, 150, 155
Clarke, L. 96
Claxton-Stevens, C. 4
Clay, C. 14
clock-cases 13–14, 44, 49, 133–4, 153, 161
Cobb, J. 3, 14, 15, 137, 155
Cock, C. 17
Coleridge, A. 4
Colley, L. 37–8
Colonial Williamsburg Foundation 126
commodes 16, 19, 23, 38–44 passim, 153–4, 157; see also Southwick Park commode
Cookson, R. 63
Cooper, J. 123
Courtenay, Sir W. 8–10, 14, 15, 109, 113, 134, 140, 141, 150, 155, 159

Cox, J. 44
Coxed, G. 16–17, 59
Crace, E. 11
Cressent, C. 40, 42, 44
Crosse, R. 4, 11, 133, 143
Culme, W. 5, 9, 13
Cuvilliés, F. 87

Daille 23
Danzig 31
Dashwood, Sir J. 106
Defoe, D. 29
Deickard, H. 31
Delamere family 82
desks 1, 16, 17–19; see also tables and desks
Dundas, Sir L. 114

Edwards, R. 1, 3, 147, 151
Elizabeth Christina, Queen 35
Erddig 17, 37, 147, 155
Eriksen, S. 44
Evans, P. 102
Exeter 5–8, 10, 13, 154

Falck, J. 31
Fenwick, A. 10–11, 141
Fiennes, C. 7–8
Fine Arts Museums (San Francisco) 79
Fletcher, H. 64
Fitz-Gerald, D. 4
Fitzwalter, Earl 31, 149
Fitzwilliam Museum 96–7
Fonthill 91, 94
Fryer, S. 10
Führlohg, C. 31
Furber, R. 4, 5, 6, 20, 64, 66, 154

Gaudreaux, A-R. 40
George, R. 21
Gérard, N. 41, 42–4
Gibbs, J. 15
Gillow, R. 114
Gilpin, T. 56
Girouard, M. 3
Goltzius, H. 15, 26, 103–5, 154
Gomm, W. 25, 106, 114
Good, A. 60
Goodison, N. 29, 44
Gordon, Duke of 70, 126, 136
Gordon, J. 20–1, 70–3, 121–3, 126, 127, 136, 137, 155, 156, 159
Grahl, J.G.H. 34
Graveley, J. 3, 21, 62–3, 64, 79, 80, 81, 136, 157
Graveley, M. 21
Greber, J.M. 25, 26

INDEX

Griffin, B. 57
Guest, A. 99

Haddo House 76, 137
Hallett, W. 14, 96, 106–7, 137, 155
Hamburg 24, 31
Harache, P. 44
Harache, T. 44
Hasert, P. 32
Hawksmoor, N. 21
Hayward, H. 4
Hayward, J. 2–4, 63, 102, 106
Hazard, J. 16
Hepplewhite, G. 29
Herrnhag 25, 26, 27
Hewer, E. 17, 147
Hintz, A. 27, 148
Hintz, F. 1, 2–3, 21, 26–9, 36, 59, 65, 67, 78, 79, 114, 117, 119, 125, 131, 132, 136–7, 147, 148
Hoare, Sir R.C. 20, 147
Hobhouse, H. 70, 73, 134
Hoese, P. 29
Holford, Sir G. 91
Holkham Hall 76
Hornby Hall 4, 11
Hubert, W. 14, 18, 147, 154, 155
Hughes 10
Humphries, J. 10
Huth, H. 25, 26
Hyde Park Antiques 79

Ince, W. 3, 113, 137, 148
Ince Blundell table 79, 85, 137, 158
Irwin, Lord 126

Jackson, R. 10
Jean, D. 44
Jensen, F. 16
Jensen, G. 14, 15–16, 59, 155
Jensen, I. 16
Johnston, D. 4, 31
Jones, J. 134
Jourdain, M. 1, 3
Joy, E. 31, 37

Keir, W.S. 84
Kelsey, J. 20, 48, 84, 147
Kennet, R. 23
Kent, W. 15
Kenwood House bureau-cabinet 1, 15, 50, 51, 52, 67–9, 96, 137, 158
Kerin, G. Ltd 102
King, C. 32
Knight, L. 82
Köster, J. 34
Kümmel, M. 29–30, 156

Landall, T. 20–1, 70–3, 79, 121–3, 126, 127, 136, 155, 156, 159
Langley, B. 15, 67, 70, 153, 158
Langlois, P. 23, 31, 44
Lee, R.A. 4, 134
Lehmann, C.F. 34, 35
Leverhulme, Lord 1, 91, 106, 131
Lewis, J.A. 99
Lieutaud, F. 41, 42, 44
Linnell, W. 47–8, 51, 114, 136, 147
Lomax, J. 4
London 2, 3, 13–23, 38, 54, 96, 99, 131;
Clerkenwell 20, 25; Holborn 19, 20, 48;
St-Martin's-in-the-Fields 6, 8, 10, 31, 138; St Martin's Lane 3–18, passim 44, 64, 102, 138, 154, 155
Loveday, J. 37
Lovelace, J. 13–14, 153
Lowman, H. 16
Ludwig VIII, Landgraf of Hesse 25
Lumb, C. & Sons 124

Macquoid, P. 96, 150
Magniac, C. 44
Malton, T. 113
Marienborn 26, 28
Marot, D. 155
Marsh family 79, 81, 158
Mawley Hall 144–5, 151, 153, 161
Mayhew, J. 4, 113, 137, 148
Mercer, Col. 21
Metcalfe, A. 113
Mildmay, B. 31
Mondon, F. 41, 149
Montagu, Earl later 1st Duke of 16, 155
Morgan, C. 8
Moser, G.M. 21, 56
Moss Harris & Sons 2, 96
mounts 39–45, 56, 150, 153
Murray, Sir W.K. 1, 87; cabinet 1, 4, 26, 36–54 passim, 87–91, 94, 96, 135, 137

Nestfell, J.G. 33, 156
Neuwied 2, 26, 27
Nicholls, J. 40, 149
Norman, S. 47–8, 51

Ochtertyre 1, 87
Okeley, J. 26, 27
Oppenordt, P-M. 40
Orme, C. 59, 133

Page, Sir G. 79
Painsun, L.S. 41
Palling family 70–1
Palmer, G. 11, 138
Palmer, W. 57–8
Paris 31, 38, 42, 54, 56, 99
Parker, R.L. 64
Parker, T. 10, 146
Partridge (Fine Art) Ltd 64, 70, 96, 134
Piffetti, P. 30
pillar and claw tables, see tea tables
Pine, J. 58
Pineau, N. 67, 70, 135, 153
Pinto collection 126
Poitou 41
Pott, Lady 59
Potter, T. (?) 19–20, 26, 27, 36, 48, 74, 84, 99, 147, 155, 156
Potter, W. 20
Powderham Castle 3, 8, 9, 13, 15, 51, 109, 135, 140, 150, 155, 159; bookcases 3–15 passim, 33–9 passim, 46–57 passim, 70, 82, 106–13, 129, 135, 137, 140, 154, 159
Pryer, C. 126

Reading, A. 8
Renshaw, J. 18–19, 20, 48
Robinson, Sir T. 23
Rocque, J. 7, 14, 154, 155
Roentgen, A. 2, 3, 4, 24–9, 31, 34, 84, 106, 148, 156
Roentgen, D. 24, 29
Roentgen, L. 24–5
Rosenborg 34, 35
Rotch, C. 2
Rotterdam 24, 31
Roubiliac, L.F. 14, 21, 154
Roussel, F. 44
Rummer, M. 26
Russell, W. 114, 131

Saunders, P. 47–8, 147
Scadding, J. 12, 139, 147
Schleswig-Holstein 34
Scott, W. 11, 126, 143
Searle, R. 58
Serena, F. 144
Shephard (of Millom) 134
Slodtz brothers 40
Sloutt, E. 16
Smith, F. 144
Sonneman, B. 30
Sophia Dorothea, Queen 29, 30, 156
Southwick Park commode 2, 38, 45, 52, 54, 96
Spindler, N. 31
Stanhope, Sir W. 17–18, 19, 59, 147
St Aubyn family 129, 130–1, 137
Steinberg, J. 1
Steinfeldt, H. 31
Stone, J. 8
Stumbels, W. 134
Sturmer, M. 45
Sudley Art Gallery 106
Sun Fire Insurance Co. 10, 21, 143
Sutton Scarsdale 127
Symonds, R.W. 1–2, 24, 59, 60, 79, 87, 91, 114

tables and desks 17, 21, 23, 74–85, 153–8 passim; see also tea tables
Taitt, J. 121
tea-chests and dressing-boxes 1, 20–1, 56–7, 121–6, 136, 151, 160
tea tables 1, 2, 21, 25, 49, 113–20, 154, 158, 159
Temple Newsam House 2, 4, 49, 96, 129
Thistlethwayte family 2, 96
Thornton, P. 4
Tipping, H.A. 144
Topsham 24
Toro, B. 15, 103
Towne, A. 12, 138, 139
Towne, M. 12, 138, 139
Treslove, T. 11, 143
Trotter, J. (?) 21
Tucker, R. 10
Tweed, H. (Antiques) 126

Vandenberghe, F. 16
van Risemburgh, B. 54
van Somer, P. 87
Vardy, J. 15, 21, 22, 156
Vassalli, F. 144
Vaultier, S. 44
Vernon, T. 23
Victoria and Albert Museum 4, 19, 21, 49, 96, 106, 131; bureau-bookcase 19, 30, 51; cabinets 3, 15, 18, 20, 34–41 passim, 60–3, 99–102, 135, 157, 159; chair 126; library table 38, 39, 40, 54, 56, 57, 91, 154
Vile, W. 3, 14, 15, 44, 137, 155

Wakelin, E. 126
Weddell, R. 114
Wilcocks, H. 13
Williams, N. 13, 134

Williamson, E.H. 10
Woster, T. 16–17, 59
Wunderlich, J. 30

Yorke, J. 4

Zinzendorf, Count 26
Zurcher, F. 29